DRASTIC DYKES AND ACCIDENTAL ACTIVISTS

DRASTIC DYKES AND ACCIDENTAL ACTIVISTS

Queer Women in the Urban South

La Shonda Mims

THE UNIVERSITY OF NORTH CAROLINA PRESS

Chapel Hill

*This book was published
with the assistance of the
Fred W. Morrison Fund of the
University of North Carolina Press.*

Set in Miller and Klavika type
by codeMantra

Cover illustration courtesy of Adobe Stock.

Library of Congress Cataloging-in-Publication Data
Names: Mims, La Shonda, author.
Title: Drastic dykes and accidental activists : queer
women in the urban South / La Shonda Mims.
Other titles: Queer women in the urban South
Description: Chapel Hill : The University of North
Carolina Press, 2022. | Includes bibliographical
references and index.
Identifiers: LCCN 2022023742 | ISBN 9781469670546
(cloth) | ISBN 9781469670553 (paperback ;
alk. paper) | ISBN 9781469670560 (ebook)
Subjects: LCSH: Lesbians—Southern States. | Sexual
minority community—Southern States. | Lesbian
activists—Southern States. | Lesbians—Georgia—
Atlanta—History—20th century. | Lesbians—North
Carolina—Charlotte—History—20th century.
Classification: LCC HQ75.6.U52 S655 2022 |
DDC 306.76/630975—dc23/eng/20220607
LC record available at https://lccn.loc.gov/2022023742

For T, who lived this book

CONTENTS

ILLUSTRATIONS

ACKNOWLEDGMENTS

I have imagined this section of my book since 2009. We might be having drinks or sharing a meal at a conference, and it seems like I am listening to you, yet I am also imagining how I will thank you. You took time out of your life to consider my work and my struggles, and you valued our friendship. Perhaps I am sharing time with you on your porch during a delightful summer respite and there I am again—imagining how I will acknowledge your kindness. How will I make the time and say the right words to let you know that I recognized that when you asked, "How's the research going?" you did not want an hourlong answer. But you stayed. You listened. You offered distraction, love, support, and most importantly a break from the chaos of academia.

Of course I told myself to jot down your name as soon as I was able. I never did. Of course I know that you should not put off the best part of your book until the last minute. I did.

Now I am here at the final hour desperately hoping that I will not forget you all. But please know that when we are connecting, I am always thinking about how grateful I am for you. Writing is indulgent. Somewhere along the way, you supported that self-indulgence. Thank you.

It was not until I applied for the Coordinating Council for Women Historians' Prelinger Award that I considered what it meant to be non-traditional or first generation in academia. The Prelinger paid for my first and only "time off" (away from teaching 4/4 loads) to write and research. I continue to be overwhelmed by the generosity of this award and its life-changing effect on my career.

The Sallie Bingham Center for Women's History and Culture at Duke University awarded me a grant for this research, and there I worked with Kelly Wooten. I am grateful for her sustained attention to my work. Kelly introduced me to the delightful Julie Enszer, who has been an advisor and friend. Her commitment to women's publishing and artistic energies is incomparable. Perhaps most importantly, she makes me laugh and sends handwritten lesbian-feminist greetings, which I treasure.

At the Atlanta History Center (AHC), I met Wesley Chenault. I was a green PhD student who came to Wesley with a desire to write about southern lesbians. He turned my desire into reality. He generously shared his time and extraordinary knowledge of queer Atlanta, as well as the resources of the AHC, without restriction. In the final days of preparing the manuscript, I benefited from my meetings with the Georgia LGBTQ archives group and deeply appreciate Kate Daly, Jena Jones, Leah Lefkowitz, and Serena McCracken at the AHC for their help with images and manuscript collections.

Emory University's Stuart A. Rose Manuscript, Archives, and Rare Book Library awarded me a week of research support. Its collections shaped the trajectory of this project. The University of Georgia's Franklin College of Arts and Sciences and the Department of History generously funded international conference travel and research at the Lesbian Herstory Archives. It was an absolute dream to immerse myself in the collections there. The staff at the University of North Carolina at Charlotte's Special Collections patiently responded to my many requests for help. I am grateful to Christina Wright for her commitment to Charlotte's queer community history and willingness to help track down images in the final days of production. The rich collections at Georgia State University offer a vibrant, and digitally accessible, landscape of queer southern life. The supportive staff in the archives division of the Auburn Avenue Research Library on African American Culture and History helped me target sources and amplify Black voices.

It is possible that I would not be a professional historian if I had not met Cindy Kierner. At our children's summer preschool outing I expressed to her an interest in graduate school. Two short months later, I was pursuing an MA in history at the University of North Carolina at Charlotte, thanks to her encouragement. Cindy believed in me when I did not believe in myself. It still surprises me that my intimidating historiography professor is now my intimidating (and dear) friend.

At UNC Charlotte, my MA committee was *the* dream team: Donna Gabaccia, Heather Ann Thompson, and David Goldfield. Donna Gabaccia was a model thesis advisor, turning my unprocessed content into meaningful writing. Even now, she continues to offer validation and encouraging words. The faculty of UNC Charlotte are outstanding. Steve Sabol is the king of the "woman-up" speech. I am certain he never planned to mentor a graduate student who studies lesbian history, but here we are. Peter Thorsheim treated me to many meals and kindly listened as I rambled about my work and worried about my future. He is proof that historians can be exceptionally kind people. Dan Dupre always showed an encouraging interest in my work and professional path. Gregory Mixon, Christine Haynes, John Smail, and Cheryl Hicks did the same. I am grateful for their support during my time as an MA student and when I returned to the department as a lecturer. Karen Flint and David Johnson are absolutely the dearest of friends. Both offered critical advice as I prepared for the job market, and Karen and I spent long hours writing together. Many of these folks shared regular lunches and invited me to join. I especially enjoyed my time with the brilliant UNCC lunch bunch, including Carol Alexander-Higham, Shep McKinley, Bethany Johnson, and Maren Ehlers. They taught me a lot about teaching. We also laughed uproariously.

The University of Georgia (UGA) kindly allowed me to join its fantastic program after a substantial personal delay.

I am grateful to my stellar and exacting advisors: Jim Cobb, John Inscoe, Reinaldo L. Román, and John D'Emilio. When Jim Cobb agreed to take me on as a student, I felt like I had scored a date to the prom with the captain of the football team. He took the work seriously and offered his very best to make sure that I centered southern history in my work. John Inscoe and Reinaldo L. Román opened important avenues of research, which improved this book. Both remained committed to my success long after I left Athens. I met John D'Emilio while pursuing my master's thesis, and for some reason he stayed with me and this project. I am deeply grateful for his willingness to support me from afar.

Ian Lekus and Pamela Voekel welcomed me to the small queer family at Georgia. They reassured me in my tenuous first weeks at UGA; Ian offered important advice, and when Bethany Moreton arrived, she and Pam became confidantes. The grad students made UGA an amazing space to do history and build lasting friendships. Many of these folks are now my closest friends. I'm so glad I met Blake Scott and Levi Van Sant and am happy that we continue to connect in meaningful ways. During one of my first grad seminars at Georgia, I sat across from someone whom I misjudged. I cautiously introduced my research topic and thought he hated everything I presented. A few weeks later, he came to my office after class and offered some of the most helpful comments I had ever received from a fellow graduate student. That man became my dearest friend. We talked or texted almost every day, sharing personal struggles and a hatred for Mumford & Sons. That person was Jason

Manthorne—a brilliant scholar and beautiful human who embraced our family, watched our dog in his home, and befriended our son (introducing him to Pink Floyd and intelligent filmmaking). Jason left us far too soon, and I will never laugh the same way again. My research and writing are better because of him, but my life is now incomplete in his absence. To Jason's Beer Team, I owe all my appreciation and love. Steve Nash, Jim Gigantino, and Zac Smith give me hope that there are truly lovely men in the universe. And there is no finer group of women in the universe than the women's caucus of JBT, Kathi Nehls, Jennifer Wunn, and Jenny Schwartzberg. Y'all mean the world to me.

When I arrived in Baltimore, the fine folks at Towson University welcomed me, read my work, funded my travel, and offered me the opportunity to teach in my field. My deepest thanks go to Akim Reinhardt, Alhena Gadotti, Christian Koot, Mike Masatsugu, Ben Fisher, Ben Zajicek, Erik Ropers, Tunde Oduntan, Kimberly Katz, Ronn Pineo, and Kelly Gray. Each of these folks welcomed me for office chats, tea, and laughter. Alyse Minter was a friend and an extraordinary librarian, researcher, and teacher. Tiffany Packer regularly lifted my spirits. It was a special joy to work with Pamela Frock in the history department.

Kennesaw State University's College of Humanities and Social Sciences granted me a manuscript completion award wherein I worked with a fabulous writing group. Bert Way, Shane Peterson, Miriam Brown Spiers, and Ebony Glover offered valuable comments and patient ears as I wrestled with writing problems. The interdisciplinary studies department afforded a warm welcome (especially Cherie Miller), and there I made many friends, including Laura Davis, Robbie Lieberman, and Rebecca Hill. My junior-faculty cohort, Rudy Aguilar, Miriam Brown Spiers, and Liz Miles, was the most fun. These three tolerantly listened to my concerns and offered constant support. Liz became my indefatigable texting buddy and a dear friend. She has offered countless hours of advice and listened to countless hours of my blather. Toward the end of my book project Liz moved to Japan, where she selflessly texted to make sure that I was surviving the copyediting. While at Kennesaw I reconnected with my UGA graduate friends Tom Okie and Ivy Way. They always had time to answer questions and share a laugh. The history department at Kennesaw offered invaluable financial support for this book.

I am happy to now call Middle Tennessee State University home. Kind colleagues, including Kelly Kolar, Ben Sawyer, Becky McIntyre, Jae Turner, Lisa Swart, and Jen Petit, welcomed me with encouragement and good humor during a pandemic year. Emily Baran has been a spectacular mentor. MTSU has also generously supported my research. Thanks go to Ashley Riley Sousa, Kris McCusker, and Susan Myers-Shirk for helping me to find my way. I look forward to more fun times with Ashley Valanzola and my fellow UGA grads, Katie Brackett and Andrew Fialka.

Because of the Southern Association for Women Historians, I have a career. Rebecca Sharpless offered me the SAWH keynote address in 2013. She refused to consider that I was too young in my career and pushed me in front of a microphone at the Southern Historical Association's annual meeting. I felt like a rock star. Because of this opportunity, I met my editor at the University of North Carolina Press, Mark Simpson-Vos. He has been extraordinarily patient, and I am sure he will be thrilled to see this project completed. Mark stayed with me for years, always answering emails and encouraging me to continue. I owe him and the entire UNC Press team an enormous debt of gratitude. This book is better because of María Garcia and Jessica Newman, who offered guidance and reassurance and spent hours thinking about this project. Julie Bush painstakingly edited my final draft (except for this sentence), and Valerie Burton patiently guided me through the editing process. UNC Press chose a first-class team of reviewers for *Drastic Dykes and Accidental Activists*. Because of their careful comments and recommendations on structure, I now have a publishable book. Many fine SAWH folks have cheered me on and supported my work in a variety of ways, including Janet Allured, Diane Miller Sommerville, Karen Cox, Megan Shockley, Melissa Walker, Joan Johnson, Pippa Holloway, Bea Burton, Anne Tucker, Kathryn Tucker, and Jessica Brannon-Wranosky. Through the SAWH I also met the dearest and most hilarious human: Nick Syrett. Thanks go to him for always answering my random texts immediately and for a lifetime of toasted rav humor. Nick introduced me to the fabulous Will Kuby and Aaron Lecklider, who have both been generous with their time and support of my professional endeavors. While working with the National Park Service's LGBTQ initiative, I built connections with fine and encouraging scholars, including Megan Springate, Paula Martinac, Julio Capó Jr., Christina Hanhardt, and Katie Batza.

Over the years of work that have gone into this book, I have benefited from the advice of generous scholars, including Glenda Gilmore, Bryant Simon, Deirdre Cooper Owens, Marc Stein, E. Patrick Johnson, Donna Jo Smith-Perry, and Jennifer Dominique Jones. I have had the pleasure of working with several students who shared my keen interest in queer and women's history. This book is better because of them.

At the beginning of this project, I was part of a vibrant queer community in Charlotte, North Carolina. Jim Yarbrough, editor of *Q-Notes*, opened his office and private collections to help me with my research. Many folks offered thoughtful comments on this project, and some were kind enough to share their stories as narrators for my research. I am deeply appreciative of the gift of oral histories that guided my work. My Charlotte book club allowed me to temporarily escape academic reading, and with those folks I enjoyed excellent conversation, wine, and cheese. Thanks go to all of them for kindly devoting a meeting to offer comments on a chapter draft. I invited my new colleague at UNC Charlotte, Sonia Robles, to this book club, and our time there together became a natural extension of our blossoming friendship. Pretty soon I introduced her to another new friend and colleague, who is now her spouse. Aaron Shapiro and Sonia Robles have read portions of this work, cooked for me and my family, and kindly invited us to share in their lovely wedding celebration in Mexico City. Also in Charlotte, my family became happily entangled with the Hall-Hertels, and I hope we never shake loose. They are our family now too, and I am so grateful for their love and support.

Baltimore is home to some amazing folks. There I met the lovely Deanna Bourassa and Joyce Fishel. We shared decadent meals, laughter, and conversation. Andrea and Mike Karolkowski are the absolute best neighbors, and I am so lucky to count them among our closest friends. We got to know Emma Bidwell and Bernie McCarthy, in the other Baltimore (the Irish one), via the Lesbian Lives conference; they will never get rid of us. Annette Snapp, my lesbian mentor, research partner, and builder of my personal lesbian archive, is magnetic. I thank my friends Kathleen and Jennifer, whom I have known the longest, for always believing (even if they only pretended) that I would get this done.

My parents were accidental activists who taught me that anything was possible for women. They thrust me into spaces that were not designed for me. As a result, I was exposed to a world that allowed me to nurture my passion for women's history, which sprouted from a deep belief in the tenacity of women. The formative women in my life, my grandmother and my mother, did not understand or embrace feminism, yet they were indeed feminists. This was also true of my father. My dad, who has always championed my education, did without so that I could live a life of the mind. If only my mother were alive to see this accomplishment. I miss her every day. My brother always respected my thoughts and carefully considered my arguments, even when I suggested that he should do the heavy lifting of cleaning our room. He read drafts of this project and would read the entire book if he were still here.

Copeland sacrificed time with me over and over again so that I could do this academic work. He encouraged me by offering profound advice and insightful comments, and when he was little he regularly asked what page I was on. Being his parent is the best work.

As you will read in the first sentences of the introduction to this book, my husbian, T Rosser, is a drastic dyke. Her love is constant and she has given more to this project than anyone.

DRASTIC DYKES AND ACCIDENTAL ACTIVISTS

INTRODUCTION

In 2002, I planned to attend a wedding in Augusta, Georgia, where my partner would be a bridesmaid. Although we arrived in Augusta, we never made it to the actual ceremony because she was kicked out of the wedding, and ultimately her family of origin, when family members deemed her appearance too masculine for the event. The father of the bride, her uncle, called my partner just a few hours before the service. He lambasted her—after having taunted her appearance at the rehearsal dinner by calling her "Little Boy Blue"—and warned that unless she could conform to family norms, do something about her (clearly too-short) hair, and uninvite her guest (me), she should not attend the ceremony.

This traumatic story framed the argument for my early work on the meanings of southern femininity and lesbian identity in the South. By examining the historical underpinnings of these identities and the expectations that often surrounded them, I endeavored to tease out the historical meaning of white southern, lesbian, and feminine identities and also to settle my own identity frustrations as a native southerner, the granddaughter of Pentecostal tent-revival preachers, the daughter of white working-class Republicans, and a lesbian. My first encounter with southern identity came as a teenager at summer camp in Vermont. I distinctly remember how foreign my fellow campers seemed. I was acutely aware of my appearance (think big, teased, soap-opera hair and a young face painted with neon eyeshadow and sparkly pink rouge) in contrast to the other barefaced girls. Because we had not encountered peers from outside of our geographic region, my camp friends and I quickly conflated our differences in appearance with our regional identities as northern or, in my case, southern. They represented North to me, and I was The South to them. We were the embodiments of our regions, mine still tied to the Civil War past in conversations and casual jest.

Identity for southerners and for lesbians is messy. The boundaries of identity are malleable and extremely personal. Many women who love women do not self-identify as lesbians, and historians have not fully come to grips with what qualifies as a singular lesbian identity over time. In recent decades the rise of lesbian visibility in popular culture has further muddied the boundaries of lesbian identity. In the 1990s, tongue-in-cheek books like *Lesbianism Made Easy* or the unapologetic comic strip series Dykes to Watch Out For shared bookstore shelves with *Vanity Fair* magazine's showstopping August 1993 cover photo of hyper-feminized model Cindy Crawford performing a barbershop shave on the face of the masculine female singer k.d. lang and *Time* magazine's April 1997 cover featuring entertainer Ellen Degeneres declaring, "Yep, I'm Gay."[1] Because lesbian, like southern, is an identity infused with several meanings and cultural images, understanding the limits and definitions of historical presentations of southern and lesbian identity is fraught with problems, though this question of identity provides an important methodological foundation for the stories presented in this book.

Drastic Dykes and Accidental Activists is a book about southern urban identity. The main characters acted as principal players in the economic, political, and social world that was the southern metropolis.

City leaders in Charlotte, North Carolina, and Atlanta, Georgia, competed to claim icon status in the New South. Southern women who loved women shared these carefully crafted New South metropolitan identities presented by city leaders and immortalized in popular culture, and they defined themselves in accordance with these urban markers. The way a city defines itself imbues its residents with certain identity markers. People who reside in Baltimore know that they have had the best crab cake and are hyperaware of their city's reputation for crime and poverty as epitomized in the television series *The Wire*. Folks who relocate to Denver know that they are the envy of all their outdoorsy friends and of those who are marijuana enthusiasts—perhaps they are even the same friends. Hipper-than-thou Austinites know that they have access to the best up-and-coming musicians, and people envy their residency when they tune in to *Austin City Limits*. Urban environments like those of Atlanta and Charlotte define cultural perceptions and influence how residents view themselves.[2]

Drastic Dykes and Accidental Activists introduces the lesbian voice to southern urban history by ushering in new southern women, exposing different New South experiences, and queering the southern historical landscape.[3] Lesbians shaped urban spaces in Atlanta and Charlotte, and they tell us stories about money, class, and the privileges that whiteness affords. The intertwined categories of race, region, gender, and class defined women's lives—in addition to, and sometimes independent from, their sexual identity.[4] Confined by these qualifiers, women harnessed their sexual identities to form the urban spaces they frequented.[5] New South lesbian life unmasks the role of religious, corporate, and political leaders in defining urban spaces for queer people.[6] Atlanta and Charlotte challenge the dominance of urban northeast metros. They prove that urban centers are also southern. Approximately 250 miles apart, the two cities are connected by a single major roadway, Interstate 85. By the late twentieth century, this road served as a conduit for queer people seeking sanctuary in the enormity of Atlanta Pride celebrations.

In its earliest years, Charlotte served as a trading hamlet with an official city charter signed in 1768 and a nickname, the "Queen City," harking back to Queen Charlotte, the wife of King George III.[7] Although the city of Atlanta dates to 1837, almost seventy years after Charlotte's founding date, it formed around the final railroad stop for the Western and Atlantic lines and in less than a decade was linked to the entire Southeast by rail.[8] As Atlanta's railways connected it to the surrounding region, Charlotte remained a tranquil, isolated, and agriculturally focused village for over a century.[9] At the dawn of the twentieth century, the two cities were on divergent paths. By 1900 Atlanta's Fulton County was more than double the size in population of Charlotte's Mecklenburg County.[10] Yet by the last decades of the twentieth century, lesbians found a variety of opportunities in both urban New South centers to meet other women socially and engage in queer activism.

Lesbians, like the city of Charlotte, have frequently been excluded from historical inquiry. Few scholarly monographs are devoted to the Queen City's history, but when Charlotte does make an appearance, the comparison with Atlanta is hard to escape.[11] For example, in the 2010 edited collection *Charlotte, NC: The Global Evolution of a New South City*, Matthew D. Lassiter emphasizes the city's wannabe status in the chapter "Searching for Respect," while Stephen Samuel Smith demonstrates that Atlanta is "the paradigmatic New South city with which Charlotte, in the eyes of its civic boosters, has long been playing catch-up."[12] In the epilogue, Owen J. Furuseth names Atlanta as Charlotte's perennial rival.[13] Civic leaders in Charlotte were intently interested in this competition as Charlotte boosters endeavored to replicate Atlanta's success, especially after World War II, while city leaders in Atlanta focused on positioning their city as the New South's urban leader. By the 1970s, however, some chamber of commerce leaders in Charlotte, whose metropolitan population had reached three-quarters of a million compared with metro Atlanta's 2 million, recognized that perhaps a middle path of controlled growth was both better and more realistic, since Atlanta obviously outpaced the city.[14] In recounting his decision to move to Charlotte, future mayor Harvey Gantt remembered his own comparison of the two cities. He recalled that Atlanta was "too big" and Charlotte was "growing," which he perceived as an opportunity.[15] Growth has always been at the heart of city management, and moderation would not satiate Charlotte's growth-hungry business leaders for long.[16]

Competition with Atlanta permeated the mindset of Charlotte business owners as they built their persona in opposition to Atlanta, against whom they were often defined.[17] Twentieth-century Charlotteans bragged about growth, noting that they led the way in the Carolinas and followed just behind Atlanta, the exemplar of urbanism in the Southeast.[18] Whether gay or straight, Charlotte businesses used Atlanta as both a measure of success and a tool to woo patrons. In a 1981 *Charlotte Observer* article, staff writers who hoped to uncover Charlotte's "gay community" noted that patrons at a relatively new gay men's bar in the city boasted of its status in comparison to the presumed gold standards of heterosexuality and Atlanta: "Classier than any straight bar in Charlotte, they say. As nice as any gay bar in Atlanta, they say."[19] Three years later, a new Charlotte gay bar attempted to attract customers based on the presumed standard of queer bars in Atlanta, declaring that it was "shooting for a light show that's better than the Limelight's in Atlanta."[20] Profiled in the *Charlotte Food and Wine* magazine, a restaurant owner excited by his establishment's new location in Charlotte's posh South Park neighborhood deemed it "the 'Buckhead' of Charlotte," referring to Atlanta's wealthy upscale shopping district—an area labeled by Atlanta's tourist industry as the "Beverly Hills of the East."[21] Charlotte's business owners repeated the oft-heard refrain that positioned Charlotte as a city yearning to reach the height of New South urban identity as idealized through the image of Atlanta.

In this search for New South superiority in the late twentieth century, Charlotte's political and business leaders crafted a city with no distinctive identity. Perhaps for this reason the Queen City's history seems inconsequential to residents. Many who call Charlotte home are in the city to make money and enjoy the excellent weather but have historically avoided building community or identifying with the city's past.[22] In *Drastic Dykes and Accidental Activists*, this tangential relationship between Charlotte's residents and their home city is transparent in the stories of lesbian and gay activism, as the Queen City's queer organizers often encountered apathetic members who lacked an allegiance to Charlotte. Lesbians made a home there and formed transient communities, but a lesbian collective built around a shared urban identity was slow to form among citizens who demonstrated a limited loyalty to place.

A brief examination of desegregation in Atlanta and Charlotte provides a useful framework for understanding the subsequent experiences of lesbians there. Charlotte's city leaders created a successful plan built on an understanding that race and class are inextricably linked. Racial integration would require socioeconomic diversity, which could be achieved only by demanding that some suburban areas join the city. In Atlanta, a successful annexation campaign in 1952 resulted in the addition of suburban areas, including the wealthy and predominantly white Buckhead, which both prevented Black dominance in the metro area and increased the city's tax base.[23] Suburban annexation earned the Queen City a near-bottom slot in a ranking of the fifty largest cities in the United States in 1980.[24] Both cities created exceptional models based on the politics of moderation in the 1960s aftermath of *Brown v. Board of Education*. Yet as Matthew Lassiter has argued, it would be the triumph of busing in Charlotte, forced by the 1971 Supreme Court decision in *Swann v. Charlotte-Mecklenburg Board of Education*, undergirding the boosterism of city leaders who portrayed Charlotte as the "prosperous and progressive embodiment of the latest New South."[25]

In its quest for exceptional city status, Charlotte's business leaders embraced the "Charlotte Way," a political middle ground on issues of race and economics. They enjoyed temporary success as a beacon of New South race relations until the Fourth Circuit Court of Appeals upheld a 1999 decision ending busing to achieve integration in the Queen City.[26] Fueled by corporate interests, including the booming NationsBank, the repeal silenced the busing turmoil while allowing business leaders to focus on luring unconcerned Black and white northern workers to Charlotte.[27] The city faced resegregation exacerbated by the tremendous suburban growth that continued the trend of residential segregation, making it difficult to maintain school integration.[28] City leaders followed the wishes and demands of suburban families who did not want their privileged children attending school with children who resided in housing projects.[29] Just as corporate leaders wielded power and ultimately oversaw the return of segregation to Charlotte, religious leaders asserted their dominance in the face of a growing and visible gay community in the 1990s and into the next decades. In contrast to the post-*Brown* desegregation battles, the moderate Charlotte Way did not apply to the city's lesbian and gay citizens, even as Charlotte's exploding banking industry demonstrated substantial support for lesbians and gay men. If Charlotte's leaders aspired to rival Atlanta, they were willing to concede on queer livability.

City and corporate leaders in Atlanta often welcomed, and even fostered, the growth of gay visibility and the resulting queer tourism. No matter how much Charlotte's leaders promoted growth and longed to be like Atlanta, this move was not imitated. A year after the uprising led by bar patrons at New York City's Stonewall Inn, members of Atlanta's Gay Liberation Front organized a Christopher Street Liberation memorial in 1970, while Charlotte's queer citizens did not celebrate a community Pride event until 1981.[30] In 1993, when Atlanta participants in the lesbian-organized Southeast Lesbian and Gay Business Expo rallied around the power of the gay, albeit elite and primarily white, dollar, the *Atlanta Journal-Constitution*'s coverage of the expo recognized that many lesbians and gay men were wealthier and better educated than their heterosexual counterparts and would certainly use that affluence for targeted entertainment and business options.[31] Supported by what would become the first gay chamber of commerce in the United States to be recognized with 501(c)(3) status, the Atlanta Gay and Lesbian Chamber of Commerce welcomed the 1994 business expo with the slogan "The Gay Buck Stops Here."[32]

A pattern of significant and sustained growth in Charlotte meant that its well-chosen chamber of commerce slogan, "A good place to make money," proved true for many queer people.[33] Yet their financial success in the Queen City did not buy them a supportive community, as city politicians avoided opportunities to tap the burgeoning gay market. Republican mayors and their interconnection with the religious right created a hostile environment for queer people. The most egregious of these alliances led to waves of revitalized activism among queer Charlotteans.[34] For example, Charlotte's fledgling Pride festival moved to a private venue funded by Bank of America in 2006 because of virulent protests by the conservative religious group Operation Save America, whose leaders urged Charlotte's mayor, Pat McCrory, to remove the festival from its previous location in a public Uptown park.[35] While Charlotte's Gay Pride happening proceeded in Bank of America's privately owned and concealed Gateway Village space, corporate sponsors such as Delta Airlines, Bank of America, Coca-Cola, and Bell South openly embraced Atlanta's celebration in centrally located Piedmont Park—home to lesbian softball and bars in the 1950s and 1960s.[36] Atlanta's Pride festival rivaled celebrations in San Francisco and New York City by 2011, with an estimated attendance of 300,000, and Atlanta's Black Gay Pride was among the largest in the world.[37] For many lesbians and gay men, Atlanta lived up to Mayor William B. Hartsfield's promise that his was a city "too busy to hate."[38]

We must recognize that the borders of the South are permeable and its regions as varied as New Orleans, Houston, Baltimore, and Miami, so the cities of Atlanta and Charlotte are not representative of all southern lesbian communities. Yet these two cities offer unique opportunities for historical comparison, in part because of their urban rivalry (look no further than the 2006 fight for the NASCAR Hall of Fame) and their geographic proximity. After Charlotte won the Hall of Fame battle, Mayor McCrory acknowledged that the city had "learned from Atlanta's mistakes" and that city leaders had enjoyed the advantage of "growing up second" behind Atlanta.[39] In a 2010 *Atlanta Journal-Constitution* blog post titled "Charlotte Who? Mayor Kasim Reed Says Atlanta Still on Top," the increasing competition between the two cities was palpable—especially in Reed's recognition that Atlanta would indeed lose ground to Charlotte if it did not "make strides on transportation, education, water and the arts."[40] The often one-sided urban rivalry reveals a fertile environment for city leaders, corporations, and southern lesbians to position themselves as change makers in the urban New South.

Lesbians carved out space for identity formation in a region often dismissed wholesale by those looking for a queer place to be or a queer history to explore. Popularly portrayed as belles or magnolias—"Real Housewives" even—but not dykes, white southern women are conflated with Hollywood's southern characters like Scarlett in *Gone with the Wind* and Truvy, M'Lynn, Ouiser, Clairee, and Shelby in *Steel Magnolias*. They are the white belles of country music, epitomized by Loretta Lynn, Dolly Parton, and Patsy Cline. As one popular magazine proclaimed, southern women "are forever entangled in and infused by a miasma of mercy and cruelty, order and chaos, cornpone and cornball, a potent mix that leaves us wise, morbid, good-humored, God-fearing, outspoken and immutable. Like the Irish, with better teeth."[41] Black southern women face a different set of stereotypical media portrayals under the white gaze, having been historically cast for white consumption as racist caricatures like the Mammy or Aunt Jemima and more recently, and controversially, as Aibileen and Minny in the novel and movie adaptation of *The Help*.[42] The Mammy crossed the color line between the worlds of Black and white in the South, and she sacrificed self-directed femininity and sexuality for a role that simultaneously supported white women's pedestals while also being defined by them.[43]

Like white women, Black women's culturally created identities were often imposed *upon* them. Because Black lives are less visible in the archives and popular culture, it can be a struggle to locate authentic sources when constructing a history of Black southern lesbians.[44] Indeed, as LaToya Eaves argues, research on Black southern queer women requires a wholly different approach, while Rochella (Roey) Thorpe demonstrates that Black queer life happened independently of white people.[45] When considering Black queer lives, Black people are often presented as an appendage to queer sexualities. Lesbian and gay historical studies typically focus on white actors, even as they engage comprehensive language like "lesbian history" or "queer history." In fact, Black queer historical studies are often written as stand-alone works, suggesting that blanket identities such as lesbian have not fully included women of color. This means that Black and queer are not integrated identities, as Siobhan Somerville has demonstrated.[46] Cherrie Moraga and Gloria Anzaldúa, along with other queer women of color in the 1970s, named this problem when they penned *This Bridge Called My Back* and demanded that Black queer women tell their own stories because they were not being written. Even in twenty-first century research efforts, like oral history projects devoted to lesbian life, Black lesbian experiences are explored separately from those of white lesbians.[47] In *Drastic Dykes and Accidental Activists*, race plays a central role. An interrogation of whiteness permeates this book, with a recognition that Black and white worlds have often remained separate in the lesbian South; the handful of Black lesbian voices and experiences presented in these pages do not fully portray the rich history of southern Black lesbians.[48]

Southern women are the stuff of Hollywood and popular culture. They are tied to their troubled racist past of identity entanglement. Universal portrayals of southern women also define lesbians who call the South home—women who are lesbians *and* southerners. But lesbians in the South identify with "southern," "queer," "Baptist," "African American," "feminist," "wife," "lesbian," "parent," "banker," "Latina," "activist," and all of the countless other identities that we might imagine. Because these are not fixed and indisputable, this book grants women who loved women a central place in history without naming or characterizing their identities ahistorically.[49]

Southern women deserve "a shared sense of a common past," which is necessary for group identity formation. They warrant historical examination on their own terms—independent from the "oppositional identities" that often frame our understanding of southerners and lesbians.[50] If identities are understood in contrast to a culturally defined Other, lesbians who identified as southerners are positioned against a prevailing conception of a presumably normative, northern identity, just as their queer identity might be placed against the hegemonic identity of heterosexuality. Questions of historical identity and naming frame an important historiographical debate in the history of sexuality.[51] The troubling nature of lesbian identity and "the lesbian" in history creates a conundrum for scholars in the field. Tracing identity across space and time can often paralyze researchers.[52] As Jack Gieseking has shown, to find the spaces claimed by lesbians and vulnerable queer people, it is useful to consider "constellations." Less affluent and lacking gay-male (particularly white) power, lesbian and queer people rely on transient spaces, identifiable only in relation to each other. Locating their precarious urban movements requires unique approaches.[53] Efforts to organize research by grouping people based solely on erotic affections and desires prove frustrating, and even pointless at times, while trying to historicize a group of people under one identity label is fruitless. One thing is clear: the lesbian past is scarcely analyzed and difficult to locate.[54]

Drastic Dykes and Accidental Activists centers lesbians in southern U.S. history. It is not a generic history of some lesbians somewhere, but it is the history of specific women who sometimes identified as lesbians, or who engaged other women sexually, or who loved other women, or who sought the company of women in queer venues—all in two archetypal New South cities. These individual stories, constructed through a variety of sources including oral histories, offer a glimpse of lesbian southern life.[55] These vignettes are partial and complex due in part to the use of oral history sources and the limitations of memory intrinsic to these sources.[56] Some narrators in this book might remember stories and events through a queer lens simply because oral historians and the projects that they created were identified as specifically queer or lesbian and gay.[57] The work of conducting oral histories for my research meant meeting narrators where they were comfortable—in bars, restaurants, and a trailer home at the Charlotte Motor Speedway. When turning to archival sources, the instability and lack of funding that curse queer organizations, which typically have no long-term repository for records, resulted in my visits to private spaces that were meant to remain confidential. Owners of gay publications in Charlotte, for example, stored mimeographed newsletters from the 1970s on the floor of a nondescript office, home to a long-standing queer newspaper whose editors were reluctant to let any publications go to an archive due to a lack of trust in heteronormative repositories.

During the process of researching and writing this book, the field of queer history blossomed. Both Atlanta and Charlotte gained queer archives in the 2010s, and once-reluctant donors, like the aforementioned editors, contributed their collections. When I began this project, many of my queer South sources were not digitized. As of 2021, almost all are. While a map of queer history at the dawn of the twenty-first century appeared southless, two decades later we are on the cusp of a southern queer reckoning. Activists and scholars have joined universities in Atlanta and Charlotte to create vital queer repositories. Included in these collections are indispensable oral histories that will transport the queer past beyond the archival scraps that I joined with a few oral histories to create *Drastic Dykes and Accidental Activists*.

Shared bonds of queer identity rarely trump realities of difference. As a result, lesbians and gay men were often separated by the many divisions that separate all women and men.[58] The same is true for Black and white queer people. Gay men's histories are privileged in the archives in part because they had the economic means to fund many long-standing publications devoted to gay men's experiences. In addition to gay men's archival material, Atlanta's better-preserved lesbian stories provided access to the history of lesbians in Charlotte. This necessarily means that Atlanta occasionally receives more attention in my work due to the sheer availability of sources. For example, the first chapter of this book is devoted to women in the Atlanta region because there is little documentation of lesbian life in Charlotte prior to 1970. Research teams focused on queer life and aligned with university archivists did not join forces in Charlotte until the 2010s.

Stretching from the 1940s to the early years of the twenty-first century, *Drastic Dykes and Accidental Activists* considers lesbian life in five different ways: opportunities for intimate liaisons, connections in social spaces, visibility of lesbian feminists, Pride festivals and the urban environment, and institutions that shaped metropolitan identity. Chapter 1 traces the opportunities and connections that some white southern women exploited in their efforts to find lovers and queer friends in the pre-Stonewall South. New South lesbians located social spaces that they could claim as lesbian spaces in the 1950s and beyond. Chapter 2 offers an in-depth tour of some of these spaces—especially bars and eating establishments—while exploring the difficulty of finding the places where other like-minded women might be. The visibility that lesbian feminists embraced in the 1970s New South is the focus of chapter 3. Lesbian-feminist communities blossomed in Atlanta and Charlotte, with visible forms of activism evident in the Atlanta Lesbian Feminist Alliance and Charlotte Women's Center and political acts of lesbian publishing, like the lesbian literary journal *Sinister Wisdom*, which originated in Charlotte. This chapter offers an alternative view of lesbians who chose to leave the often-veiled space of the bar for the visibility of lesbian-feminist identity in the South. In many metropolitan areas, including Atlanta and Charlotte, Gay Pride celebrations served as a barometer of the environment for lesbians and gay men. Whether or not lesbians participated in—or even attended—the events, the history of Pride celebrations in chapter 4 demonstrates the level of queer acceptance and community in each city. Along with these festivals, both Atlanta and Charlotte gained national attention through scandals that would spotlight lesbian lives in the New South at the end of the twentieth century. Chapter 5 is focused on recent lesbian urban history as shaped by institutions like community policing, politically minded social groups, universities, corporations, professional sports, and religion. This chapter pinpoints the importance of urban institutions in defining social spaces and economic opportunities while crafting Atlanta's and Charlotte's national reputations for southern lesbians in the post-Stonewall New South.

Lesbians shaped the New South in drastic and accidental ways as they adapted to the urban climate and the accompanying regional mandates on sexual behavior. When Charlottean Kate Mullen came out for the first time, it was as a white debutante recognized by a celebration of "southern brunches and southern punches," but when she came out again, as a lesbian to her elite family, there was no celebrated southern tradition to follow. When white Atlantan Donna Jo Smith-Perry moved back to the South from San Francisco, she thought it would be a difficult lesbian life. Instead she found herself joining "Gay Pride Day with Atlanta's Lesbian Avengers, in nothing but a push-up bra and cut-offs, pausing in front of the First Baptist Church only long enough to moon the goonish security guards placed outside by its notoriously homophobic pastor, Rev. Charles Stanley." As the first to graduate in her family, Dawn

Heard found that as a Black woman she had "next to zero chance" of fostering "a meaningful relationship" with white people in the South. Her Blackness defined her in a way that her lesbianism did not. Although she met many white folks in Charlotte and they were "friends all day long," she understood that she would not be invited to their homes to meet "their momma and daddy."[59] And when lesbian feminists bemoaned that southern dykes lived life in an "oppression sandwich," faced with cruelty from southern men and criticism from non-southern lesbians, they understood that their activism would include a distinctly southern flavor.[60] From intimate letters to bawdy bars, from political lesbianism to the visibility of Pride, whether drastic or accidental, southern women made choices while negotiating the borders of their varied selves—but none with as scant a common past as the identity of lesbian.

I wonder if ever a woman will love me,
and answer the part of me that so needs to
be answered. —Carson McCullers

1 OPPORTUNITIES

Famed southern writer Carson McCullers did not claim a lesbian identity, yet her life opens a window into a pre-political southern queer world. Celebrated in her family as a nonconformist, McCullers became known for her eccentric southern characters—outsiders with unique relatability.[1] She represented, with shocking insight, the lives of Black Americans in the South through her multilayered characters. In fact, Richard Wright praised McCullers as a white author who produced Black characters with "as much ease and justice as those of her own race."[2] Even decades after its publication, a 1968 stage production of McCullers's *Member of the Wedding* allowed a memory of a "happier time" and a chance to highlight Atlanta's Black actors, according to the African American *Atlanta Daily World* newspaper. With her scathing portrayals of southern whiteness, she raised the ire of the Ku Klux Klan. In reaction to her publication of *The Heart Is a Lonely Hunter*, the organization deemed her a "n——r lover." When she tackled homosexuality in her 1941 *Reflections in a Golden Eye*, a suspected KKK member placed an anonymous phone call to her family home, labeling her "a queer" and threatening her life.[3] In her storytelling, McCullers regularly positioned the New South of her childhood as a character confronting the Old South.[4]

I begin this journey into the queer New South with McCullers because her personal musings on sexuality and desire are enmeshed with her southern fiction. McCullers hailed from Columbus, Georgia, and traveled in the spaces central to this book: Atlanta, Georgia, and Charlotte, North Carolina.[5] She created the archetype of the sexual-outsider tomboy in the South. Her sexually ambiguous characters challenged the traditional femininity of the mythical southern belle. As Jack Halberstam notes, McCullers's novel *The Member of the Wedding* is "remarkable" for having come from the "repressive cultural climate of the American South."[6] McCullers's gender nonconforming protagonist, "Frankie," came of age in the author's mind, which was firmly planted in the southern culture of the 1940s. It was a world where Black and white relationships labored under the oppressions of Jim Crow. It is here that I place McCullers: in the company of outsider women in the South, interlopers who mirror her queer characters.[7]

The women I introduce in this chapter—Carson McCullers; Mary Hutchinson and her partner, Dorothy King; and Ginny Boyd— represent the varied ways that white women located and loved other women while living in the changing landscape of the urbanizing New South. This chapter uses only three personal stories because they are all we have in the pre-political queer South. These women each explored opportunities defined by their race, region, and social class to understand their passionate desire for relationships with other women. Class status determined the nature of their relationships and the ways in which they negotiated these liaisons, but their race provided access to queer opportunities available only to white women. These are white stories not because Black stories do not exist but because Black women lived separate lives from white women, as they often still do. Following the paths of Black women's lives presents an entirely different history, which deserves to be investigated on its own terms. White privilege undergirds the lives revealed in this chapter, providing evidence for something we know little about: how women who loved women navigated the South to find one another and build their lives together, working within the cultural confines of the region.[8] Yet the borders of the Black South and the white South are adjacent, so we learn a little about the separate world of Black lesbian sexuality as these white actors cast a light on Black southern lives through literature, art, and social spaces.

This chapter creates new knowledge on pre-political lesbian life in the South, a region often perceived as closed to queer people. By examining the lives of white women who loved women before an organized lesbian rights movement existed, we catch a glimpse of homosocial and homoerotic life outside of queer bar communities. Southern women built queer lives prior to the 1950s and the formation of the first political lesbian organization—and in the culturally conservative South. Class shapes the stories I tell in this chapter. We know McCullers and Hutchinson because of their artistic successes and public lives. The third woman profiled, Ginny Boyd, affords a rare look at a southern working-class woman's story. It is available only because of Boyd's longevity and the practice of queer oral history. Since a wealthy archive of southern queer women's lives does not exist, the stories privileged here are remarkable.

Writing candidly about her struggles to understand sexuality, Carson McCullers identified herself as a sexual invert.[9] She sought inspiration in the work of sexologist Havelock Ellis, who was active in an early twentieth-century community of sexologists. Ellis advocated for placing sex outside of the procreative realm and linking sexuality with personal identity. In Ellis's work, McCullers found confirmation that her "inversion" was inborn, functioning at the core of her authentic self.[10] She regularly turned to Ellis's writings for understanding and clarity.

In his *Studies in the Psychology of Sex*, Ellis asserted that homosexuality in women usually took on a masculine cast, much as homosexuality in men would show itself in a feminine display. Ellis suggested that homosexuality in women mirrored the findings on homosexuality in men.[11] Yet homosexuality in women would be harder to detect, according to Ellis, because homoeroticism between women was often overlooked or deemed acceptable. He argued that women might not understand how to process their affections, noting that "a woman may feel a high degree of sexual attraction for another woman without realizing that her affection is sexual, and when she does realize this, she is nearly always very unwilling to reveal the nature of her intimate experience."[12] Ellis's positions on inversion served as a guide to McCullers, who confronted her own masculinity by developing boyish female characters, wearing mannish clothing, and setting aside her given name, Lula, to adopt the masculine name "Carson."[13]

In passionate letters to her friend David Diamond, a successful American classical music composer, McCullers revealed her internal dialogue as she wrestled with her own desire.[14] Having studied music as a child, she originally traveled to New York to pursue her education in piano. Although she transferred her artistic energy to a pursuit of writing, she remained fascinated by classical music. In Diamond, McCullers found a shared love of music but also a fellow queer traveler, to whom she detailed musings on her own sexual tumult.[15] She expressed to Diamond a gnawing need for love and recognition; her turmoil became the basis for her famously troubled tomboy character and queer icon, Frankie, in *The Member of the Wedding*. Writing to Diamond in the early 1940s, she confided the details of her crumbling marriage to Reeves McCullers. She described a "brotherly" love for her husband but a passionate love for Annemarie Clarac-Schwarzenbach, a married Swiss scholar and writer for whom she felt an immediate affinity.[16]

Yesterday I read Havelock Ellis's *My Life*. His wife was an invert, and there was so much in her situation that is exactly my own. What a great man Ellis was! But even he could not help her at the last, and she went mad. I think about Annemarie often here, I shall always love her. I play Mahler and Schubert. I wonder if ever a woman will love me, and answer the part of me that so needs to be answered. But I ask so much, and expect to give so much—I am so deadly serious about such things.[17]

Schwarzenbach, who was famously connected to many female lovers, displayed an androgyny and "physical fearlessness," which fascinated McCullers.[18] Her infatuation consumed her imagination, drawing her attention away from her husband. When she could not spend time with Schwarzenbach, McCullers turned to bars and bourbon for comfort. Longing for meaningful companionship with others and obsessed with Schwarzenbach, she distanced herself from her husband.[19] Schwarzenbach's death in a 1942 bicycle accident devastated McCullers, leaving her divorced from her husband and permanently separated from a passionate love.[20]

Because she had no children, and her milieu, "dominated by gay editors and writers," allowed for unconventional freedoms, McCullers indulged her troubled mind.[21] Her class status consistently offered access to privileged outlets where her queer appearance and interests were a matter of fascination. At private parties, in her travel to Europe, and during summers at the Yaddo artist colony in Saratoga Springs, New York, she surrounded herself with bohemians who, like Diamond, sympathized and supported her as she grappled with her loneliness, mental health, and queer emotions.[22]

To Diamond, McCullers expressed substantial concern when Reeves McCullers faced a term of service in World War II. His impending military requirement would play a role in Carson and Reeves's eventual reunification. Yet in the four years between their divorce and remarriage, Reeves McCullers enjoyed an intimate relationship with Diamond. Carson McCullers loved Diamond but was also aware of a deep connection between the two men, writing to Diamond, "I don't know just what your relation is with each other . . . and I would not ask. I only sensed that there was something for me to withdraw from."[23] Queer desire surrounded McCullers and shaped her view of the world.

Because of her class status, her occasionally forgiving (and also queer) husband, and her artistic community, McCullers did not need to navigate a path for her queer sexuality in her work or in her home. Yet she still sought companionship and understanding in her search for female lovers. She found it in her passionate friendship with Diamond and in her readings of Ellis. To label her as a lesbian would be inaccurate. McCullers struggled with queer sexual desire but without a connection to the growing and visible queer community during the 1940s.

What Elizabeth Lapovsky Kennedy styles a world of quiet lesbianism seems the best description for McCullers's gender fluidity and sexual outsider status.[24] On the cusp of a burgeoning bar culture for lesbians and gay men in the economically resurgent wartime and postwar South, McCullers tied herself to an increasingly dated view of lesbian desire as inversion inspired by Ellis. Antiquated ideologies about gender roles were in flux during the 1940s and 1950s, offering an increased visibility for women as workers and individuals independent from husbands and families. Yet McCullers chose a queer life outside of the traditional postwar queer narrative.

Through her writing, McCullers challenged the stringent gender prescriptions of the time, while she existed outside of an embryonic queer social world in her native Georgia. As Lori J. Kenschaft argues, "In her texts, homoerotic interests do not form a basis for human connection and collective activity as they do in many actual lesbian and gay male communities," and when she connected with other gay people, it was often with gay men.[25] McCullers did not embrace an accidentally activist, or drastic, lesbian identity.[26] Similarly, the southern activist Lillian Smith and her longtime partner Paula Snelling (contemporaries of McCullers) lived a life of quiet lesbianism. Unlike McCullers, Smith remained in Georgia throughout her life, where she hid her lesbian desire. Margaret Rose Gladney endured a "scholar's nightmare" as she worked to fully integrate Smith's public life with her private. Throughout their relationship, Smith and Snelling burned their letters to one another to protect their love. Although Snelling affirmed their intimacy in later years, and notably after Smith's death, Gladney struggled to place the women in historical context while Smith's family expressed their disdain for the work. In the end, Gladney named Smith's sexual desire as part of a complicated and complete life.[27] In Jenn Shapland's "autobiography" of McCullers, the author admits to appropriating Carson for her research cause. I am doing this too, because, as Shapland notes, we must often find lesbianism (and certainly southern lesbianism) housed in straight narratives where a lesbian identity has been "dismissed" as a possibility. This is true of so many queer subjects in the 1940s and 1950s.[28]

McCullers did not seek public opportunities to explore her affections for other women. Instead, she processed her queer mental turmoil through the characters in her novels. Shapland unveils McCullers's queer desire through conversations exchanged with her therapist, Mary Mercer, whom she also loved.[29] As an emerging writer and participant in an avant-garde artist community, Carson McCullers found space to be queer. Perhaps she was at a disadvantage in corralling her attractions for women because she existed separate from a lesbian community, but it is also true that she could not afford the risks of a public lesbian identity—and perhaps did not want one.

In the 1940s, Mary Hutchinson and Dorothy King began a passionate relationship, lasting until Hutchinson's death in 1970. Their life together paints a picture rarely seen in lesbian history of the 1940s and 1950s—an intimate sexual bond existing outside of a queer bar scene and outside of a butch-femme community. Born in 1906, Hutchinson grew up in Atlanta during the 1920s. She was a successful artist who departed for New York City in the 1930s and spent several years in Franklin D. Roosevelt's Works Progress Administration's Federal Art Project as an art teacher. As an artist, she was most proud of her affiliation with the Independent Painters and Sculptors of America in New York City. Through this organization, she realized her belief that art should be taken out of the "luxury class" and placed squarely in the domain of daily life.[30] Hutchinson had her first solo art show in New York in 1934. In Atlanta, the newly formed High Museum of Art celebrated Hutchinson's work, holding her first solo exhibit there in 1932 and purchasing two of her works in 1934.[31] Her paintings often featured everyday people, frequently including African American subjects. In fact, she would maintain a working relationship with Atlanta's Black artists throughout her life.[32]

While in New York, Hutchinson had significant lesbian relationships with two women: Joanna Lanza and Ruth Layton, sharing ten years of her life with the latter. In letters home to her mother in Georgia, Hutchinson was effusive about her attraction to Lanza, expressing to Minnie Belle Hutchinson that she did not want, and would outright reject, a marital relationship with a man.[33] Throughout her life Hutchinson was enmeshed with her mother, sharing frequent letters and openly displaying her emotional concerns. She credited her mother with helping to ignite her passion for art, and their mutual affection was a constant point of discussion in press interviews and personal letters.

Shortly after the Works Progress Administration came to an end in 1943, Hutchinson returned to Atlanta to be with her mother at the time of her father's death. Her return coincided with the beginning of the end of her ten-year relationship with Ruth Layton.[34] Upon her arrival in Atlanta, Hutchinson actively pursued a relationship with Dorothy King, a music teacher.[35] Hutchinson managed both her emerging desire for King and a bombardment of affection from her previous partner, Ruth Layton. The result was a dramatic triangle of desire punctuated by Layton's struggle with mental illness, her efforts to understand her own sexuality, and her partnership with Pete, a man who would eventually become her husband. Layton desperately wanted to care romantically for Pete but noted to Hutchinson that "he is not as good looking as you are and does not have lovely eyes as you do." Layton expressed to Hutchinson the hope that "someday we will be together" and often sought Hutchinson's reassurance that she wanted this future too. By 1946, Hutchinson had established a passionate relationship with King in Atlanta. Nevertheless, Layton was excited to visit her there. Cautious in her planning, Layton wrote, "Frankly, do you want me to come. I can cancel my reservation and get my money back if you don't. On the other hand if I get frightened about it and just can't make it the last minute, you will have to understand. I do feel strange about it and afraid at times. I can't explain it all very well but it would be so nice to see you." Appended to her typewritten letter was Layton's handwritten plea: "Just a sec. Rec. your letter. Answer me *truthfully*—Will it be hard on Dorothy or on you & Dorothy if I come? I realize I must not interfere with anything—it would not be fair from any point of view. Be sure about this because I am nothing for future & she may be."[36] Although the details of the Hutchinson-Layton-King triangle are not entirely clear, Layton remained an important figure in both Hutchinson's and King's lives. Layton penned an emotional letter at the time of Hutchinson's death, noting that she missed Mary "deeply over the years since we lived in New York."[37]

Like McCullers, Layton struggled with what love, expectations, passion, and sexual desire would mean in her life. In considering her relationship with Pete, she pined, "I love him in the incarnation of you and for his kindness and constant re-assurance. But I love you with my soul and when I went to live with you I knew then I would never truly love anyone else. I also knew that you did not and were not capable of loving me as deeply."[38] In passionate letters to Hutchinson in Atlanta, Layton promised Hutchinson to not tell Pete about their relationship, hoping to savor it on her own and to protect herself from potential heterosexual backlash. These poignant and occasionally painful struggles to forge loving relationships, face their sexual desires, and balance their emotions with the daily expectations of heteronormative respectability demonstrate the emotional turmoil and sacrifice of privileged white women who loved women in the middle of the twentieth century.

Although Hutchinson and King would eventually live together with Minnie Belle Hutchinson in Atlanta, for the first few years of their relationship both often resided separately with their mothers.[39] This living arrangement was certainly characteristic of the 1940s and in keeping with socially appropriate norms for unmarried women, who were expected to live at home until marriage or as singletons. Daily letters traveled the approximately thirty-eight miles between Hutchinson in Atlanta and King in Newnan, Georgia. They lived for occasional visits with one another, as both women struggled with the responsibilities of caring for their mothers. Attention to their mothers was a constant in their lives, as both regularly shared information on their mothers and exchanged good wishes, food, and gifts from each woman's mother to the other. At the close of their letters, both regularly communicated affection from their mothers to each other. Hutchinson begged for King to write more letters and arrange more visits. The four women often visited together, even sharing holidays together. The two daughters longed for more time together as a couple, but their obligations to their mothers did not inhibit their ability to foster a loving and passionate relationship.

Remarkably candid intimacies occasionally seep through the lines of Hutchinson's letters. Hutchinson hoped to soon be sleeping with King— "as it should be"—and she imagined during one of their frequent separations what it would be like to have King there with her to "take her in" on her shoulder.[40] She conveyed her love to King by signing letters with "more feeling from me than can be spelled by a four letter word— or any word" and expressed her pain at their separations: "miss you so much it hurts."[41] On one occasion, after a missed opportunity to talk by phone, Hutchinson was blatantly coy: "I was so disappointed not to speak to you at least on Saturday, even if I didn't see you. It was my regular Saturday tub time,—and I was *really* all wet!"[42] A sassy warning in another letter states, "As for you, . . . I'll tell *you* a thing or two when you get back about what I think of *you*, and I won't stand for any back talk, either."[43] Hutchinson teased King with playful comments about sharing meals and feeding her by "slipping you a mouthful now and then," or wishing that King would feed her cake by hand.[44] Hutchinson's references to "Jessie," a domestic worker who performed various tasks for the

Hand-drawn doodle by Mary E. Hutchinson. This is typical of the fanciful drawings that Hutchinson regularly included in her correspondence with Dorothy King. Mary E. Hutchinson and Dorothy King Papers, 1900–1988, Manuscript Collection No. 1096, Stuart A. Rose Manuscript, Archives, and Rare Book Library, Emory University, Atlanta.

household, confirms her upper-class status. During a holiday separation, Hutchinson wrote to King, "Jessie has just rung the bell for our warmed up turkey—I can hardly bear to go in without you. In fact, I won't. I will just take you with me!"[45] Perhaps most captivating in the letters from Hutchinson to King are her skilled artistic iterations of her declarations of love: signing her letters with often swirling versions of "MTE," meaning More Than Ever, and fanciful doodles of flowers, hearts, and King's name.

Hutchinson's career as an artist was successful and nationally recognized, but her identity as a southern woman upstaged her identity as an artist in southern newspaper coverage. The *Atlanta Constitution* claimed her as an "Atlanta girl" while anticipating the High Museum of Art's acquisition of two of her paintings, and South Carolina's *Spartanburg Herald-Journal* featured Hutchinson in a 1940 article series titled "Southern Accent in New York."[46] The opening of the article mentioned her "disheveled and freckled" appearance and her "blue slacks," along with her "blonde, tall and lanky" features.[47] By highlighting her decision to wear pants, the article noted a fashion choice with significant implications for women. Hutchinson wore pants in 1940, prior to the common practice of women publicly wearing pants during World War II, due to wartime factory work. "Pants panic" multiplied during the war because the attire denoted masculinity and possibly lesbianism.[48]

Wearing slacks, though certainly more common, at least temporarily, during World War II, remained an issue of concern for lesbians, women in the South, and women in the United States generally. When lesbians wore slacks, however, it was understood as an assertion of butch identity, especially in the butch-femme bar culture of the 1940s and 1950s.[49] World War II created the opportunity for "lesbians to more openly express their erotic interest in women through their clothing. Since all women were now able to wear pants to work and to purchase them in stores off the rack, butches who wore pants only in the privacy of their homes in the 1930s could now wear them on the street."[50] In the 1950s, wearing pants was a butch signal in the lesbian community. And butch lesbians were culturally perceived to be the most dangerous to normative gender roles.[51] When describing her identity in dating relationships, one lesbian recalled that when her partner wore dresses, "I obviously was the butch since I had on pants."[52] Hutchinson continued to wear pants beyond the war. King worried about getting slacks for Hutchinson and hated for her to manage this task alone. This further signals a butch or masculine identity for Hutchinson, as King viewed the purchasing of the pants to be her caretaking duty in their relationship. When Hutchinson and McCullers wore slacks, they challenged the long-standing expectation that the white southern woman was a southern belle. With the belle label came the expectation of femininity, often signaled by dresses or skirts.

In spite of the explosion of the gay bar subculture taking place in cities like New York and San Francisco, which according to Lillian Faderman made it "immeasurably easier to be a lesbian" immediately following the war, some women who were "far from the nascent pockets of the lesbian subculture" would maintain "the innocence of an earlier era" in their relationships.[53] Hutchinson and King maintained this innocence, avoiding the label of lesbian. In describing a similar coupling in Nebraska, Faderman shows that the pathology associated with lesbianism did not jibe with the affectionate and passionate relationships that women shared. One woman's "knowledge of the medical texts that described lesbianism as a physiological or psychological problem gave her no information about her own experience, which she knew was not sick, and did nothing to reveal to her the growing society of women who were creating a lifestyle around their affectional preferences."[54] After World War II, the pathologizing of lesbianism continued in the Cold War era of heightened gender conformity and consensus.[55] The 1950s were not propitious years for women to explore or claim a lesbian identity, as an increased focus on the lesbian as a "sicko" abounded. Stoked by the newfound independence of women during World War II, a desperate need to return to normalcy drove the psychoanalytic argument that lesbianism was a condition to be cured and one that could never truly lead to fulfillment or satisfaction.[56]

Conformity in the Cold War era compounded the regional expectations of gender normativity for white southern women. Like McCullers, Hutchinson and King practiced what Elizabeth Lapovsky Kennedy termed "private lesbianism"—with no interest in moving their identities to a public space.[57] Restraint, respectability, and a quiet lesbianism defined their entire connection. For example, after Hutchinson's death, King reflected on their twenty-five-year interaction as lovers. She wrote a letter to herself expressing enormous grief and struggling with her inability to contain her emotions in the way Hutchinson would have wanted: "I must work to practice the restraint that she so naturally lived . . . because my continued lack of restraint could be so easily misunderstood—as indeed it might well already have been."[58] Their letters, and those of their other friends and lovers, often recall the coded and passionate language of Victorian-era female "friendships." As Carroll Smith-Rosenberg uncovered in her examination of the Victorian female world, women occupied an "emotional centrality" in each other's lives, gripped by "isolation and despair" when they were separated.[59] Hutchinson and King's letters demonstrate these same sentiments a generation later. Scholars note that we should not relegate these women to the nineteenth century, as "remnants" of the Victorian era, but instead should see them as something altogether different.[60] Their privacy seems an obvious but also purposeful choice; it was not necessarily about shame but an acceptance of the rules of respectability. Their lives were not about public activism or identity claiming, yet many women, not all of them lesbians, participated in Hutchinson and King's community as part of this quiet lesbian world.[61] By refusing a visible lesbian identity, Hutchinson and King enjoyed comfort, "status[,] and power" in the female world of daughters, mothers, and teachers.[62]

Mary Hutchinson's decision to live with her mother helped keep her femininity, and the perception of heteronormativity, intact even as she challenged some feminine appearance codes in her personal presentation. She longed for time alone with King, writing, "If I could just see you and talk with you, without it being a mater party."[63] The possibility of time alone together for the couple increased with King's purchase of a new car. It seems purposeful that the particular letters offering careful descriptions of this important acquisition were preserved and passed on through kinship networks orchestrated by King, because in comparison to Hutchinson's letters to King, there are very few letters from King that remain.[64]

King rang in the New Year with the purchase of a 1954 light blue Chevrolet and was eager to share minute financial details with Hutchinson. The thorough discussion of the financial arrangements regarding the car suggests that in spite of their middle- or upper-class existence, financial security was not easily attained for women who remained unattached to men—especially when performing monetary transactions. In the end, King had to rely on an uncle to ensure the purchase, which included a $356 down payment with a trade-in and a $1,300 bank loan. She cautioned Hutchinson not to share the details of the financial arrangement. King noted that the new Chevrolet would have "absolutely no 'fandangles' of any kind . . . no clocks—no ash tray."[65] But she was eager to replace her other car and clearly eager for Hutchinson to approve. A car often provided many lovers a private space to enjoy sexual intimacy, and King excitedly anticipated a new year and perhaps the opportunities a new car would bring to her relationship with Hutchinson. The car represented independence to King, as it did to the American automobile consumer of the 1950s.

The impact of the automobile in the South was markedly different than in more established cities in the Northeast. In a growing and industrializing midsize metropolis like Atlanta, the city adapted its built environment and infrastructure based on the needs of automobile transport.[66] At Atlanta's Piedmont Park, for many years a site for intimate connections, automobiles became a major concern in the 1950s. Heterosexual couples parked here to engage in intimate activity, which brought an increased visibility to gay men who also appropriated the park's space for cruising and sex.[67] In fact, according to John Howard, by installing lights in Piedmont Park in 1956 in an attempt to curb primarily heterosexual intimacies, the city literally exposed the park as a site for homosexual intimacies as well. Exposing gay men in the park ultimately created a larger sense of gay community in general, as these men were able to rally around a shared identity in their search for sexual space.[68] Yet this visibility would not have been possible for lesbians, as their very presence in a public space without a male escort would have raised suspicion. Though increased policing would challenge gay men's ability to use the park as a public sexual space, women alone in the park after dark would be problematic largely because they were women without men, no matter their behavior or activity. Dorothy King's new Chevrolet allowed her independent, safe, and reliable travel to be with Mary Hutchinson, but their visibility as two women without male escorts remained socially constrained.

Middle- and upper-class queer white women might be read as invisible lesbians, yet their invisibility was a choice and often a privilege. Upper- and middle-class women could afford safe space for their queer lives and did not mix across class lines or venture to sketchy areas where bars existed.[69] But safe space could also be restrictive, limiting options for lesbian socializing. It is unlikely that Hutchinson and King frequented women's bars in 1940s and 1950s Atlanta. Avoiding the bar scene would be necessary to maintain their jobs. This was of concern particularly for teachers working with children, as both women did. Much of the social world inhabited by King and Hutchinson was private and primarily heterosexual. Public and private, heterosexual and homosexual spaces were fluid before the queer activism of the late 1960s and the ironclad queer closet. Kennedy argues that "all sexuality was a private matter" at this time, which allowed quiet lesbians to enjoy some privileges of the heterosexual world while operating under an upper-class assumption of heterosexuality.[70] Mary Hutchinson's papers happen to include intimate snapshots of her vibrant and passionate relationships with Dorothy King and her previous lover Ruth Layton. Her papers are primarily those of an artist, a southern woman artist who identified herself as such but did not openly identify as a lesbian. Yet King and Hutchinson seemed to have enjoyed a vibrant network of friends, mostly women and a few men. One brief reference from a New Year's letter suggested that King and Hutchinson shared friendship with another lesbian and her partner—a partner who would be referred to simply as a "friend," just as King would refer to Hutchinson as she grieved her death in letters.[71] Their letters suggest strong familial ties and support, a social life, and a passionate love, which they chose not to label. Where some lesbians found support networks in the bars, King and Hutchinson built their own in postwar upper-class Atlanta.[72]

Hutchinson's story is strikingly different from the stories we know of working-class white lesbians during World War II. She and Carson McCullers participated in a world of white privilege and quiet lesbianism. Both sought the comfort and anonymity of the world of the outsider, which in the South often meant Black lives. Hutchinson portrayed Black life in her art and worked within the Black art community when she returned to Atlanta. She judged African American art shows and served as an art consultant at the West Hunter Branch Library, "Atlanta's African American Carnegie Library."[73] This relationship is evident in the pages of the *Atlanta Daily World*, Atlanta's oldest Black newspaper, where Hutchinson made several appearances.[74] The newspaper covered Hutchinson's show at the Castle Galleries, located in an area of historic ties to the Atlanta arts community, where her art included "Negroes used as subjects . . . on their own merit." Of particular note in the newspaper's coverage was *Duet*, her painting of a "handsome couple." The writer celebrated Hutchinson's skill by noting her "marvelous collection of prize-winning Negro subjects."[75] Both McCullers and Hutchinson connected the outsider status of gender and race. Using Black subjects to demonstrate this bond, they built their lives within the margins of southern respectability.[76]

On a stormy Atlanta night at the Bobby Jones Golf Course on Northside Drive, two young women shared their first kiss together: "And, boy, ooh! All the pins and needles, all the carrying on!" Ginny Boyd's mind raced with excitement and confusion as the driver of the car asked her, "Have you ever been in love with a woman?" Boyd managed to squeak out, "I think so." She had cared for girls in junior high school, was always protective of them, and even used church as an opportunity to hold hands and pursue a neighborhood classmate. But on this stormy night, now she knew. "All these obvious things that I had done and felt, didn't know what I was doing, didn't understand why. All this is running back and forth through my head." The year was 1942, and at the age of eighteen, Ginny Boyd suddenly understood her attraction for women.[77]

Boyd was born on May 4, 1924, in Atlanta and died there on March 28, 2006. She graduated from high school in 1942 as the class valedictorian and was soon working for Southern Bell Telephone Company, which offered Boyd her first real chance to connect with a woman, date her, and ultimately understand her own intimate desires. As early as elementary and junior high school, Boyd wanted to be with girls, but she had "no idea at the time"; it just seemed natural. "Let's see, I was in the fourth, fifth, and sixth grades. And she was a year behind me. I'd walk her to school. I'd help her with her homework. Turned out her mother was an alcoholic. So she spent almost all her time down at our house. And I protected her. Oh, I tell you, had no idea what I was doing!" But while at Southern Bell, she met a woman who would ultimately lead her to that first kiss on Atlanta's Northside Drive.

I went to work at Southern Bell in the accounting department, and there was a girl that worked there . . . she and I just sort of hit it off. And she said, "Let's go to a movie one night." Sounded great to me. So we went to a movie, and we held hands through the movie. I tell you, when I look back, everybody that came in contact with me knew, must've thought I was the dumbest human that ever walked around on two legs. So, bless their hearts. So we went back to a movie . . . the next week.[78]

Ginny Boyd's coming-of-age story is similar to other white southern working-class women's stories of the 1940s and 1950s. In some ways, the paths she followed were typical. Boyd made choices on these paths, however, that led to love, connection, and intimacy with other women. Although a traditional southern woman, she challenged that mold balancing desire for women with her other identities. Boyd, a new kind of Rosie the Riveter, illustrates the story of Atlanta's women in the World War II era and highlights a southern lesbian past, intertwined with the industrial development of the New South.

In the same year that she came to understand her love for women, at the age of eighteen, Boyd shot herself in the back. Overcome by the painful nature of her relationship with a lover and after a verbally abusive exchange, she shot her lover's gun into her own back. "I know that sounds ridiculous," recalled Boyd, "but I picked the gun up, walked in there where she was talking on the telephone, and I had it in my hand here, leaning up against my back, with my thumb against the trigger. And I walked in there, and I said, 'Will you please tell my parents that I love them?'"[79] If this relationship was indicative of what it would be like to date women, Boyd decided she would rather die. After her arduous recovery she could have returned to work at Southern Bell where her boss held her job during her recuperation. Instead, she sought work "where there wouldn't be people that knew" her, probably fearing rumors after the shooting.[80] Boyd threw herself into her work at what would later become Lockheed Martin, the Bell Aircraft Corporation.

Bell Aircraft offered better pay and improved advancement opportunities when compared with other employment options for women. The Bell workforce also included a relatively high concentration of women, employing approximately 10,000 women out of 28,000 workers during the war. They were, according to Clifford Kuhn, "Atlanta's versions of Rosie the Riveter."[81] World War II radically altered the economic landscape in Atlanta with the help of the war industry effort. Not only did manufacturing corporations, like Bell Aircraft, bring new jobs, but the influx of soldiers who passed through Atlanta on the way to Fort McPherson, located at the edge of the city limits, and Fort Benning, in nearby Columbus, Georgia, stimulated Atlanta's local economy. Black workers were able to move into positions previously unavailable to them because of their race. As a result, they enjoyed an increase in earnings, which boosted their economic participation in Atlanta's growing wartime economy.[82] The importance of Bell Aircraft to the Atlanta metro region cannot be overstated, as it permanently altered nearby Marietta, Georgia, from rural county seat to industrial Sun Belt center. Bell's new work opportunities for women also permanently altered, and queered, Boyd's life by placing her in a same-sex work environment where she built intimate relationships with women.[83]

In 1945, Boyd left Atlanta and Bell Aircraft to join the military. Segregated by race and gender, the same-sex military environment offered her liaisons with other women under the umbrella of her white privilege. Like many of her female contemporaries, Ginny Boyd would find opportunities to pursue her attraction for women at Fort Des Moines, Iowa, the first training location for the Women's Army Corps (WAC), and Camp Atterbury in Indiana.[84] She joined the WAC at the age of twenty-one, training as a surgical technician. Her goal was to impress the base leadership in order to earn weekend passes. For example, when she served as an acting sergeant of her barracks during her training, she aimed to challenge a general who was strongly opposed to women in military service. An authoritarian with other women in her barracks, Boyd recalled, "The girls hated my guts, because I'd make them work their butts off when we were gonna have a white glove inspection. Out of the three barracks we were the only ones that passed, so we got a weekend pass to go into town and the other two barracks had to stay on base. So all of a sudden they couldn't buy me enough beers."[85] Boyd used these passes to travel off base where she would socialize with women who were "gay" and those who were "straight as a stick." She sought out clubs that were considered off-limits and occasionally found female officers there dancing with each other. She would join them in dancing, where their shared secret was understood: "You don't tell on them, and they don't tell on you."[86] Boyd participated in a coded understanding of queer urban spaces that allowed her to locate like-minded women and engage in erotic behavior.

Although serving in the army allowed for queer opportunities, life in the WAC also posed danger for lesbians. Even when enjoying sexual connections off base, lesbians could never abandon caution.[87] A handbook distributed at Fort Des Moines warned against public dancing with other women while in uniform or wearing haircuts that were too masculine. The butch lesbian faced more danger and punishment than the femme, who was thought to be helpless at the hands of an aggressive butch. Perceived mannishness was believed to be the biggest threat in the WAC. The 1943 handbook for women at Fort Des Moines labeled "'mannish haircuts' and 'dancing together in public places in uniform' as 'taboo.'"[88] Masculinity was a particular problem at the Fort Oglethorpe WAC post in Georgia, possibly heightened by cultural perceptions related to southern femininity.[89] Religious observers were dispatched to Fort Des Moines and Fort Oglethorpe, where the biggest lesbian investigation occurred. Investigators aimed to ensure the training sites were appropriate, respectable, and spiritually safe spaces for women.[90]

Efforts to quash lesbian activity in World War II not only were unsuccessful but sometimes served to foster lesbian identities and communities. When lesbian Pat Bond arrived at Fort Oglethorpe, she was glad to be included among a group of recognizably butch women.[91] Warnings about mannishness issued at Fort Des Moines were similarly issued at Camp Lejeune in North Carolina, but they were often ignored once basic training was over. Lesbians in the WAC developed cliques, identifying a community of women with whom they could socialize and develop intimacy and who also could be trusted to protect acts and conversations that might be labeled as homosexual.[92] Although it was clear to Boyd who was gay and who was not, she worked hard to claim ignorance when pushed on the issue: "They couldn't force me to say what I knew."[93] She used the space for her intimate opportunities and protected it from the army's threats and witch hunts.

Women in the corps were charged with maintaining feminine respectability and avoiding masculinity, which was the biggest concern for the army.[94] The sexual respectability required by the army focused on keeping heterosexual desire in check but often did not consider the possibility of same-sex desire among women. Lesbians experienced the most freedom in the army while off base. They moved freely in cities, even in masculine uniforms with pants, and were able to maintain their respectability required by the army because they were not interested in seeking male company.[95] Two women renting a hotel room did not raise suspicion, allowing lesbians the freedom for erotic and intimate connections. This intimacy was substantially harder for Black women or interracial couples to enjoy, because hotels did not rent to Black people. Most of these couples relied on word of mouth to locate safe spaces willing to rent to Black women or mixed couples, such as one woman at Fort Oglethorpe who remembered finding out about a tourist site out of town where mixed-race couples could connect.[96] Queer Black women in the WAC faced segregation and racism on base and in the community where they were stationed. Although the army committed to following the racial codes of the surrounding communities where bases were located, this was not the case at Fort Des Moines, where women were segregated by race in eating and sleeping areas in spite of Iowa's law against segregation at the time.[97]

A national and gendered "coming-out experience" for lesbians and gay men, World War II set in motion a variety of cultural changes that permanently altered lesbian and gay social life.[98] Lesbians and gay men would bring newfound awareness of their sexuality home after the war, and in the South—as in other regions of the country—this was met with varying degrees of acceptance.[99] For lesbians, the war meant newly created jobs and "a social atmosphere which encouraged women's independence." Sudden control of leisure time and personal finances, as well as safer and "more congenial" urban spaces populated by women, moved "white lesbian social life from private networks to bars in the 1940s."[100] Although the culture of the home front during World War II may not have propelled all women who loved women into the public spaces of the bars, the women-only spaces in the civilian sphere allowed for increased visibility and independence. Socialization outside the home became a possibility for women without the risk of "endangering their reputations."[101] Boyd eagerly explored and found queer opportunities before her military service, yet she enjoyed more opportunities for a gay social life because of World War II. Boyd's story of her sexuality and military service during the war era is a classic example of the war's impact on white lesbians and gay men. Her life followed a familiar trajectory of paid work, military service, and a return to paid work in a city where a lesbian community could be found for those who had the drive to seek it out. The same-sex environments available during the war fostered opportunities for women and men to explore homosexual feelings and create public spaces for socializing. For Ginny Boyd, World War II brought dramatic changes both in her career and in her ability to create sexual and deepening bonds with other women.

Boyd described herself as a protector of women while she served in the military, continuing her junior high interest in protecting bullied female classmates. She was a tough woman who was not afraid of being discovered as a lesbian. "You have to—to be afraid, you have to care.

And I didn't care. For a long, long—most of my life. After that—after shooting myself, I didn't care." Boyd dated women and actively sought their company while in the military. In describing her sexuality at the time, she actively chose the word "gay" instead of "butch," "dyke," or "femme," labels that Boyd dismissed. "I've never wanted to be a man, in other words. I've never wanted to be a male substitute. I liked a woman because she was a woman. And I wanted her to like me because I was a woman. Not a male substitute, or vice versa."[102] Navigating the military expectations of respectability and femininity, Boyd engaged in masculine behaviors as an acting sergeant demanding excellence from her peers and as a suitor courting women while off base. She navigated these roles and gained the approval of her male superiors, exploiting the WAC's opportunities for lesbians and maintaining the femininity necessary to avoid military suspicion.

Fear of mannishness among women was also prevalent in civilian spaces during the war. With the southern belle ideal portrayed as the cure, the dramatic 1942 *New York Times* article "Wives—but without Husbands" detailed the supposedly sad state of women abandoned on the home front during World War II. One of the nameless women in the article, who worked as a secretary in a wartime munitions factory, bemoaned her husband's exposure to the flirtations of the stereotypical southern belle while he was stationed at Fort McClellan in Alabama: "'If a marriage weathers this, it's foolproof,' declares a 21-year-old bride, with a drab aside on 'the Southern belles' in Alabama, where her husband of three months is stationed."[103] The article demonstrates a tendency to automatically associate the South with southern belles—eager to steal other women's husbands with their wily, feminine charm. A 1945 *Washington Post* article portrayed southern belles as the ultimate solution to the wartime threat of "aggressive" and masculine women: "Servicemen who have been complaining in magazines and in their own publications of American girls' self-absorption and aggressiveness may be heartened to know that social prophets foresee women here, as their marriage bargaining power declines, developing more of the continental social deference toward men. Also, surveys of women both in service and in war plants indicate that postwar competition for husbands will top that for jobs. Certainly the present craze for feminine finery suggests a revival of southern belles rather than an upsurge of Amazons."[104] Women's work during World War II threatened white women's femininity, but once they put their "Rosie the Riveter" experience behind them, southern women confronted a distinct expectation of femininity attached to the southern belle myth.

When Boyd returned to Atlanta, she continued to navigate the cultural prescriptions of gender, finding social space to resume her same-sex liaisons. In describing her time with a nurse named "Bebe," Boyd refused to label their connection a "relationship." Instead she described their involvement as intimate, and there was plenty of "fooling around. We were just having a good time. And we would go out with a lot of different people. We'd go to all these different places. I think the main place that I can remember going, that I knew was where gay people congregated was out on Peachtree."[105] This place was the Tick Tock Grill.

Ginny Boyd "practically lived" at the Tick Tock Grill because she knew that gay people would be there. From 1948 to 1959, the Tick Tock, located at 1935 Peachtree Road Northwest in Atlanta, was owned by Martha Louise Allen, but Ginny knew her as "Lou." When Allen's father had a heart attack, Ginny waited tables (something she had never done before), collected the money, and closed the restaurant at the end of the night. Boyd was not employed by Allen, but the owner was comfortable leaving her business in Boyd's hands. Allen trusted Boyd, and Boyd was comfortable at the Tick Tock. It was "like a Waffle House," a diner with a bar, booths, a jukebox, and a short-order cook. The Tick Tock offered Boyd and her peers—nurses, interns, and office workers—a place to be gay. "When there was nobody straight in there you'd get up and dance in the little bit of room you had on the dance floor, you know. And, oh, I did love to dance." Boyd "got a lot of mileage out of dancing," and she danced sexily, slowly, and with "close bodily contact." In spite of the occasional "stray straight couple" that might wander in, the Tick Tock Grill was a site for lesbian community and connection.[106]

The Tick Tock Grill was not strictly a lesbian bar, nor did it advertise to gay clientele in any way. Yet, Boyd's memories of a restaurant resurrect a southern lesbian history that could just as easily have been laid to rest with Boyd in 2006. The Tick Tock was one of many places where alternative sexual identities were often unrecognizable to a heterosexual majority.[107] When Ginny Boyd, a native Atlantan, danced sexily with other women at the Tick Tock Grill in 1950s Atlanta, she was a rebel and certainly not a traditional southern belle. Boyd's behavior at the Tick Tock challenges the historical monolith of southern women's history: a history about straight women, often focused on women's activism, a history that has only recently included Black women, and one that has yet to expand its definition to include gay women.[108]

Boyd's memories highlight a largely white southern lesbian history. The majority of Boyd's social public spaces during the 1940s and 1950s were probably limited to white patrons and heterosexual women with male escorts. Finding a safe and comfortable place to dance was vital. She frequented a heterosexual bar near downtown Atlanta where a police officer (related to a woman in Boyd's group of friends) offered protection from straight men's unwanted attention. She also spent time at an African American bar, which provided a safe and accepting space. Boyd eventually bought a house not far from the same area, in a subdivision "available only to ex-service people," but unfortunately did not recall the name of the Black night club.[109] In retelling the story of her time there, the importance of her white privilege—her separation from Black people generally and Black lesbians specifically—is clear. "There was a Black night club close by there, and we'd all sort of gravitate with, finally wind up with one or two cars with eight or ten or twelve people [laughs], and we'd go to that Black night club a lot. And dance with each other." When asked if "they" (the Black patrons) minded the white lesbians coming in, Boyd said that they were so nice that "you'd have thought we were some kind of queens, you know."[110] It is possible that she and her friends were attracted to the Black bar not only because it was nearby and tolerant but also because there was no risk of being seen or bothered by other familiar white people.

Boyd and her friends took advantage of their whiteness in crossing this boundary, one that could not be crossed in the reverse.[111] Speaking to her place of white privilege, she remembered feeling welcome and that she and her friends were treated as "queens." Boyd used the Black night club as a low-risk venue for connecting with her gay friends. Boyd's social circle did not regularly include Black lesbians in the 1940s and 1950s, in part because the anonymity provided by Atlanta's growing populace extended only to white lesbians who could pass as appropriately feminine or seek out protection to enjoy straight spaces that would allow for lesbian socialization. This anonymity did not extend to Black lesbians who had to contend with their vulnerability both as Black women and as lesbians. Their visibility came at a higher risk.

Boyd eventually moved away from the neighborhood, but when she and her friends returned to the Black nightclub, "they" would "have a fit"—so happy to see Boyd—and "they" would just "carry on."[112] Perhaps Boyd and her friends viewed themselves as neutral on race, as Roey Thorpe suggests, assuming their "experience of living as lesbians in straight society created a common ground with lesbians of color that was more powerful than their differences."[113] In recalling her postwar lesbian life in Atlanta, Boyd remembered the names of the clubs that were primarily white but not the Black club they patronized. If she indeed felt a kinship with Black lesbians, it was not strong enough to earn a comparable place in her memory next to white queer spaces.

Elizabeth Lapovsky Kennedy and Madeline Davis have demonstrated the importance of private spaces for Black lesbian social life, which was necessary for safe queer social life.[114] In their study of Buffalo, New York, they connected these safe spaces to population growth, which provided greater anonymity for Black lesbian socialization. Atlanta was a city with a sizable Black population in the 1940s. By 1959, 36 percent of Atlanta's city population was African American.[115] Compared with Buffalo in 1940, Atlanta's Black population was almost six times greater—potentially allowing for a Black lesbian and gay community that was somewhat socially visible.[116] Black lesbians in Atlanta likely found public spaces for lesbian socializing in the 1940s and 1950s, perhaps at a nightclub like Boyd encountered or, more likely, at house parties. During this time period in Detroit, Thorpe found that lesbians of color relied primarily on house parties.[117] The same was probably true in Atlanta, where the Black population was sizable enough to support a substantial Black lesbian community but where Black women required spaces that allowed for social secrecy and did not threaten family networks.

Black bars in general would have been harder to open and maintain because of liquor licenses and the structures of Jim Crow in the South, limiting Black access to the full realm of citizenship and protections under the law.[118] White safety in lesbian bars did not equal Black safety. Boyd's connection with a protective cop would not have been possible for African American lesbians seeking safety at a straight bar. Even in queer-friendly spaces, like the Black nightclub Boyd frequented, the assumption was made that Black was a separate identity from lesbian, leaving Black women on the outside of community based on race and sexuality.[119] A Black lesbian bar would have been impossible to sustain in Buffalo due to the threat of racist violence. The same would also have been true in 1950s Atlanta and the South.[120]

Black lesbian anonymity and secrecy often meant separation from a white lesbian community and a Black straight community. Atlanta was "home to the South's largest population of college-educated African Americans and a crucial birthplace of the reform vision that drove the new generation of Black elites." This generation was "unified in its devotion to uplifting Black Atlantans."[121] W. E. B. Du Bois's "talented tenth," a concept embraced by Black elites at Morehouse College in Atlanta, acted as a liaison between the uneducated and less savory Black community and the white power structure. Respectability was crucial to Black elites, but this respectability of course would exclude the "legions of African Americans who did not and could not conform to the gender roles, public behavior, and economic activity deemed legitimate by bourgeois Americans but which the forces of Jim Crow white supremacy sought to prevent Black people from achieving."[122] Black lesbians seeking community through a public identity would be separated from members of a Black elite, who were focused on larger societal acceptability through uplift. They were shut out by their race from a burgeoning lesbian community and by their class from a powerful Black elite community.

The stories detailed in this chapter demonstrate the importance of class and race in southern lesbian communities. Kennedy and Davis illuminate the stark contrast between lesbian socializing and gay male social spaces, which frequently allowed for "erotic cross-class socializing." As women, lesbians had much to fear, whether white or Black, when it came to social exposure and job vulnerability.[123] Socializing across class lines, whether in bars or in other social settings, was not common for lesbians or most southerners during the 1940s and 1950s.[124] The bars that Boyd frequented were primarily populated by white working-class women— nurses, interns, and office workers.[125] Lesbian bar networks offered Boyd comfort and a space for her queer identity. These networks were increasingly vital to lesbians in the growing bar culture of the 1940s and 1950s. New social groups formed around bar communities allowed women to determine how they defined lesbian identity and how they would navigate the demands of family and a queer social life. Women who limited their queer social activities to a private world rarely encountered these issues, according to Kennedy and Davis's research.[126] But perhaps such a community would have provided queer affirmation for Carson McCullers, a confirmation that she could find only in scholarly texts on inversion. Even in their private networks, white women like McCullers, Mary Hutchinson, and Dorothy King likely considered ways to balance their social networks and their sexuality. It is hard to say whether this balancing act was agreeable to them, but certainly they strategized about ways to create small arenas of support for their lesbian identities—even if they were indeed private. Their paths were significantly different because their social status dictated the types of social spaces that they would frequent.

While it is true that public lesbian socializing defied southern gender norms, whether or not working-class white lesbians like Ginny Boyd consciously meant to challenge society is a separate issue. Similarly, we should not dismiss the challenges that women like Hutchinson and King and McCullers posed to southern gender norms, even if not always in a public venue. Claiming public bar space was not the only way to challenge heterosexual dominations of social spaces. Choosing to live as an independent woman, without being married to a man, as Hutchinson and King did, or choosing to wear cropped hair and masculine dress, like McCullers and Hutchinson did, sent a different kind of societal message, as well as a powerful internal message to lesbians in different social classes who chose these paths.

The less visible the claim to a lesbian identity, the less visible the lives of women who desired the intimate company of other women become. Historical research on lesbians often depends on a personal commitment to lesbian visibility—a commitment that lands subjects in an archive or leads one to participate in an oral history research project specifically focused on lesbian or gay topics. Women who were socially prominent, like McCullers and Hutchinson, or willing to be visible in the archive, like Boyd, are most likely to appear in lesbian histories. The coming chapters highlight visible manifestations of lesbian identity in the dynamic post–World War II South. They focus on stories privileged in the archives, which include women who were willing to participate in an increasingly public lesbian sphere. Personal choices to join these activist movements or to participate in a growing and identifiable bar culture, coupled with the pace of economic and demographic change, defined opportunities for lesbian community. Political activism and engagement in lesbian separatism merged in the coming decades. As the next chapter shows, lesbians created spaces and visible activisms that they shared across regional borders in the growing, soon-to-be Sun Belt cities of Atlanta and Charlotte.

*The next thing they know Piedmont
Tavern wasn't a straight bar anymore.*
—*Ginny Boyd*

2 CONNECTIONS

Vera Phillips ran Atlanta's Mrs. P's, also known as Piedmont Tavern. To those in the know, it was a lesbian hangout. Like the Tick Tock Grill, frequented by Ginny Boyd, Mrs. P's was an example of the bars and diners appropriated by white lesbians in the 1950s and 1960s. Phillips's husband, a preacher, would come in after delivering his sermon to help her manage the crowd. "It was fun," one patron recalled, "and we used to get a big kick out of Mr. P coming in from having preached earlier in the evenings, putting on that apron, taking off those . . . glasses, getting behind the counter, and Vera could say, 'I got help.' It was a small place, small place. It was a one man, one woman operation, then from that . . . it just became her business."[1] Although the bar eventually moved to Atlanta's Ponce de Leon Hotel, its lesbian clientele did not follow. Like most bar patrons, lesbians who were looking for a comfortable place to socialize and drink after softball games also prioritized convenience when it came time to locate the best watering hole.

Although queer bars sometimes served as sites of activism, most women in Atlanta and Charlotte stopped at the bar seeking comfort and anonymity in a chosen queer community, but not necessarily an activist or even a concerned one.[2] As one gay North Carolinian noted, "'Even when, on Thursday of Gay Pride Week, there was trouble over the bar's liquor license . . . was there a riot anywhere near that of the Stonewall? Hardly. Everybody simply went up to the other bar in Chapel Hill for the weekend and resigned themselves to the circumstances during the week.'"[3] In their research on feminist activism, Finn Enke notes that "the movement was built by more than the people who embraced the name."[4] The same is at least partially true in the lesbian South. Some activists proudly claimed labels and welcomed visibility, while some simply sought comfort, convenience, and anonymity. If taking up public space to forge erotic same-sex connections connotes activist behavior, then many women were accidental activists. They paved a way for future organizing opportunities, but New South lesbians focused on daily survival and queer social connections.

The history of the gay bar is a history of making space—a history of creating public room for social interactions so that lesbians and gay men could find one another. Bars offer anonymity and same-sex spaces that allow lovers and friends the time and leisure to meet, build community, or simply share a drink after a long day of work or play. Bar-built social connections were essential to lesbian urban socializing, as historian John D'Emilio has observed, because bars served "as the only clearly identifiable collective manifestation of lesbian existence." In short, lesbian bars moved "lesbianism into the public sphere."[5] Prior to the 1960s, Elizabeth Lapovsky Kennedy and Madeline Davis argue, they were "truly the only places that lesbians had to socialize."[6] This chapter reveals how bar spaces offered community to some southern lesbians, how local newspapers helped women locate these spaces, and how money often defined access. As in other metropolitan regions in the decades following Prohibition, lesbians created community, forged queer identities, and developed lesbian consciousness in New South bar spaces.[7] These spaces were overwhelmingly white and occasionally imbued with southern tropes.

White lesbians built their bar communities on the necessity of disposable income, urban spatial access, and safe movement in city spaces. Black women did not enjoy these privileges. Compared with white women, Black women were especially vulnerable to police violence and arrest. They carefully negotiated a variety of obstacles based on race, class, and gender, and as a result of safety concerns and economic limitations, Black lesbians often socialized separately at house parties.[8] In places like Buffalo and Detroit, parties drew queer Black women from nearby cities where they constructed a queer Black entertainment marketplace.[9]

Audre Lorde recalled the segregation in New York City's midcentury lesbian scene, noting that Black house parties were vital for nurturing Black culture. For example, Black and white social spaces remained separate due in part to music differences. White music generally did not appeal to Black women for dancing and sexual connections.[10] At house parties—or dollar parties, as they were often called based on the one-dollar admission—Black women "circumvented the problems created by a racist, homophobic society."[11] Based on the sizable Black population in Atlanta at midcentury, party life for queer women there probably mirrored nightlife in Buffalo, Detroit, and New York City in that era. Private spaces remained economically important, and limited racial mixing occurred in urban environments.[12]

Black and white lesbians might have been the only Black and white women communicating with each other in New York City in the 1950s, Lorde recalled, and when they did mix at bars it encouraged a cohesive gay culture.[13] But while there was often a sense of shared gay community, especially by white women, this came at a price for Black women because it obscured "the distinctness of the Black experience."[14] For Lorde, an invisibility permeated her existence in racially mixed lesbian communities.[15] The perceived "sacred bond of gayness" sensed by white lesbians was insufficient for Lorde.[16] Black women did not find that a shared gay bond trumped their desire for the camaraderie of Black community. The "gay girls" of Lorde's world in the 1950s believed they were bound together against the outside "other" world. Even Lorde's white girlfriend believed that as lesbians, their shared oppression meant that "we're all niggers."[17] But as much as they hoped they could ignore the problems of the world, lesbianism did not free them from the divisions and boundaries of "capitalism, greed, racism, classism, etc."[18] In other words, lesbian community did not supersede the need for Black community—in spite of white women's belief that it did.

In mid-1960s Atlanta, when Scotti Hooper began frequenting white gay bars, she was turned off by the options for lesbians. She found Mrs. P's to be "awful," but in spite of the "rough" crowd there, Hooper wanted to go out "and meet friends and have a drink or whatever." Just down the street was a bar named Dupree's that Hooper remembered attracting "mostly women. I think guys were afraid to go in there, and I don't blame them. It was just rough, dykey women." The first location of Dupree's Grill was at 640 Glen Iris Drive, Northeast, in Atlanta, and when the bar moved, it relocated to 715 Ponce de Leon Avenue, just a short walk around the corner, where it hosted "masculine" and "butch" women. Both spots were in Atlanta's Old Fourth Ward, a largely African American neighborhood less than two miles from the Auburn Avenue birthplace of Martin Luther King Jr. By the 1960s, the once-thriving neighborhood was in disrepair, due in part to highway construction and an exodus of middle- and upper-class Black residents.[19] White women in Atlanta, and in the South generally, were taught to avoid being alone in public, but especially in Black areas like the Old Fourth Ward.[20]

Being at a bar "in the mid-twentieth century no longer defined a woman as beyond the pale," as John D'Emilio has demonstrated, but in the South it defied a particular brand of white respectable femininity and "bore connotations of disreputable behavior."[21] This "disreputable behavior," combined with the likely racial and sexual tensions created by white women cavorting in a predominantly African American Atlanta neighborhood, is indicative of the risks that some white women took to find companionship. The "tough bar lesbian," described by Kennedy and Davis as "street-wise and able to handle a difficult environment," aligns with the type of women whom oral history narrators remember at Dupree's in Atlanta.[22] Rough bars often meant working-class bars and integrated spaces. Racial mixing took place among the "tough" lesbian bar crowd of the 1950s in Buffalo, New York, and occasionally won out over racial division because it was often the only space available. This would have also been possible in the 1960s at Dupree's—a bar in a predominantly Black neighborhood that white lesbians and bar guides labeled as "rough" and "dykey," yet as distasteful as it was, white lesbians like Scotti Hooper went there without recognition of the racial dynamics at play.[23]

When Dupree's "moved around the corner onto Ponce de Leon" Avenue in the mid-1960s, it was anything but a refuge for Hooper. "It was a women's bar, but it was awful. . . . It was kind of scary at the time even. It was one of those, you go in and you just think somebody's going to pull out a gun or a knife or whatever. And you certainly don't want to be seen going in one of those places. Because there really was a threat of being fired from your job." A 1969 guide to gay establishments labeled Dupree's as "AYOR," meaning "At Your Own Risk." The guide further described the "AYOR" label by noting that "you might like the people there, but it is highly questionable that they will like you."[24] In the underground world of queer connections, travelers and urban residents used such guides to point them toward safe spaces, but it is likely that white men who wrote the bar guides constructed this perception of safety based on their own gendered and racist understanding of safe space.

Also located in the Old Fourth Ward, "The Tower" restaurant opened in Atlanta at 735 Forrest Road (later known as Ralph McGill Boulevard) in 1957—the same year as Dupree's.[25] It was a neighborhood bar and grill with a pool table in the back, and it catered to lesbians. In the 1968 thirtieth anniversary program for the Lorelei Ladies, a women's softball team in Atlanta, the owners of the Tower, Denny and Charley Gamas, ran an advertisement in support of the team—"The Tower: The Place Where Nice People Meet and Eat."[26] The owners of the Tower "took care of the girls," even bailing them out of jail when necessary.[27] The Tower maintained a long-standing connection to the lesbian community, as both a local hangout and a sponsor for its softball teams. By the 1980s, the Tower supported its own team—the Tower Tornadoes—in the Atlanta Gay Pride celebration tournament at Piedmont Park.[28]

Scholars like Lillian Faderman have recognized women's softball as a magnet and haven for lesbians, but it is rare to find historical evidence of the connection between lesbians, softball, and their sponsors who participated in an economic exchange of mutual benefit. The Gamases' support for the Lorelei Ladies and another advertiser's reference to being "Next Door To Tower Restaurant" highlight the importance of the bar for women—especially lesbians—who connected publicly through softball and at the bar. Faderman's oral history research shows that patronizing establishments, especially bars that supported their teams, was common for lesbian softball players.

> "We had no place to go after the games but the bars." The bars were often even the team sponsors, providing uniforms and travel money. And it was "an unwritten law," according to a Nebraska woman who played during the '50s, that after the game you patronized the bar that sponsored you. Young and working-class lesbians who had no homes where they could entertain and were welcome nowhere else socially were held in thrall by the bars, which became their major resort, despite attempts to escape such as the formation of athletic teams.[29]

Nell Stansell played softball for her Atlanta employer, Retail Credit, and spent time at the Tower because the "ballplaying girls really do drink pretty heavy." While softball opened the door for many women, like Stansell, to lesbian connections, others found this path objectionable and even frightening. When native Atlantan Barbara Vogel returned to Atlanta after college in the early 1960s, she had the opportunity to play for the Lorelei Ladies and the Tomboys. Vogel avoided these teams because she thought they were "very gay, very lesbian, very activist," and she did not want that kind of "lifestyle." The bars associated with softball teams were clearly just as distasteful to Vogel, who felt that simply by entering Dupree's or the Tower, "you took your life in your hands." Softball players wanted to play ball and socialize, but as Christina Hanhardt argues, a "sweaty softball game" could also be "part of the struggle." Socializing might turn political when players had to challenge limitations on their access to ballparks or bars.[30]

The Tower advertised in a thirtieth anniversary celebration program featuring members of the Lorelei Ladies softball team (*pictured on next page*). This is significant because although the Tower was a lesbian hangout, especially after softball games, it could not risk advertising itself as a queer establishment at this time. This ad served as a quiet nod in support of the Tower's lesbian softball clientele. Thirtieth Anniversary Program, Lorelei Ladies Softball Team, 1968, accessed from the Atlanta Lesbian and Gay History Thing Collection, MSS 773, Kenan Research Center at the Atlanta History Center.

FRANCES COX — RIGHT FIELD

This is Frances' first year with the Lorelei Ladies. She has played slow pitch in Macon, Georgia for many years. We think she is your "young lady to watch" in the years to come in fast pitch softball.

SHIRLEY FIENE — CATCHER

This is Shirley's first season with the Loreleis. Her home town is Higginsville, Missouri, and she has played in the past for the Greenville Travelers. Her profession is Oral Surgeon Technician with Veterans Hospital

SANDRA WELLS — SHORT STOP

This is Sandra's seventh year with the Lorelei Ladies. This is her first year playing short stop. The previous six years she played in the outfield and did an excellent job for the team.

BOBBIE DAMRON — THIRD BASE

Bobbie Dee has played third base for the past six years. She has done a most excellent job. Her attitude toward the team is the greatest. She is a Physical Education teacher at one of the county schools.

MARTHA MOORE — LEFT FIELD

This is Martha's second year with the team. She is the most improved player on the team in the last year.

JANICE WHITE — CATCHER

Janice has been on the Lorelei team for the past four years. In 1966, she made All Star National Tournament Catcher. She does a very outstanding job for the team

PATSY ADAMS — SECOND BASE

Patsy has done an outstanding job as our second baseman for the past five years. In September, she will begin her senior year at Georgia State College where she is studying to become a Physical Education teacher.

KAYE LEWIS — FIRST BASE

Kaye has played for the past six years on the team. She previously played right field. In 1967, she moved to first base and has done an excellent job.

The original Piedmont Tavern became a gay gathering place due to the frequent patronage of lesbians, especially women who played softball in Piedmont Park. Lesbians made Mrs. P's a gay bar, and Ginny Boyd spent a considerable amount of time and money there.

> I was going to art school on the GI Bill, and this was while Jean and I were together, and I'd go down there to Piedmont Tavern . . . facing the park at lunch time. Because I had very little money, and she served a big bowl of chili for the money. So, and then I got to where sometimes after classes, I'd go down there, and Jean would come on down, or other friends that I'd talk to would come there, [and] the next thing they know Piedmont Tavern wasn't a straight bar anymore. It was a gay bar.[31]

Increased policing of Piedmont Park in the 1950s meant that Ginny Boyd's time at Mrs. P's tavern on Piedmont Park was potentially suspect.[32] Lesbians like Boyd needed the safety provided by Mrs. P's, since their very presence as women alone or coupled with another woman in the park would be viewed as socially irregular. Boyd could seek the shelter and community provided in the bar off Piedmont Park with her fellow softball-playing lesbians, but it is probable that the bar community was not an appropriate or even desirable option for many lesbians. Boyd was in her thirties when she frequented the bar. Age and class most likely played a role in her willingness to be visibly associated with a lesbian bar and softball culture. Lesbian recollections reveal adamant opinions about the bars as lesbian social spaces. For Nell Stansell, bars were for a particularly defined group, not just in terms of race and social class but also in terms of age. "There's no old people bars. That's not where they hang out."[33]

According to Ginny Boyd, class-based bar choices were available to two tiers of lesbians in Atlanta—nurses and office workers frequented the Tick Tock, and factory workers frequented bars in the "country." These women did not have the same "educational background," and they favored locations where they would find women with similar experiences. Similarly, Vogel recalls that "nicer" lesbians did not frequent Dupree's or the Tower because of the clientele. Vogel's comments speak to her commitment to invisibility as a lesbian.[34] Embracing lesbian identity was of great concern and a great struggle for Vogel. Perhaps her disdain for the regulars at the Tower was based on social class or race or perhaps her own discomfort with being publicly associated with lesbians. Bars offer a place to gather, where people have "traditionally exercised" and enjoyed the "freedom to associate."[35] For some lesbians, however, this association was too great a risk, or simply not desirable.

Like Hooper, Stansell remembered Dupree's as a "rough" bar, actively policed for serving alcohol to minors.[36] In the 1960s, Stansell took her partner Carol to Dupree's, a bar so close to Carol's mother's house that Carol ducked when people passed the door of the bar. Dupree's and the Tower were butch-femme bars where primarily working-class lesbians often presented themselves in hypermasculinized (butch) or hyperfeminized (femme) roles. Lesbians used these roles as an organizational tool within the bar community and as a means of presenting to the outside world. Butch-femme roles also allowed women in the bars to locate friends and lovers, as butch women fraternized with other butches but sought femmes as lovers, and vice versa.[37] Jack Strouss visited the Tower and quickly recognized the butch-femme dynamic in the dress of the lesbian patrons and felt uncomfortable as a gay man in a lesbian bar. "The bar was on Ralph McGill and we went in there one night and I said, 'Oh.' I looked at the gals and they were having a wonderful time, but at the bar I saw some gorgeous young-looking men sitting up there and I thought, 'Oh boy.' But then I got closer, they turned around, and they were not men, they didn't have mustaches or beards." Strouss was "surprised" and felt out of place, and he viewed the femme-butch scene as a signal to leave the bar. In Strouss's queer world, it was rare for lesbians and gay men to commingle in the same public space.[38]

Lesbian feminists in 1970s Atlanta—women who were largely educated and white but were also occasionally unemployed—flocked to the Tower. The bar was conveniently located within walking distance of Georgia State University, where some of these women were students. They did not concern themselves with the social or political implications of being visibly associated with a bar or other women. In fact, they embraced this association. Though many of the women in Atlanta's vibrant lesbian-feminist community were white college students, they preferred the Tower in the 1970s—in spite of its location in a primarily African American neighborhood. The presence of educated lesbian feminists at the Tower suggests that the social-class stratification Boyd recognized in the 1950s changed over time in some venues.[39]

The favored gathering spots for lesbians in cities like Atlanta often reflected the class, geographic, and political affinities of the patrons. Lesbianism sometimes united women, but often class and race won in dividing women in the bar scene.[40] Black lesbians found safety and Black community in house parties and social spaces that were separate from those of white people. Ginny Boyd also created a semiprivate space for her and her friends, limiting their circle to a respectable and class-based group of predominantly white lesbians. In fact, Boyd opened her own private club in the 1970s. It was a house "sort of off in the woods." Patrons paid five dollars to enter but had to be approved by all six people who managed the club, which Boyd remembered kept the "troublemakers" out. Concerned about avoiding trashy people and also about respectability—not being too gay in front of straight people—Boyd and her friends made decisions when granting club membership, which probably limited the space to white lesbians.[41]

As expanding bar options in Atlanta offered women various choices, they frequented bars offering a sense of family. The Sports Page, a popular women's bar in 1970s and 1980s Atlanta, sponsored a women's softball team and is remembered as a nice place—as THE place—to go.[42] When Dorothy Muse was injured playing for the team, she was forced out of work temporarily. The team held a benefit at the bar to support her, and it was covered in the local gay magazine, *Pulse*, which was a unique publication in that it attempted to reach both women and men in its local coverage. Similarly, the Sports Page bar was unique in that it advertised events for "guys & gals together"—combining drag nights with softball team sponsorship and nights exclusively devoted to women's bands. The images in *Pulse*—a magazine with obvious connections to the Sports Page bar—suggest that a majority of its readership and community, if not all, was white. In Atlanta and elsewhere, for white women, a nice place to go often meant a white place to go.[43]

Like most bars in the South, lesbian bars were white spaces because their white owners, usually male and heterosexual, had the necessary viability and political, economic, and police connections to exist. Gay bars in Atlanta and Charlotte existed because white owners were willing to use their connections to maintain a queer social space—and happy to take queer dollars from a targeted clientele who offered a guaranteed flow of financial support. Patrons remained loyal to these bars, finding comfort, camaraderie, and a stand-in family when so many were ostracized from their biological families. Facing little competition, bar owners enjoyed a dependable clientele who found few options for queer socializing— especially lesbians. Across the country, women's bars proliferated in the 1960s and 1970s, and they became, as Finn Enke demonstrates, "primary locations for newly politicized enactments of social segregation; the assertion of gender, race, and class hierarchies among women; and the publication of a newly defined feminist subject."[44] Black women who sought the company of other women did so with fewer options, as outsiders in relation to the hierarchies of white economic power who could not afford to pay police for protection or persuade them to look the other way when nightclubs catered to homosexual dancing. The cost of drinks was high at these bars in order for owners to afford the lease payments and payments to law enforcement.[45] As in other metropolitan areas, primarily white lesbians in the New South committed time and money to bars supported by the power of a heterosexual white identity.

Scotti Hooper's earliest recollections of bar life included her white friend circle. She never knew any Black gay people and assumed that because there were so few gay people in the world, perhaps being gay was simply a foreign concept to Black people. It was not until the 1960s or 1970s, Hooper remembered, that she frequented some bars on Atlanta's Southside, where she became aware that a Black gay nightlife existed.[46] These recollections and snapshots of southern queer bars defy the tempting myth that lesbians were always united by their deviance as lesbians— or with gay men in their deviance as gay people. For example, in one gay men's bar in Greensboro, North Carolina, the unsanctioned policy was "no dykes and no blacks allowed"—suggesting that bars occasionally worked to divide lesbians and gay men or at least accommodated prevailing social/cultural divisions on issues of class, race, and gender at the same time that they created space for identity and community for some.[47]

Perhaps in response to such divisions, the Atlanta bar Ms. Garbo's opened its doors on August 27, 1976, under new management. The remodeled bar advertised itself as the "Southeast's First Bar for Professionals." The new menu offered steak and lobster, and the bar was actively seeking a particular class of gay clientele. The women who frequented Ms. Garbo's were known to be "upwardly mobile," and they existed in a separate social realm from lesbian feminists who preferred the more familiar comfort of the Tower.[48] As noted in *Cruise* magazine, a 1970s guide to southeastern gay life published in Atlanta, Ms. Garbo's was newly open to gay men, having previously been a private club for women. This move boosted the bar's ability to stay afloat financially.[49]

Lesbians, and women in general, would require an influx of male financial support for enduring public social spaces. It is unclear exactly how lesbian earnings compared with gay men's during the 1960s and 1970s. Prior to the 1990s, national statistics on how much women made are thin, suggesting a lack of interest in women's earnings generally. Men were the primary breadwinners, and understanding women's pay rates offered little value to number crunchers interested in economic analyses. A Bureau of Labor Statistics report examined the sluggish rise of women's wages relative to men's, noting that "the overall sex earnings ratio . . . was 62 percent in May 1967 and had risen only to 64 percent by . . . 1981."[50] Women's average weekly earnings in 1981 were $224; men's were $347.[51] At least one economist suggested that educational differences had little impact on this disparity but argued that occupation played the greatest role, noting the overrepresentation of female workers in low-paying sectors. In 1982, for example, 78 percent of all clerical workers were women. Women's earning potential also peaked at a much earlier age than did men's. After their early thirties, few women could hope to continue improving their income.[52] Although it is hard to say how lesbians and gay men in the New South compared with national averages, it is likely that women in the cities of Atlanta and Charlotte reached the peak of their earning potential during their prime bar years. Lesbians who frequented bars did so with less money and less long-term earning potential relative to gay men and were often unable to sustain private social spaces. The ability to sustain Black women's bar spaces would be substantially harder due to racial discrimination in all economic sectors.

When Ms. Garbo's opened its doors to men, it was clear that a lesbian and gay professional population with a certain amount of economic clout had arrived in Atlanta. The commentary in *Cruise* was particularly interesting in its assessment of class at the bar and of the opportunity for lesbians and gay men to interact in a bar setting:

> As straights are now accepting gays, so are the gay women now accepting the gay men and the group that attended the cocktail party to celebrate their reopening contained a lot of both. The record turnout of professional businessmen and women drained the well stocked bar and it had to be replenished in the middle of the night in order for the fun and festivities to continue. I think this all goes to prove that men and women with a tish of class can gather in this newly decorated bar with its understated elegant atmosphere and drop their inhibitions.[53]

Gay men's bars dominated the Atlanta gay bar scene in the 1970s, and this commentator's presumption that women and men *should* be mixing in the bar community certainly ran counter to the active Atlanta lesbian-feminist movement of the 1970s, but the economic success of Ms. Garbo's ultimately depended on opening its doors to the gay male dollar. Separate bar space for gay women was crucial in forming their identity as lesbians and as women, and the above assessment of Ms. Garbo's opening suggests some gay men's lack of understanding for this need, simply reading Ms. Garbo's policy change as progress of acceptance of gay men within the lesbian community.

In the same issue that *Cruise* magazine celebrated the mixed crowd at Ms. Garbo's, the Tower's advertisement read "Where the Women Come First," recognizing the desire for differentiated women's bar establishments and now quite openly claiming its place as a lesbian bar. Yet, the Tower could not compete in the same league as Ms. Garbo's. Charlene McLemore remembered arriving in Atlanta in 1978 and finding the Tower was still a "dive"—too questionable for her partner at the time to patronize.[54] Six months after reopening, Ms. Garbo's received an Atlanta Bar Award for "Best Women's Bar." In the previous year's awards, no category existed for a women's bar. It is worth noting that this award, probably the first given for a women's bar in the Atlanta gay bar scene, was granted to an establishment that *Cruise* (primarily a gay men's bar guide) celebrated in its welcoming of gay men. By opening their bars to gay men, lesbians enjoyed improved notoriety and celebration in the gay male press. For Jack Strouss, it was a great place to mingle with gay women and men in a restaurant atmosphere. Strouss remembered Ms. Garbo's as not "overtly gay" but just a "lovely restaurant" where he and his partner could enjoy the company of their lesbian friends, a space that was historically hard to find for these couples.[55]

Ms. Garbo's created a space where a professional lesbian population could associate with other women but avoid overt lesbian-feminist activists. By the mid-1970s, some upwardly mobile lesbians were disinterested in lesbian-feminist activism, or at least in a working-class bar like the Tower. When Ann McKain came out as a lesbian, it took her several years to feel comfortable being out in public with another woman. As a professor at Georgia State University, McKain was concerned with seeing students in the community, yet she and her partner decided that they could no longer hide from an open life together. She remembered Ms. Garbo's as her first foray into a gay bar scene. It is interesting that Strouss and the male writer at *Cruise* magazine identified Ms. Garbo's as a bar that brought gay women and men together, but McKain's memories of Ms. Garbo's are focused on women being together in public and being able to eat together in a public place. Notwithstanding the eventual male presence at Ms. Garbo's, the establishment was clearly important to McKain as women's territory.[56] Because of her career as a nurse at Grady Hospital, Barbara Vogel, like McKain, worried about being out and being recognized publicly as a lesbian: "I did not talk about my life outside of the hospital. There were very few people that knew. There were maybe about half a dozen people that knew."[57] Vogel thought of overt lesbian bars with disdain, and McKain sought out socially comfortable lesbian spaces while waiting to "fully" come out as a lesbian until after she left her position at Georgia State University. Both women maintained a commitment to their semi-closeted lifestyle and chose lesbian social spaces based on their professions.[58]

In spite of the lesbian closet, often viewed as a professionally necessary space, by the 1970s queer travel guides celebrated Atlanta as the gay mecca of the South. Throughout the decade, their coverage of lesbian bars increased as they actively labeled identifiable women's bars, or bars that primarily attracted women, while appropriating New South rhetoric to sell Atlanta's thriving gay men's bar scene:

> You may or may not have heard of the "New South." This refers to a rapidly progressing economic and social climate in this warm and lovely region of the country. To be sure the old south of extreme poverty and ignorance can still be found; however, signs of exciting changes are evident in the more urbanized sections. Atlanta is sort of the Star of the Fleet in this progress and has emerged in the last decade to be one of the United States' most rapidly advancing cities. Southern boys have always had their charms. . . . Here both southern boys and their charms abound.[59]

Just two years after this proclamation, gay men in Atlanta celebrated the weekend-long Hotlanta Hoedown, welcoming revelers from places like Charlotte, Chicago, Houston, Los Angeles, and New York to celebrate the Old South. The event culminated in a rafting trip on the Chattahoochee River, where a Charlotte attendee remembered the moment when the event's organizer "unfurled a Confederate flag he'd managed to keep dry and started raising that beautiful banner over the river. All those Northerners and Westerners whooped with Rebel yells and joined us Southerners in the most rousing rendition of Dixie you've ever heard." Later in the evening, the primarily white partiers ate barbecue and danced in downtown Atlanta waving miniature Confederate flags as a Charlotte "Hoedowner" brought out a larger version of the flag on the roof of the host hotel.[60] Memories of the Old South dovetailed with the 1979 Hotlanta Hoedown despite the city's reputation as a progressive southern city with a healthy racial climate. The "city too busy to hate," as its boosters promoted Atlanta, was still not a great place to be Black. Black people witnessed scant changes in their day-to-day lives in the decades following the promising racial uprisings of the 1960s. The travel guide writer's celebration of a New South Atlanta that had moved on from ugly past scars overlooked the "extreme poverty and ignorance" that continued to shape life for many of Atlanta's Black citizens.[61]

Both Dupree's Tavern and Ms. Garbo's received attention in the *Falcon World Gay Guide*'s celebratory section on Atlanta. The guide listed both establishments as "G," which was defined as "Girls, means lesbian action. Only in a few places, generally larger cities, are the girls' bar[s] so exclusive that a guy would feel unwelcome. Frequently, bars that cater to both guys and girls are the wildest."[62] The guide also noted eateries, such as the American diner chain Denny's, located at 621 Ponce de Leon, and the Prince George Inn, at 114 6th Street, as welcoming to "gay guys and girls."[63] Although Jack Strouss recalled few "girls" at the Prince George, McKain remembered the Prince George and another meeting place, Gene & Gabe's on Piedmont Avenue (located in Midtown Atlanta's gay-friendly shopping center, Ansley Mall), as part of a growing group of gay eating establishments emerging in 1970s Atlanta. These businesses also catered to a straight clientele and supported music appealing to lesbians or gay men, engaging a varied audience in an establishment not solely focused on selling alcoholic beverages. For McKain it was significant that "we were gathered around a content that was separate from gender or you know sexual orientation. It was around music."[64] The ability to interact publicly was a triumph for Atlanta's lesbians and gay men.

Queer travel guides from the time period confirm that there were bars like Dupree's in Atlanta's sister city in the New South, Charlotte, but unlike Dupree's, none were identified as strictly women's bars. In 1973, three gay bars in Charlotte were near Charlotte's City Center in its Uptown district—a hot spot for "men in shiny cars and expensive clothes" who cruised for male lovers.[65] A 1966 guide listed four gay bars in Charlotte and eight establishments in Atlanta, but by 1972, when Charlotte's metropolitan population stood at 773,600 and Atlanta's had reached 1.9 million, the *International Guild Guide* listed nineteen "gay fun places" in Atlanta and seven for Charlotte.[66] Atlanta's rapid metropolitan growth—especially during the first three years of the 1970s—enabled the growth of gay spaces, which blossomed well beyond the decade.[67] Queer spaces grew because of local queer networks of newspapers and newsletters promoting their existence.

In addition to gay travel guides, one of the best ways to understand the culture of queer spaces in the South is to examine the newspapers and guides publicizing these establishments. A vital resource for locating queer people and safe spaces, these media outlets established communication networks for lesbian and gay identity formation and helped readers locate gay-friendly places for forging connections: "By the early 1970s there existed a highly complex yet widely known homosexual geography of the United States that had points for national meccas, regional capitals, and small-town outposts and lines drawn around gay enclaves, other safe zones, and dangerous places."[68] Atlanta was a "regional capital," to be sure, and gay southerners were apprised of Atlanta's gay community through a variety of communication networks. In the 1960s and 1970s, an increasingly common way of finding bars like the Tower was through local gay magazines and newspapers. Printed material in gay guides such as *Cruise* or the *Falcon World Gay Guide* also served this purpose by making it easier for lesbians and gay men to locate one another and identify establishments where they would feel welcome. Based on the advertising and images used in the publications, this welcome extended primarily to white queers.[69] Gay publications in Atlanta and Charlotte cross-advertised, as did gay bars. They recognized the importance of connecting these two gay communities and their role in assisting lesbians and gay men who traveled between the two.

With an initial circulation of 5,000, the *Atlanta Barb* newspaper premiered in the early 1970s. The *Barb* was the "Groovy Newspaper serving Atlanta and Surrounding Cities," and like most gay newspapers it primarily promoted bars for men. Occasionally, a lesbian bar—such as the Tower Lounge—could afford to place a few printed lines in the classified advertisements section of the *Barb*, but the quarter-page advertisements (often handwritten) were devoted to bars that catered to gay men who could afford the economic cost and the price of social visibility. Neither cost was regularly feasible for lesbians.[70] Going to a bar "implied a comparatively open acknowledgement of one's sexual identity." For gay men this level of visibility could be reached in "stages by participating in street cruising and other forms of public liaisons," but similar "transitional opportunities" were not possible for lesbians.[71] In addition to the challenge of social visibility, lesbians faced the substantial economic challenge of lower earnings compared with men.

The *Barb* actively supported gay community in Atlanta, whether it meant gathering at a bar or at a church. At the opening service for the new home of the primarily gay Metropolitan Community Church in

Mrs. P's and Powder Puff Lounge advertisements in the queer newspaper *Atlanta Barb*. Mrs. P's went through several name changes but was identified by Ginny Boyd as a space that lesbians claimed as their own. The *Barb* regularly carried religious news in support of the local queer-friendly Metropolitan Community Church, as well as advertisements for regional bars that welcomed patrons on Sundays. *Atlanta Barb* 1, no. 1 (1974), accessed from the Kenan Research Center at the Atlanta History Center.

Atlanta's cosmopolitan Virginia Highlands, flowers donated by the *Barb* adorned the Communion table.[72] Yet Chattanooga's Powder Puff Lounge boasted in the *Barb*, "You Bet Your Sweet Ass We're Open on Sunday." Both queer social spaces found an opportunity to reach their parishioners and patrons in the pages of the *Barb*, as the paper represented the growing cosmopolitanism of Atlanta and its gay citizens. Politics occasionally made an appearance in the *Barb*, but queer newspapers were often torn between a focus on politics and activism or on social spaces and drag performances.[73] In Atlanta, both the *Barb* and the 1980s bar guild paper *Phoenix* serve as examples of publications that bridged the gap between religion, bars, politics, and occasionally racial issues.

Massive ads dominated the pages of the *Atlanta Barb* featuring "The Showplace of the South," the club known as the Sweet Gum Head. Charlene McLemore and Barbara Vogel were impressed with the club: "The Sweet Gum was primarily a purely gay bar, and predominantly male. The females sat kind of on the left side, and the guys kind of at the right side, in the back."[74] In between the drag performances, couples would take to the floor to dance. They saw it as a good place to take straight people and noted that there were often more straight patrons than gay. The Sweet Gum "maintained a decorum that was above, quite a bit above, the Tower and DuPree's," the couple recalled. Although it catered to men, there was a butch-femme lesbian scene at the Sweet Gum, and lesbians frequented the club because it was one of the best options for queer space in 1960s and 1970s Atlanta.[75] Bars featuring drag entertainers, like the Sweet Gum, could be found throughout the Southeast. James T. Sears recognized these entertainers as "heroes for midseventies southerners." Instead of "gay liberationists with queer placards and clenched fists," queer southerners embraced drag queens as "heroines adorned with rouge and rhinestones."[76] This was certainly true in Charlotte, where drag quickly took over in the 1970s and show bars regularly welcomed and entertained lesbians in the Queen City.[77]

One of the most memorable Charlotte queer spaces was Oleen's Lounge.[78] Oleen's predated Atlanta's Sweet Gum Head, opening on May 9, 1970, and hosted equally big-name drag entertainers. While Atlanta bars regularly advertised to the Charlotte and regional queer crowd, Oleen's was one of the few establishments that advertised to an Atlanta crowd in queer news outlets. Operated by Martha Oleen Love, remembered as "the mother of gay Charlotte," and her husband, Don, Oleen's was born out of the Brass Rail—a 1960s straight bar co-opted by gay men and managed by Oleen herself.[79] Ed DePasquale, a patron of both Oleen's and the Brass Rail, recalled that at 10:00 P.M., the Brass Rail changed over to a gay bar "as though a switch was thrown."[80] Oleen noticed the frequency of gay male customers and began to reserve tables for them. It was at the Brass Rail that an idea for Oleen's gay bar developed. By 1976 the bar claimed its legacy as "The Oldest Show Bar in the Southeast" and as "Charlotte's 1st and only SHOW BAR," catering to a professional and national drag-performing community. Oleen offered gay people "refuge" from their often-closeted lives: "A solitary outside bulb barely illuminated 'Oleen's' written on the door. Patrons squeezed through [a] narrow portal, cramped into an entryway to pay and get stamped. No neon here, but people always found it anyway. It was magnet to our bi-polar, duplicitous lives. Sanctuary, even."[81] Oleen's regularly played up its southern identity by hosting "Hee Haw" and country and western nights, yet it was one of the only establishments to promote queer Black entertainers in Charlotte.[82]

Oleen's was known primarily as a drag bar, but it also hosted special events that catered to lesbians. In November 1975, the bar welcomed female folk singers Jill and Marty from Atlanta to entertain the lesbian clientele, signifying the important connection between these two cities and their gay communities. Oleen's hosted a Thursday night for women in the 1980s, offering free admission and drink specials, recognizing a need for women's space in Charlotte, a city that struggled to support separate spaces for queer women and men.[83] A memorable night at Oleen's could provide an unforgettable story:

> You walked in the back door and had a person sitting in a window kind of set-up that took your ID and money and then buzzed you thru a door. Once you walked in there was a big round burgundy chair with a high round back on it that multiple [people] could sit on all around in a circle facing outward. The floors were black and white checked. There was a runway for the drag queens. This was a mixed bar [for] men and ladies. . . . One of my most vivid memories was: one night my friend Chere and I were doing upside-down Margaritas. It was the week of Hurricane Hugo and the National Guard came busting in checking IDs. They had their M-16s waving around harassing everyone. They especially were picking on Chere because she looked younger. I remember one of the female National Guard members was really bothered by the way some of her

counterparts were acting. She did not say anything and could hardly look us in the face. It dawned on me that she must have been gay. I will never forget that moment as long as I live.[84]

Charlottean Sarrah Kelly remembered Oleen's as a rough bar, a good place for a "Friday night fight." The brawls usually centered on "somebody trying to talk to somebody else's girl," and the end result might be a high-heeled shoe "popped" at the offender's head.[85]

Like Atlanta, Charlotte's queer community supported promising gay newsletters. Within these periodicals a fledgling bar scene advertised regularly, while the publications documented their struggles to survive and their successes in fostering a lesbian and gay community. These print media efforts serve as evidence of an organizing lesbian and gay community. As its economy and population grew, Charlotte boasted media outlets, activist groups, and bars that all suggested a vibrant group of queer citizens. One of the most enthusiastic 1970s gay media ventures was the *Charlotte Free Press* (*CFP*), published every two weeks. Featuring stories on bars, disco music, cinema, plants, and "homosexuality," the editors noted that "gay people do have interests that have nothing at all to do with homosexuality and hopefully the Free Press will be able to pick up on what some of those interests are" by treating "gays indifferently" instead of "differently."[86] The paper promoted its "straight" advertisers, recognizing them as an indicator of its distinctiveness when compared with other gay publications at the time. "The inclusion of straight advertisers in a predominantly gay newspaper is a sign of the changing times. Every advertiser in the *CFP* knows it is a gay paper and wants to advertise to gays. That's good news!" Distributed in Charlotte, Raleigh, and Chapel Hill, the *Charlotte Free Press* began with a circulation of 1,000. By 1976 the editors celebrated its distribution "all over North Carolina"; in Charleston and Columbia, South Carolina; and in Atlanta, boasting a total circulation of 3,500. The *CFP* distributed over 600 papers in Atlanta every two weeks and used these numbers to encourage its Atlanta readers to pay just one dollar for a classified ad that could "reach as many as 2,000 people in the city of Atlanta alone!"[87]

Unlike many gay publications at the time that were owned and operated by gay men, the *CFP* covered news of interest to lesbians, although this coverage was most likely contributed and written by lesbians. In its coverage of 1976 planning meetings for a lesbian community center in Charlotte, the paper noted that the center would be for lesbian women only—"men would not be allowed, period."[88] The oblivious

Most Gay Publications Are Boring.

A LOT OF GAY NEWSPAPERS HAVE BAR NEWS AND TOKEN WOMEN'S STORIES. BUT I DON'T WANT TOKEN STORIES. I WANT A PUBLICATION THAT REALLY CARES ABOUT BOTH MEN AND WOMEN. FOR ME, THE *FREE PRESS* REALLY CARES!

ENTER MY SUBSCRIPTION:

Name _____

Address _____

City_____ State_____ Zip_____

FOR ONE YEAR SUBSCRIPTION
ENCLOSE $8 CHECK OR MONEY ORDER
AND MAIL TO:
R & J PUBLISHING CO
BOX 2550
CHARLOTTE, N. C. 28234

ALL SUBSCRIPTIONS ARE MAILED IN PRIVATE, SEALED ENVELOPES.

16/May 16, 1977

This *Charlotte Free Press* subscription advertisement targeted its women readers, which was rare among queer periodicals, and claimed that it offered more than "token women's stories." *Charlotte Free Press*, May 16, 1977, accessed from Atlanta Lesbian Feminist Alliance Periodicals Collection, 1962–1994, RL.00024, Sallie Bingham Center for Women's History and Culture, David M. Rubenstein Rare Book and Manuscript Library, Duke University, Durham.

tone of Atlanta's *Cruise* magazine, in its coverage of Ms. Garbo's 1976 opening to gay men, is nowhere to be found in the *Charlotte Free Press* article focused on lesbian community. While the bar-focused *Cruise* magazine celebrated a supposed long-awaited lesbian "acceptance" of gay men in the reopening of Ms. Garbo's, ignoring men's ability to utilize public spaces for socializing in a way that women often could not, the more political *CFP* recognized the importance of separate lesbian space. Its article on the new lesbian center ended with a cheer, "Let's get it together, Lesbians of Charlotte!"[89] Very few establishments identified themselves as exclusively devoted to lesbians, and none portrayed Black women in their advertising. In fact, the *CFP*'s photos, drawings, and advertising depicted only white people. In Charlotte and the New South, lesbians gathered regularly during the 1970s, yet the cost of advertising likely limited their visibility. Advertising costs were prohibitive for Black women's gatherings, and the paper's lack of Black faces suggests that Black queer people would not have looked to the *CFP* to locate community. In a full-page advertisement, the male editors reached out to women readers by featuring a picture of a white woman proclaiming, "A lot of gay newspapers have bar news and token women's stories. But I don't want token stories. I want a publication that really cares about both men and women. For me, the *Free Press* really cares!"[90] A bar advertisement for the Greenhouse read, "A Bar For Females (Males admitted as guests only)." The Greenhouse opened every day but Monday, required a membership, and boasted of a game room and a "Female Disco DJ."[91] In nearby Durham, North Carolina, the Blueberry Hill Disco advertised the opening of "N.C.'s 1st Exclusive Women's Club," which shared the same complex as the primarily gay male bar. Women would have a separate front entrance, a game room, and the "Latest Lesbian Music."[92] Community newspapers like the *CFP* performed the quiet work of sharing white lesbian community information and promoting regional lesbian public spaces.

Just two miles out of Uptown Charlotte, and not far from the eventual location of its chief competitor, Oleen's Lounge, the Scorpio advertised in the *Charlotte Free Press* and other gay publications in the Southeast. The oldest operating gay bar in Charlotte as of 2022, the club opened in the South End neighborhood of Charlotte. In 1974 the bar briefly moved to 4316 Tryon Street, farther from Uptown in an area known for gay men's cruising.[93] The Scorpio moved to its long-standing Freedom Drive site to celebrate its third anniversary, located just west of Uptown near the historic and crime-infested Wesley Heights neighborhood.[94] The Scorpio anniversary party made the cover of the June issue of the *CFP*, and an advertisement for the new bar read, "Scorpio invites you to the most exciting new DISCOTHEQUE in the SOUTH!!" The Scorpio hosted drag shows, offered giveaways, and even served a southern Sunday dinner, boasting a holiday menu of ham, chicken, potato salad, bean salad, baked beans, sandwiches, and pineapple/cheese/marshmallow salad. Queer bars often served as replacement family for ostracized queer people, and places like the Scorpio cultivated this sanctuary. Continuing the tradition of softball and bars, in June 1981 the Scorpio celebrated the first community Gay Pride event in Charlotte by supporting the winning and predominantly white coed softball team "The Stinging Scorpians."[95]

Thriving bar communities in Atlanta and Charlotte relied on solid outlets in the 1980s for advertising in the gay news media, easing the process of locating queer-friendly spaces. A 1981 *Charlotte Observer* exposé on Charlotte's gay community mentioned "at least six bars [that] cater to gay patrons" but also noted that "gay life in Charlotte remains less obvious and less open than in larger cities." One of the most significant bars to open in Charlotte was the Odyssey in 1980 — a dance bar that welcomed women and men, although the majority of the crowd was gay men. It was recognized regionally as a chic bar that put Charlotte on the gay map and was heralded by the *Charlotte Observer* in its coverage of the growing gay community in Charlotte: "The Odyssey is more than just another gay bar. Even those who seldom go, who find it too loud, who disdain the hunting ground it affords gay men seeking partners, speak of the place with pride. Classier than any straight bar in Charlotte, they say. As nice as any gay bar in Atlanta, they say. The Odyssey . . . is part of an emerging gay life, part of Charlotte's coming out."[96] As this writer noted, Atlanta's queer bar scene set the standard for other gay bars in the region, including those in Charlotte. Recognizing the important class and gender divisions that divided the mythically united gay community, however, one Charlotte lesbian remembered the bar less fondly, describing it as "snooty" and primarily welcoming to gay men.[97]

As in many urban centers, political action happened at gay bars in Charlotte. When a fire caused the owners of the Scorpio to undertake a major renovation, the *Charlotte Observer* took note. "When the new Odyssey . . . opened last winter," the *Observer* recognized that "it placed Charlotte at a new level of sophistication in bars — gay or straight. Now the city has another at the same level: the new Scorpio." The article covering the renovation noted the importance of Martha Oleen Love's presence at the Scorpio private opening party and an "impressive" flower arrangement sent to the party courtesy of the Odyssey, suggesting that the "vague tension" that divided the Charlotte bar owners for years was now giving way to more "cordiality."[98] Later that year a group known as the Gay/Lesbian Caucus of Charlotte organized a voting drive in the Charlotte gay community by working directly in the bars, recognizing these establishments as vital to political organization and action for gay people. A political action group known as Queen City Quordinators put the degree of cordiality among bar owners to the test. The group convinced the bar owners in Charlotte to come together and promote a St. Patrick's Day event at the Odyssey in support of political action for lesbians and gay men in Charlotte.[99] These events were only marginally successful, however, and by the end of the 1980s, the Odyssey, the caucus, and the Quordinators were all kaput.[100]

Charlotte's exclusively lesbian bars came and went in the 1980s, some lasting just a few months. A 1984 ad for the Charlotte lesbian bar Diana's warned, "Sorry, gentlemen, but Diana's is for women only."[101] This women's-only space would not last long—Diana's did not advertise regularly, and no oral history narrators recall the bar. Four years later a columnist in the Charlotte-based gay newspaper *Q-Notes* noted her concern for community among Charlotte's lesbians as yet another exclusively lesbian bar closed:

Last month I talked about the need for more organization and activities in the Lesbian community. That column hadn't gone to press when Flamingo's, our only all-women's bar, closed on December 31st. I happened to stop in about 1:00 with some friends . . . and the first thing I heard was, "This is their last night." It was a sad beginning to the New Year. I looked around and remembered the evenings I shared with friends there in just the three short months Flamingo's was open. I really felt comfortable there. I liked the bar area where you could have an intelligent conversation without shouting. I liked the music because I recognized the songs . . . and I enjoyed slow dancing, which I was beginning to think was taboo in Charlotte. The pool tables and the video games and pin-ball weren't always so crowded that by the time you found one you lost interest. . . . Maybe it wasn't the immediate success y'all envisioned, but I think from that will be born other ideas and other places that will capture the community spirit that was starting to build there and carry it to new heights this year.[102]

When Flamingo's closed in 1988, there were no women's bars left in Charlotte, including Diana's. Shortly before Flamingo's demise, Steven's opened to "fill three needs of Charlotte's gay community: an after-work bar close to downtown, a restaurant, and a 'quiet' bar with no dance floor."[103] Just two years later, in 1989, Steven's was no more; but Liaisons Restaurant opened for business in the same site. Lesbian owners Linda Swinson and Pat Sizemore hoped to offer something new to the gay community in a comfortable restaurant setting with an upscale menu of "French Continental Fare."[104] A national guide to lesbian travel listed Liaisons as a very popular restaurant and bar with a lesbian following. There were no Charlotte bars mentioned in the publication exclusively devoted to women or even receiving the guide's designation of "mostly women."[105] The food concept did not last at Liaisons, but the bar did. Affectionately referred to as the "Pink House," Swinson ran Liaisons until it closed twenty years later.[106]

Although both Charlotte and Atlanta boasted promising queer bar communities by the 1980s, in larger, more cosmopolitan Atlanta, options for women worked out better. The budding gay marketplace in Charlotte did not portend a steady and continuous growth pattern for the future of queer visibility in the Queen City.[107] Perhaps Charlotte missed the gay economic boat in the post-Stonewall potentiality of the 1970s. The 1969 riot at the New York gay bar the Stonewall Inn catapulted the gay rights movement into a national spotlight, at least momentarily. The riot also galvanized New Left and gay activists across the country. These activists were willing consumers ripe for a dynamic gay marketplace that materialized rapidly in Atlanta, but Charlotte's queer economic and political growth floundered in the decades following Stonewall.[108] It is difficult to say whether the history of lesbian social spaces prior to 1970 in Atlanta is similar to that of the New South city of Charlotte, North Carolina.[109] Based on the marked growth of lesbian hangouts in Atlanta by the 1980s and the dearth of similar places in Charlotte at that point, it is clear that over time women in Atlanta found more accessible opportunities to forge lesbian connections. Choices of bar spaces were not always possible in Charlotte. There were very few gay-friendly bars, and for lesbians who wanted to be out in the scene, this meant that they primarily frequented gay men's bars prior to the 1980s. Charlotte's lesbians found ways to divide along lines of race, gender, and class, as discussed in the next chapter, but in the bar scene this was not always a possibility due to their limited options.

When a "long-anticipated" bar named Arney's opened in 1981 on Cheshire Bridge Road, known to some as Atlanta's "Great Gay Way," it welcomed both women and men. Several bar owners and clientele attended the opening parties at Arney's, including women from the Sports Page bar, located just down the road.[110] Arney's and the Sports Page faded from the lesbian bar scene when the *Damron Women's Traveller* named Atlanta "the unofficial capital of the Southeast" in 1994. The lesbian travel guide recognized Atlanta as a refuge "from the rural South and the hustle-bustle of the Northeast. The laid-back, friendly attitude here makes for easy mingling in the bars, while the big city energy breeds trendy discos and high-style-with-a-smile." The guide listed only two bars that year, Revolution and Bellissima, whose clientele were "mostly women," but also listed a "very popular" bar owned by women, frequented by lesbians and gay men, called "The Otherside: Where the Mix is Perfect!" Located just north of Cheshire Bridge Road, the Otherside joined a community of queer bar spaces on the Great Gay Way in 1990s Atlanta.[111]

The fleeting nature of lesbian bar space makes this a difficult story to tell. The silence that surrounded lesbian gathering spaces in the 1940s and 1950s continued into the 1970s and 1980s, with lesbian bars unable to afford the level of visible advertising necessary to spread the word and financially sustain the physical spaces for significant periods of time. The financial imperative of the gay male dollar made separate women's space a near impossibility. Men often escaped the responsibilities of family and children, and their ability to command a higher paycheck in the workplace allowed them frequent access to bar spaces. Gay women often remained tied to children and family responsibilities, and even in a stable lesbian relationship they could not match the financial power of a gay male couple. These complications impeded women's ability to participate in the bar community with the same regularity as gay men. Bars devoted exclusively to lesbians provided important community potential for women, but if they excluded men, these bars struggled to survive. Publications that catered to a gay audience often focused primarily on the interests of gay men, although occasional snippets of lesbian life and community seeped through the male-dominated pages. Oral histories help to identify public social gathering spaces for lesbians, but the failures of memory often lead to dead ends when attempting to reconstruct an uninterrupted story of these places.

Bars are often equated with disrespectable behavior, and they represent an effort by lesbians to disengage or separate from the mainstream sites of heterosexual power. It would be difficult to define a lesbian community in Charlotte or Atlanta based solely on bar spaces or the disparate experiences profiled in this chapter. Bars typically mirror the segregations of both local neighborhoods and larger society, and lesbians in Atlanta and Charlotte sought social spaces that would allow them to get a drink, share a dance, and maybe eat a meal in a non-oppressive but socially familiar (in terms of race and social class) environment. The local distinctions of each city defined the possibilities for "various groups with differing beliefs, symbols, identities, lifestyles, languages, and interests operating inside a common border and within a cultural context of homophobia and heteronormativity." Even though Charlotte's queer landscape lacked the diversity and structure of Atlanta, it would be incorrect to assume that queer life did not exist there in vibrant and exciting ways.[112] Lesbians enjoyed a greater opportunity for social connections in Atlanta because of the activist lesbian-feminist organization the Atlanta Lesbian Feminist Alliance, more bars regularly frequented by lesbians, and occasionally greater political and corporate support.[113] But this potential for visibility was inconsequential to some, like Atlantan Scotti Hooper. She did not equate her queer identity to a political identity; she was never a "flag carrier." "You know I am who I am. I'm a good person and what I do is nobody's, really nobody's business. . . . And you know I get calls from certain gay organizations and I do contribute some but I really, I have a hard time doing that. I feel like we're all people, we all make our own way. And probably because I had to do it. I came through and I'm like you know, OK, why should I make it even easier for everybody in the world."[114]

While some lesbians like Hooper cared little about claiming an activist identity, in the early 1970s many were eager to assume the identity of "flag carrier"—with their political agenda proudly displayed for all to see. It is now time to meet drastic dykes. In both Charlotte and Atlanta, lesbian feminists established spaces, held conferences, created print media outlets, and worked to organize a visible community that would be central to the urban identity of each city.

This is a dangerous area for women.
—Atlanta Lesbian Feminist Alliance,
1975

3 VISIBILITY

"We are gone from the Women's Center because remaining involved with the Center meant continuing to put a lot of energy into women who were in turn giving a lot of energy to men. It is much more complicated than that of course. Lots of anger, lots of hurt all round."[1] With these words, lesbian feminist Joy Justice announced the 1975 departure of the separatist group Drastic Dykes from the Charlotte Women's Center (CWC), home and meeting space for a group of primarily white feminists in Charlotte, North Carolina. The departure of the Drastic Dykes was a personal and political decision to separate from other local feminists, some lesbian and some not, at the CWC. The Dykes felt an "immediate" need to "plant" their lives in "radically different ground," or else face the destruction of the planet "sooner than anyone thought with the most vulnerable among us being sacrificed first."[2]

Choosing a temporary separatist model allowed the Drastic Dykes to follow a path of self-discovery, personal political action, and community building. As a cadre of white feminists who were successful in their separatism—as attested to by their publishing efforts, visibility, and protest of patriarchal structures—Joy Justice and the Drastic Dykes challenged the narrative of white lesbian separatism as a failure.[3] Through the group's self-published magazine, *Sinister Wisdom*, the Drastic Dykes in Charlotte united lesbian voices in print, creating a national network of lesbian feminists who depended on the publishing work of women who called the South home. The action, activism, and community-building work of *Sinister Wisdom* continued well beyond the immediacy of its original separatist lesbian-feminist vision in the 1970s.[4]

Lesbian feminism and lesbian-feminist separatism radicalized women in Atlanta and Charlotte, two archetypal New South cities.[5] Both were home to activist groups who demonstrated the increasing visibility of lesbians generally. Lesbians in the two cities forged personal and political connections across geographical boundaries through feminist print media like the Charlotte Women's Center newsletter; *Sinister Wisdom*, founded in Charlotte; Atlanta Lesbian Feminist Alliance's *Atalanta* newsletter; and lesbian-feminist bookstores, like Charis in Atlanta, that were devoted to feminist print culture, and ALFA's library that preserved it. Created by southern lesbian feminists, these connections channeled activism, erotic desire, and community, which flowed between lesbians in the two cities, offering women unique places and spaces to express their innermost desires and share activist commitments.

The story of lesbian-feminist separatism in Charlotte is not possible without an understanding of lesbian feminism in Atlanta, Charlotte's New South competitor. Lesbians in Charlotte looked to Atlanta lesbians for leadership and support, and similarly Charlotte's municipal leaders frequently looked to Atlanta on how (or how not) to do things. Both cities were home to lesbian feminists who established spaces, held conferences, created print media outlets, and worked to generate a visible community intertwined with the urban identity of each metropolis. Lesbian bookstores, publications, and community centers served as a pipeline of political action, love, desire, and support that flowed between women in these two cities, allowing them to find unique places and spaces to express their innermost desires and activist commitments. The history of lesbian feminism is a history of movement, not just the movement for equal rights and increased awareness of the plight of women but also the movement of ideas through printed communication and travel. Even when Joy Justice felt ideologically lost and the larger movement seemed personally unclear to her, she continued to hope in the pages of *Sinister Wisdom* that "we are moving."[6] The connection, both physical and ideological, between Charlotte's and Atlanta's lesbian feminists created a fluid exchange of hope, community, and ideology. Women moved in and out of spaces and places—communal houses, husbands' homes, lovers' homes—and this affected the product of lesbian feminism in Charlotte: for example, the publication *Sinister Wisdom* relocated many times due to shifting editors, shifting economics, and shifting lovers. Although fleeting and contested, the practice of lesbian feminism in Charlotte created a wide-reaching network of lesbian feminists who depended on the work of women in Charlotte, specifically the publishing work of the Drastic Dykes.

Lesbians exited the midcentury feminist movement on local and national levels in response to the movement's commitment to equality of the sexes, which often included working within the structures of the patriarchy and dismissing lesbian concerns. The most notable of these dismissals was the infamous rejection of lesbians from the National Organization for Women (NOW) by its founder, Betty Friedan. Identifying lesbians as a risk to NOW's political agenda, labeling them a "lavender menace," she yearned to gain mainstream (heterosexual and male) support for a national women's movement.[7] In response to Friedan, New York–based Radicalesbians railed against mainstream feminism because it operated within systems of heterosexuality that linked women in an ongoing relationship with their "oppressors." Drastic Dykes in Charlotte embraced this stance and the label "dyke," removing the term from a system of power that worked to "frighten women into a less militant stand" and separate them from their "sisters."[8]

During the NOW-led fight for the Equal Rights Amendment, southern gender expectations hardened.[9] Those who supported the ERA in North Carolina were readily accused of being homosexuals. ERA opponents assigned traditional and anti-gay values to North Carolina women, suggesting that they shared more in common with Anita Bryant, a religious anti-gay entertainer, than the feminist leader Gloria Steinem.[10] Unlike other southern states, where state legislators simply allowed the ratification clock to expire, North Carolina soundly defeated the ERA. In her role as coordinator of the group Georgians for the ERA, ALFA member Vicki Gabriner attended the first ERA organizing meeting in Alabama. A speaker delivering the keynote address disparaged lesbians from the platform, leaving Gabriner in tears. Yet there were familiar faces from the Alabama NOW group who shared her frustration and offered their support. Gabriner had recently gathered with these women at the NOW southern regional meeting in Alabama. When Jackie Frost of Charlotte reported on that meeting in the 1974 national newsletter, she neglected to include Gabriner's workshop on sexuality and lesbianism. A crushed Gabriner responded with a ten-page letter to Frost, copying several NOW leaders in regional and national positions, detailing her frustrations. NOW was an organization for women that included lesbians. But several at the Alabama workshop repeated the idea that NOW was not a lesbian organization. Gabriner agreed. Yet she wondered when NOW would be an organization for "lesbians qua lesbians." In detailing her frustration to Frost, she explained, "It's a drag to be the lesbian who always gets up and talks about lesbian oppression." Further, she was tired of being understood as only a lesbian: "You turn into a giant vagina."[11]

The long reign of southern belledom and the role of southern states in the anti-woman suffrage movements of the early twentieth century set the stage for continued opposition to women's equality efforts, distinguishing the South as particularly hostile to lesbians and feminists.[12] The ERA encouraged fears of androgyny, which threatened the gendered structural support of a southern house of cards built on the entrenched cultural memory of powerful plantation masters and their mistresses, women who inhabited ideological pedestals of purity and femininity.[13] In describing the South for queer women who cropped their hair, rejected southern femininity, and demanded to be treated as men, the queer southern writer Lillian Smith concluded, "There was no comfortable place for such women in the South."[14] Dykes in the South were drastic because of southern cultural confines. Some southerners viewed second-wave feminism as interchangeable with lesbianism, and this association threatened the gendered structures on which southern identity rested. For those who opposed the ERA, an erasure of gender divisions invoked fears of lesbianism. As one Tennessee man put it, ERA supporters were just lesbians who wanted to use the bathroom with men.[15]

Feminists understood that a different approach would be necessary in the South. When appealing to the North Carolina state legislature regarding ratification of the ERA, local leaders in the city of Durham encouraged national NOW leaders to be "moderate" in their appeal; local activists understood that adopting "extremely polite, very low-key, and pleasant" language would be necessary to sway southern politicians.[16] But even though the politics of respectability and moderation made sense for the feminist movement in the South, the women who made up the Drastic Dykes chose a different strategy. Working outside the systems of southern womanhood and southern feminism, they paved a successful path for radical feminist publishing, creating local and national lesbian community through *Sinister Wisdom*, which was their "political action."[17]

At the height of the feminist movement in 1971, heterosexual feminists, lesbian feminists, and lesbian-feminist separatists in Charlotte established the Charlotte Women's Center, a site integral to the roots of national lesbian culture because it served as the breeding ground for the lesbian separatist group the Drastic Dykes.[18] Few women were involved with the Dykes on a daily basis. The group's initial goals were unclear, and its lack of direction often broke down along lesbian separatist and feminist lines.

Yet the results of its organizational efforts had a lasting impact on both the local and national stage of lesbian-feminist print culture.

A cozy purple bungalow in Charlotte's Dilworth neighborhood provided the physical space where "a constant stream of women and urchins" sought to create a center for political, spiritual, sexual, and social growth for all women, although a majority were white. Located on Lyndhurst Avenue, in a primarily white neighborhood of families and communes, the founders intended the house to be a "women's commune" and a "center for subversive activities."[19] Women who frequented the CWC documented their thoughts in "a blue loose-leaf notebook" kept "on a green desk in the office." Notes from this log—a 1970s social networking tool—reflected women's disparate concerns and the mundane activities of operation. Just as twenty-first-century social networking websites record everything from the banal to the tragic, the CWC log reflected a wide range of concerns. Women met there to create feminist handouts for the annual "Festival in the Park" at Charlotte's nearby Freedom Park, and they partied on a Saturday night, playing Risk while eating and drinking too much. Women eagerly anticipated the arrival of a party featuring "turnip greens and sangria" and complained about house problems with moth infestation and "dog shit in the back room."[20]

The CWC hosted meetings such as a writers' workshop, a theater group, a television group concerned with a recently released "videotape on women's culture," and lesbian consciousness-raising groups. Discussions included the center's organizational structure, the content of the newsletter, and current events related to sexism, sexuality, women's education, unemployment, abortion rights, rape, and women in prison. A young lesbian's traumatic exit from home and her need for shelter resulted in the following entry: "A woman called, wonders what to do about sixteen year old lesbian who's moved out of parent's home—needs place to live." When "Mr. Robertson," a chemistry professor at Central Piedmont Community College, made sexist jokes and handed out sexist material in class, the center's log served as a communication board to publicize his actions and call for a feminist response. Committed to educating women about women, the CWC newsletter regularly advertised local academic classes such as "Women in Modern America," offered at the community college in 1975. Yet a frustrated diatribe in the following year's newsletter lamented the cancellation of a 1976 women's history course due to low enrollment, suggesting the lack of local acceptance for a course totally focused on women.[21]

Feminist causes of regional and national interest were paramount concerns for the Charlotte Women's Center, and occasionally it served as a hub for regional feminist organizing. Even as they appeared in and primarily attracted white circles, CWC's activist causes occasionally brought interracial solidarity. When African American and North Carolinian Joan Little was charged with murder, Charlotte's women rallied to offer their support. An indigent female inmate accused of killing a white male prison guard who tried to rape her, Little was the only woman in the Beaufort County jail at the time of the assault. Alternative and national mainstream press picked up the story, and in August 1975 Charlotte women organized a trip to Raleigh to back Little during her trial.[22] Alongside women from the CWC, groups from around the country, like the activist Third World lesbian softball team Gente, which traveled from Oakland, California, joined Little's feminist support network.[23] The case garnered interest from regional chapters of national groups like the Youth Against War and Fascism and a North Carolina–based chapter of the Black Panthers. At a Richmond, Virginia, march in support of Little, Youth Against War and Fascism leader Joan Butler insisted that rape laws were designed to "intimidate and terrorize" Black people.[24] Some Black women asserted that Little's struggle mirrored the struggle of "thousands of women" who faced similar oppression and asked "white sisters to struggle side by side with us to overcome racism and build solidarity."[25] According to *Time* magazine, "It took the six white and six Black jurors only 1 hr. and 25 min. to reach the obvious decision: not guilty."[26] Little's case exemplifies the social causes vital to the goals of the national feminist movement in the 1970s, as it united a variety of women across borders of sexual, regional, racial, and national difference.

Regional connections with other feminist groups—especially ALFA—were the lifeblood of the Lyndhurst Avenue house. The women regularly mailed their newsletter to ALFA, as was common between women's centers across the country, and when Charlotte's feminist women visited Atlanta to participate in activist causes, they stayed at ALFA's house. These types of visits were not simply politically motivated but also social calls. As other scholars have noted and feminists of the 1970s boldly proclaimed, resistance mingled with both the political and the personal. Activism, social connections, and sexual opportunity overlapped as lesbian feminists worked to advance their cause.[27] For example, when Claire from Charlotte attended a Georgia Equal Rights Amendment march in Atlanta, she especially enjoyed a "damn good women's dance!"

An intimate portrait of Harriet Desmoines and Catherine Nicholson, the lovers who founded *Sinister Wisdom* in Charlotte. Accessed from Catherine Nicholson Papers, RL.00950, Sallie Bingham Center for Women's History and Culture, David M. Rubenstein Rare Book and Manuscript Library, Duke University, Durham.

When the Charlotte Women's Center was struggling to survive at the end of the 1970s, a member included a handwritten note to ALFA when mailing the CWC's newsletter. She reported that the group was experiencing some changes but moving forward and anticipating an upcoming dance and concert to be held at the "Y.W.[C.A.]"[28] Dances such as these provided safe and defined spaces for lesbians to find one another, even across the miles that separated Charlotte from Atlanta.

Approximately 150 miles northeast of Charlotte, in Chapel Hill, North Carolina, a group of feminists began publishing the *Research Triangle Women's Liberation Newsletter*, initially funded by the University of North Carolina at Chapel Hill and named after the state's Research Triangle region anchored by the cities of Chapel Hill, Raleigh, and Durham. This 1969 newsletter was the precursor to the feminist editorial collective *Feminary*, which by the 1970s was already hailed as one of the longest-running feminist publications. Like the CWC newsletter, women created and controlled the production of *Feminary*. These periodicals functioned as a platform for women to build local and national community because they highlighted issues of local activism but also linked southern feminists to like-minded activists throughout the country.[29] As women connected regionally through the printed word, they created bonds of national sisterhood. This was indicative of a national feminist trend. In fact, these publications served as a form of feminist activism.[30]

Intimacy and sexual liaisons were an integral part of these activist associations. Just as women who frequented bars were eager to find lesbians, at the heart of lesbian-feminist print culture and its consequent activism was a deep desire to find like-minded lesbians for sexual connection. Southern lesbian poet, educator, and activist Minnie Bruce Pratt formed her national presence as a writer in the lesbian-feminist movement through ties to places like the CWC. Pratt published her first poem in *Sinister Wisdom*, and this would lead her to forge intimate connections with women in Charlotte. Pratt, referred to simply as "MB" in the center's newsletters, serves as an example of the intertwined relationship between lesbian feminists in Charlotte and the Research Triangle, where Pratt was part of *Feminary*. Pratt met her lover Cris South at a National Organization for Women conference in Charlotte. When South spoke at one of the conference workshops about her experience as a lesbian mother, Pratt was immediately drawn to her, since she was in the process of losing her own children as a result of her lesbian identity. At this same conference, Pratt remembered that several women, both straight and gay, went out to see a drag show at the Charlotte gay bar the Scorpio.[31] Her impression of Charlotte at that time suggested that the lesbian culture was vibrant, at least for educated and visibly active women: "I was living in Fayetteville, NC, at the time and there was no gay gathering space except for a couple of bars. These conferences in Charlotte made me think there was a significant lesbian presence and energy there, since 'everyone knew' that lesbian participation was very high in Women's Studies & NOW! After Cris & I became lovers, and I stayed with her in Charlotte at the Center, I had the impression that there were lesbian cultural events going on regularly."[32] Passionate sexual connections formed at the CWC fostered the creation of the lesbian-feminist magazine *Sinister Wisdom*, which emerged on the heels of a major ideological split among local women. The activism of women at the CWC and the resulting publication of *Sinister Wisdom* could not be separated from intimacy, friendship, and personal pain.

Discussion of a published journal, or possibly a collection of short stories and poems, at a 1974 writers' workshop at the Lyndhurst Avenue house

SINISTER WISDOM

VOLUME I, ISSUE 1   JULY, 1976

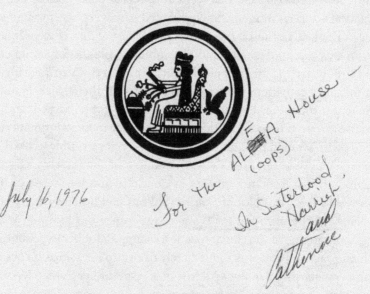

July 16, 1976

For the ALFA House (oops)

In Sisterhood, Harriet and Catherine

Editors: Harriet Desmoines
Catherine Nicholson
Contributing Editor: Beth Hodges
Technical Advisor: Jan Millsapps
Special Thanks to: Drastic Dykes,
women of the Charlotte Lesbian Center

Cover graphic by Marianne Lieberman

Sinister Wisdom first issue cover page. The journal offered special thanks to the Drastic Dykes of the Charlotte Lesbian Center, while a handwritten note demonstrated the lesbian community shared between Atlanta and Charlotte. *Sinister Wisdom* 1, no. 1 (Summer 1976), accessed from Atlanta Lesbian Feminist Alliance Periodicals Collection, 1962–1994, RL.00024, Sallie Bingham Center for Women's History and Culture, David M. Rubenstein Rare Book and Manuscript Library, Duke University, Durham.

was a standard weeknight activity. In fact, writers' workshops were typical of the larger feminist movement—an effort to find space and opportunity for women's words. As a direct result of workshops like these, and because of the feminist belief in the power of women's writing, both *Feminary* and *Sinister Wisdom* came into being. Charlotte's Drastic Dykes began to meet in January 1975, while members of the group briefly lived in the upstairs apartment of the CWC. Their residence caused substantial concern for other women at the Lyndhurst Avenue house. Although they remained in the CWC, the Dykes' presence created palpable tension and anger as they separated themselves ideologically. This split played out in the 1975 issues of the CWC newsletter. Amid this controversy and torrid love affairs, a lesbian-feminist separatist literary magazine—one that would gain national attention—began publication in Charlotte. It became a primary outlet for publishing separatist rhetoric, and it is perhaps the most significant legacy of the Charlotte Women's Center. In the wake of the split at the CWC, the newly involved lovers Harriet Desmoines and Catherine Nicholson harnessed their frustrations and their love for one another, anchoring their emotions to their literary home: *Sinister Wisdom*.

In her description of the troubled origins of *Sinister Wisdom*, Nicholson recalled that some women at the CWC wanted a different format for the magazine than what she and Desmoines envisioned: "Neither of us was interested in a local newsletter. We were interested in literature, philosophy, and theory. They thought that was elitist. So we left."[33] In fact, their departure did represent an arrogant effort led by Nicholson, who had recently resigned her teaching position at the University of North Carolina at Charlotte. She saw herself as a scholar in a man's world, where she and other women were doomed to seek male approval in their work. She viewed the university system as a tool of patriarchal domination and left her tenured professorship as a symbol of her commitment to lesbian separatism. In her defiant departure, Nicholson placed a note on her office door at the university and left a campus where the commitment to patriarchy was symbolized in its phallic Belk Tower: an "unadorned stiff prick" at the center of campus, in Nicholson's words.[34] Although Desmoines and Nicholson were aware of their class and race privilege and wrote about it often, they nonetheless left behind women at the CWC who struggled to maintain jobs and incomes and to support children and did not necessarily share the education or privileged ability to devote themselves fully to literary pursuits.

The Dykes who left the CWC were determined to live "emotionally" beyond the constraints of patriarchy, to separate from men as well as heterosexual women. Lesbian separatists sought a life that would be free of patriarchal entanglements. They broke from the feminist movement because women who were married to men or associated with them functioned within a patriarchal society. Even in their roles as sisters to brothers, wives to husbands, daughters to fathers, and mothers to sons, non-separatists were part of the patriarchy, which wielded political power over women. Propelled by their anger and determined to pursue their separation from a life dominated by men, the seven white women who formed the original Drastic Dykes each made individual sacrifices: Nicholson left her academic career, two other women quit college, and all faced challenges in separating from lovers, family, and friends. It was in this separatist mindset that *Sinister Wisdom* took shape, with a belief that the only way to achieve true feminist ideals was to be separate from all forms of patriarchal power. Women—even lesbians—who stayed at the Charlotte Women's Center struggled with the Dykes' position, in part because they could not make sense of political separatism. Joy Justice detailed her understanding of the separatist split at the CWC in an article for *Sinister Wisdom*: "We did not become separatists because we wanted to separate ourselves from the world. In fact, for the first five or six months that Drastic Dykes met, we met at the Women's Center, and were individually still very much involved with the straight women at the Center."[35] But this tense coexistence did not last: "When straight women and other lesbians were frightened and angry with us because of what we thought . . . we became more angry, until finally there were no straight women coming to the Center. We were left with the choice of continuing to run a women's center for women who would not come to meetings because we were there, or leaving. We left."[36] Justice hoped that those who remained at the CWC would come after them and beg them to stay, but instead she found that "isolation was the ultimate result."[37]

Threatened and alienated by the Dykes' separatism, women at the CWC worried about its commitment to meet the needs of all women and believed the Dykes were betraying this mission. Just three years earlier a paper presented there by a women's socialist group highlighted ten major areas of action for the women at the Lyndhurst Avenue house. Number ten was to "end the discrimination against our Lesbian Sisters." Although this was a foundational goal, by the mid-1970s it was an incendiary debate. The CWC newsletter devoted significant space to information about the Drastic Dykes, noting that by July 1975, the group no longer met at—or had anything to do with—the center. In the wake of the split, Jan Millsapps wrote in the CWC newsletter about the comfort she took in mailings from "all over" demonstrating that women's centers were struggling over separatist issues, and she lamented the labor of bringing "diverse masses of women TOGETHER to work toward common goals," which seemed overwhelming. Millsapps noted the importance of the center as a place like no other for women, but she bemoaned the fact that "only a handful seem to need facilities which can accommodate many more. . . . The house stands as a shell which once contained workshops, discussion groups, and lots of women getting down to business. The business of being themselves."[38] In 1975, "Kristin" opened the CWC newsletter with a heart-wrenching greeting:

> Dear Sister, So you women want a Women's Center. Tell me about it. Tell me about a house in Dilworth that provides space for women to go, a space where the warmth between women may be shared. Tell me about the tears of joy and pain that have been freely given, experienced and shared, and I'll tell you about a place that no longer exists. I'll tell you about bitterness, I'll tell you about hostility, I'll tell you about no cooperation, I'll tell you about weary women who no longer want to keep on telling you.[39]

Efforts to define the physical space of the center divided the women who tried to claim the space according to their sexual or political preferences. As Jan Millsapps remembered it, "friendships were shattered," and "the whole place came apart."[40] Just four years after its founding, the Lyndhurst Avenue bungalow overflowed with pain and conflict.

Although the members of the Drastic Dykes continued to live in the CWC's upstairs apartment until December 1975, they did not support the mission of the center or interact with the non-separatist members.[41] Reflecting national debates over lesbian separatism, the Charlotte Women's Center could not find sufficient common ground for lesbians, lesbian separatists, and heterosexual feminists. The center hoped to provide a space for all women, but in actuality only a relatively small and predominantly white group of women found it to be a welcoming space. Although more than seventy women were affiliated with or connected to the CWC, only ten to twenty regularly attended monthly general meetings. As Finn Enke has shown, during the early 1970s "community spaces came into being alongside activists' intense efforts to define themselves and their politics. . . . To the extent that struggles over politicized community were about generating and achieving feminist goals, they were equally about defining space."[42] Like the better-known and better-documented

Washington, DC–based lesbian-feminist collective the Furies, the women at Lyndhurst Avenue shared contentious political and activist space. In trying to explain why she was affiliated with the Drastic Dykes, Joy Justice turned to the Furies for a "lucid" and "thorough" analysis of separatism.[43] The continued dissension among the women at the center led to significant fissures that crippled their efforts to create a lasting community. CWC member and lesbian Concetta Hinceman attempted to understand the stance adopted by the Drastic Dykes. "The current residents are political separatists; now I can't explain that, except that this particular kind of separatism excludes all other people who are not of the same political ideologies, which means the upstairs residents exclude all women except women like them." Hinceman went on to argue that no one "should be living in the house that contains the Women's Center" if they were not willing to accept all women. "Just think how hard it has been letting women know that the Center is open to all women."[44]

In the two years following the split, the content of the CWC newsletter focused on community outreach, abortion rights, and women in prison. Only occasionally did a reference to a lesbian dance warrant inclusion. In a survey to determine what groups would garner the most support for meetings at the center, a lesbian group was not even listed among the options. The separatism of the Drastic Dykes effectively removed visibility for any lesbians at the center, whether separatist or not. Indeed, separatist and lesbian became discursively intertwined in the CWC newsletter.

In addition to personal sacrifices and the turmoil of personal separatist commitments, economic challenges defined the production of *Sinister Wisdom* in Charlotte. The love affair between the editors and their energetic commitment to the journal were not sufficient to sustain the publication. Minnie Bruce Pratt met *Sinister Wisdom* founders Harriet Desmoines and Catherine Nicholson when she was invited to read her poem at the Southeastern Women's Studies Association annual conference held in Charlotte in 1978. In describing her time in Charlotte, Pratt recalled, "I never went to the *Sinister Wisdom* production parties in Charlotte, but I understood . . . these were big community events—and also that participation faded so much so that Harriet and Catherine couldn't put out the magazine with regularity."[45] The editors faced substantial economic challenges and often relied on care packages from around the country, including "head food," meant to feed their bodies and fuel their minds for production. In the first issue of the magazine, Desmoines recognized that she and Nicholson enjoyed the privilege and "freedom" necessary "to edit and produce a magazine" for a year, but money would be a defining concern in moving forward with the publication. As they compiled their first issue, it was unclear to them if the magazine would ever be more than its first three issues. Anyone who was able to send $4.50 would receive those first three issues. Beyond that, they would depend on contributions to see if a second year of publication was possible.[46]

Charlotte was a place where *Sinister Wisdom*'s editors felt oppressed and isolated. At the end of the 1970s, *Sinister Wisdom* relocated to Lincoln, Nebraska, where it received support from a vibrant community of lesbians, but while in Charlotte, Desmoines and Nicholson ran the magazine from their home in a quiet Cold War–era neighborhood near the Charlotte Country Club.[47] Isolation was a term often used by southern lesbians who saw themselves in an "oppression sandwich." They were caught between non-southern lesbians on one side—who often viewed southern lesbians through a regional lens, as disorganized, ignorant, and fearfully closeted—and "repressive" southern men on the other.[48] In the idyllic Country Club Heights neighborhood they faced hostile male neighbors, including a national leader of the Ku Klux Klan.[49] They found their sloped driveway routinely littered at the top with broken bottles, which could not be seen from the road. When their cat was shot, Desmoines confronted a male neighbor who habitually watched them from his front porch across the street and remembered that when he answered the door, a rifle was visible in the entryway.[50]

Despite this harassment, just a few blocks from the Charlotte Country Club, a bastion of wealthy white heterosexual privilege, writings from Audre Lorde, Tee Corinne, Karla Jay, Adrienne Rich, Rita Mae Brown, Pat Califia, and other radical lesbians mingled in the pages of *Sinister Wisdom*. Academics, activists, mothers, a poet in Paris, an editor of the groundbreaking lesbian magazine *The Ladder*, and a founder of Daughters, Inc., who famously published Brown's pathbreaking southern lesbian coming-of-age novel, *Rubyfruit Jungle*, all came together through their words in a small home in Charlotte. Their thoughts were sustenance for an international lesbian-feminist audience. A 1976 editorial statement from Desmoines revealed the activist roots of the publication:

> We're lesbians living in the South. We're white; sometimes
> unemployed, sometimes working part-time. We're a generation
> apart. Catherine directed university plays for twenty years. . . . I was
> an erratic activist in the civil rights movement, the Left, and then

the radical feminist women's movement. . . . The consciousness we want *Sinister Wisdom* to express is . . . that of the lesbian or lunatic who embraces her boundary/criminal status, with the aim of creating a new species in a new time/space. We're using the remnants of our class and race privilege to construct a force that we hope will help ultimately destroy privilege.[51]

While the editors faced their biases and worked to "destroy privilege" in Charlotte's Country Club Heights neighborhood, some lesbians at the CWC attempted to forge a non-separatist path.

Discussions of a separate (but not separatist) lesbian center and dances to raise funds for this center received attention in the CWC newsletter, and by the fall of 1976 the Lesbian Center Group produced a separate newsletter.[52] Quite similar in format to the typewritten and xeroxed format of the CWC newsletter, the *Lesbian Center Journal* covered the group's local activism, devoted space to personal thought pieces, and hoped to form lesbian consciousness-raising meetings. When a local restaurant worker, Jennifer Justice, was fired from the Stonehenge Restaurant allegedly because she "wouldn't do sexual flirtations with her bosses and the male customers," there was some debate among members of the Lesbian Center Group as to whether they should support this action since Justice was not a lesbian, but eight women did show up at the restaurant and march against the firing.[53] They carried signs and chanted songs of protest:

> I don't know but I've been told
> waitresses are bought and sold,
> I don't know but I really feel
> man's cooked up a dirty deal,
> Dykes unite we're marching now,
> make them know we take this vow,
> To fight the state and fight the prick,
> that makes this world so goddamn sick.[54]

Although police tried to disband the protest on the grounds that the group had no permit, the women argued successfully that they did not need a permit and had access to legal counsel. The police left the protest after this exchange, and the women "arrived home safely." According to Penny, who submitted the coverage for the newsletter, the Lesbian Center women viewed the protest as successful, and they hoped that they "slowed down

. . . business that night."[55] Thereafter came calls to boycott the Stonehenge in the future and for women who worked there to demand a respectful workplace.[56] As other scholars have noted, even if actions like the Stonehenge protest occurred off the main stages of national movements, they represent a continuity of movements in 1970s queer militancy.[57]

Lesbians who sought community and visibility often wrestled with the politics of lesbian-feminist separatism. Drastic Dyke Joy Justice grappled with her own commitment to separatism. She felt frustrated by the words "anger" and "isolation" used against her by women at the CWC yet acknowledged that her separatism necessarily included both. Working through her anger was part of her separatist process, but she hit personal roadblocks, causing her to return from separatism after two years. She could not abide a theoretical position requiring her to abandon her biological sister because she was heterosexual. When she wrote about this personal turmoil in the pages of *Sinister Wisdom*, she concluded that she could live only as an "individual," without being part of a movement or a separatist community. Yet she also admitted needing lesbians in her life. In leaving separatism as an identity, Justice was unwilling to forsake lesbian camaraderie. As she put aside the label of separatist, she still embraced many of its ideals—especially with regard to issues of race, class, sex, and age. "I still need to always remember the things I learned from separatism about society, because otherwise the world would be an incomprehensible ball of goo." She "needed to be around lesbians" and found this opportunity in meetings for the newly formed Lesbian Center Group.[58]

Three years after the Drastic Dykes exited the Charlotte Women's Center, some lesbian involvement returned to the Lyndhurst Avenue house, providing the camaraderie that Justice and others sought. A few women who were involved with the Drastic Dykes and *Sinister Wisdom* frequented the CWC with the hope of avoiding former lovers and messy emotional entanglements. But the community of lesbians was too small to withstand the splits between former lovers and friends, which often trumped any commitment to activist organizing or publications. A lesbian support group met at the center, but at least one woman worried about participating in a group with women who were her former lovers. She suggested that two lesbian support groups would allow "more freedom to air feelings" and avoid inhibition by former lovers who might be forced to participate in the same group. Charlotte's lesbian population was small enough in the 1970s that the friendship pool was often indistinguishable from the dating pool. Gathering like-minded women who identified as activist and lesbian sometimes meant interacting with former lovers. As a result, the activism and amity that Joy Justice sought would have to take a back seat to sexual tensions at the center as women hoped to avoid previous lovers and find new ones.[59]

For women attempting to live independently, money was a constant concern. Financial limitations regulated many CWC activities, permeated the content of its newsletter, and would ultimately lead to its demise. If women were to be visible on their own terms, woman-run operations were vital. Yet outside funding and support was sometimes necessary for survival. As lesbian-feminist gathering places exchanged their newsletters with other like-minded women's groups, the financial and housing needs for traveling women became a frequent topic. When a San Francisco feminist singing group contacted the CWC about their upcoming tour and their desire to play in Charlotte, a note on the center log read, "Letter from women in San Francisco—touring country—singing. Will be here April 21–26. Want to play. Doesn't say anything about money. Assume feminist. Might be neat."[60] Financial struggles seeped through the pages of the center's newsletter, often controlling the content focus. These struggles were common among alternative New Left publications, yet dedication to producing voluminous amounts of written material was integral to the foundation of the movement generally. Through newsletters such as the one produced in Charlotte, matters of national and international feminisms brought women together through the written word—a staple of the movement.[61] In keeping with the national feminist movement, women at the Charlotte Women's Center sought a variety of outlets for documenting and expressing their feminist goals. One such outlet was *The Road*, an alternative newspaper based at the University of North Carolina at Charlotte. The CWC newsletter described the publishing opportunity this way: "THE ROAD needs women writers, artists, photographers for women's section of new monthly alternative newspaper. No pay, but great exposure and outlet for bursting creativity."[62] The CWC ran advertisements in *The Road* describing its center as a "life space . . . staffed by feminists" and offering a "place for all women." Jan Millsapps worked with *The Road* on its "women's content," as did J. C. Honeycutt. Honeycutt covered the Joan Little case for the paper, and Millsapps called for an integrated approach to the woman-focused content in *The Road*. She rejected a tokenistic layout, which would relegate the "woman" information to a special highlight box. Millsapps argued that women's interests were important to all readers and should be included as such. In a 1975 survey of its women readers,

The Road reported that they ranged in age from eighteen to over forty and were married, divorced, and had a lover or lovers, but overwhelmingly these women were "definitely interested in women's sexuality (69 percent responded favorably to that)."[63] *The Road* was woman-oriented but not lesbian-oriented. Although the paper advertised the CWC's openness to all women, the interests and identities of lesbians were not addressed. Revealing the need for publications like the CWC newsletter and *Sinister Wisdom*, independently managed and published by women, *The Road* abstained from using the word "lesbian," and its male-led staff controlled the presentation of woman-related content.

The unpaid labor of lesbians was the primary source of support for women's centers and publishing, and the scene in Charlotte was no exception. In 1974, the CWC newsletter highlighted the discouragement at the center and an effort to motivate "raving women" toward involvement at the center. The women "got even more discouraged when it finally dawned on us that what most women need is money, and we didn't have any of that. The only way to get money was to apply for grants, and that would take away our independence and transform the women's center into another liberal social service agency." Finances alienated the women from their mission, and the women at the CWC struggled for years with the dilemma of autonomy versus survival.[64]

In comparison with other regional southern centers, the CWC women saw theirs as a uniquely independent entity controlled "by women for women."[65] At the same UNC Charlotte Southeastern Women's Studies Association conference where Minnie Bruce Pratt met the editors of *Sinister Wisdom*, J. C. Honeycutt represented Charlotte at a featured workshop on women's centers, with other participants from Knoxville, Tuscaloosa, and Asheville. CWC member Gloria Knotts expounded on the conference for the newsletter: "Our autonomy and control by women for women, our length of existence, our focus on 'women's liberation' and consciousness-raising rather than on issues, social services, funding or 'respectability' were all facets of a different approach."[66] Knotts noted that other centers represented at the workshop suffered under bureaucratic controls, but the women in Charlotte saw their control of the CWC as vital to their comparative longevity. They understood their autonomy as a release from any societal respectability necessary to garner community or government support. Other centers received funding from the American Association of University Women and were largely supported and attended by university women. Charlotte's center was independent of UNC Charlotte, which encouraged some social and class diversity and allowed it to be located closer to the center of Charlotte proper. The university stood on the edge of the city and hosted events that were important to the CWC, but it did not serve as the primary anchor for the activities of the CWC.

Yet the center depended more on outside support than its leaders recognized. The loss of Comprehensive Employment and Training Administration (CETA) funding in 1979 came just a year after the Women's Studies Association conference, and it would cause substantial financial hardship at the CWC. The center's only stable financial support came from a CETA-funded coordinator position. Signed into law by President Nixon in 1973, CETA funding allowed many community organizations like the Charlotte Women's Center to pay for basic expenses. The funds were handled entirely at the local level, and in the case of the CWC they could be used only to support one clerical or coordinator position. Center members were eager to use the funding for basic operational costs, but this was not allowed. By June 1979, it was clear that CETA would probably cut all financial assistance by the fall and leave the center in a state of desperation: "We need to come up with possible alternatives to having a full time coordinator. We need people who are willing and able to help us deal with ceta and its 'people in power.' We need you!!"[67] The CWC faced a stark financial reality. Autonomy was no longer the priority, or even a real possibility, and the center's survival was questionable. A newsletter writer closed an issue with the following warning: "See you next month, maybe." The newsletter's writers begged for money and help in writing grants or dealing with the power structure at CETA. The loss of this funding in October 1979 was devastating. One month later the center was out of money. It was now an all-volunteer organization, and the newsletter writers desperately pleaded for help just to lick stamps.[68]

While Charlotte women labored to maintain the Charlotte Women's Center, the Atlanta Lesbian Feminist Alliance enjoyed relatively more success. If Charlotte was a hub for southern lesbian activity and organizing, Atlanta was a mecca. Boasting not only ALFA but also the successful alternative newspaper the *Great Speckled Bird*, a local chapter of the Gay Liberation Front, and the lesbian-owned feminist bookstore Charis Books and More, lesbians in Atlanta sustained a level of visible community-based activism throughout the 1970s and 1980s that their Charlotte counterparts could not achieve.

The impetus for ALFA came from women who were committed to New Left activism and frustrated with the gay liberation and women's liberation movements. Gay activist organizations were often hotbeds of sexism, with the Gay Liberation Front in both Atlanta and Charlotte largely controlled by gay men. In ALFA, "young leftist women who had joined the Venceremos Brigades and had come to Atlanta as one of the staging areas for the Brigades" found an opportunity to focus solely on their lesbian-feminist goals. In the funky "Little Five Points" (L5P) neighborhood close to Emory University, "there was a home in Atlanta for lesbians who found the women's liberation movement too heterosexist and the gay liberation movement, as well as most leftist groups, too sexist."[69] Lesbian awakening gripped Atlanta's L5P by 1971. Decimated by white flight in the 1960s, the neighborhood attracted freethinkers, political activists, artists, lesbians, and feminists who were free to pursue their "'anything is possible' view of the future" in a neighborhood threatened with further annihilation by interstate development but that offered sketchy yet affordable housing.[70] Predominantly white college students at nearby Georgia State University and Emory University engaged in political organizing and communal living led by women who defined the development of the neighborhood.

In the beginning, ALFA operated from the "Edge of Night"—a communal household, much like the Charlotte Women's Center. "The three-story wood frame structure on Mansfield Avenue in Little Five Points," a neighborhood of lesbian communal households, featured "concrete steps that led from the street past the wild garden to the front porch of this twenties-style house." The house offered a place for women in and outside of Atlanta "'to just be with other lesbians.'"[71] Eventually ALFA would move to a rented home on McLendon Avenue in the same L5P neighborhood.[72] From its formation, ALFA quieted the divisive debate over lesbian separatism. Members fought against both sexist and heterosexist strictures.[73] According to member Vicki Gabriner, "Atlanta Women's Liberation 'was too straight and the Gay liberation Front was too male.'"[74] ALFA would be lesbian-focused, but according to early ALFA organizers Gabriner and Lorraine Fontana, there would not be a "'litmus test—you don't have to pull out your lesbian ID card!'"[75] ALFA provided a space for women who hoped to escape the heterosexism of liberation (gay and women's) and the sexism of the New Left generally. According to Saralyn Chesnut and Amanda C. Gable, "For the first time in the history of lesbians in the South, there were social spaces outside the bars where lesbians could meet other lesbians and public activities in which they could participate as lesbians, without fear of persecution by police and with the knowledge that if they did encounter harassment or persecution from anyone, they had a community of strong, activist women to support and defend them."[76] With ALFA as its base camp and the alternative L5P neighborhood providing relatively safe space, queer feminist community blossomed in Atlanta.

The ALFA house offered more than refuge; it offered education. A six-dollar membership ensured, among other things, "sisterhood and good vibes."[77] ALFA managed to create an impressive library (the Southern Feminist Library and Archives) of feminist and lesbian-feminist newsletters and periodicals. Its *Atalanta* newsletter often listed these receipts and acquisitions as a community service for lesbians seeking information and regional and national connections. ALFA's commitment to the print culture of feminism meant that the history of women's centers across the world—including the Charlotte Women's Center—would be preserved.[78] The members' ability to maintain the organization and archives speaks to the relative affluence of women in Atlanta generally and to the vibrant community of artists, activists, and college students in the Little Five Points neighborhood. Women in Atlanta earned real wages—adjusted for cost of living—that were 11 percent higher compared with the combined averages of hourly wages for women in the remainder of the South's six largest metro areas at the time: Houston, Miami, Dallas, New Orleans, and Tampa.[79] Women in ALFA used what marginal resources they could muster to bolster the Edge of Night and provide feminist refuge in the South. Atlanta operated on a profoundly larger economic and population base than many New South cities, including Charlotte, and organizations like ALFA benefited from this.

Atlanta's economic climate for women boosted Georgia's position as the state with the second highest growth rate in the number of women-owned firms nationally.[80] This affluence was apparent to African American lesbian Karla Brown, who moved from Charlotte to Atlanta in the early 1970s and found the women at ALFA to be more welcoming than those at the Charlotte Women's Center. She was also keenly aware that some women at the ALFA house had their own places to live, unlike Brown at the time, and were largely middle-class white women who were older than she was and had completed their educations.[81] When Atlanta's *Pulse* periodical featured an article titled "Celebrating a Woman's Space," it demonstrated that even twelve years after ALFA settled into the Little Five Points neighborhood, its spirit was still strong. The article praised the vital role of ALFA's library in preserving Atlanta's "herstory" and the continued, if controversial, importance of providing a "male-free zone," noting that "even if the gay men didn't really want to hang out with the lesbians all the time, they resented an area that was forbidden to them."[82] Local queer publications like *Pulse* offered the women of ALFA a platform to publicize their work in the community.

ALFA and southern lesbians also benefited from the success of Atlanta's alternative paper, the *Great Speckled Bird*.[83] Promising a "radical perspective from Atlanta," the *Bird* offered significant coverage of lesbian news.[84] ALFA fought with the city's mainstream newspaper, the *Atlanta Journal*, to gain coverage of its events, making the *Bird*'s coverage even more consequential. Other Atlanta women's groups enjoyed event listings in the *Atlanta Journal* but not so ALFA. When the paper did not print notice of ALFA's 1973 Susan B. Anthony open house, the *Journal*'s celebrated editor Jack Spalding responded to ALFA member Vicki Gabriner's letter of complaint by noting that newspapers were "slow in taking up new ideas." He closed his patronizing five-sentence response this way: "Your complaints were about yesterday. Things should be better tomorrow."[85]

The *Great Speckled Bird* featured Atlanta's 1975 Great Southeast Lesbian Conference on the front page, and included a feature article that discussed the conference's focus on "Building a Lesbian Community." Notably, this effort toward lesbian community building came in the same year that the Drastic Dykes members made their exit from the Charlotte Women's Center. The *Bird*'s women writers celebrated the conference's focus on "change, change, change," moving away from "choking anger" toward an inclusiveness that was seen as refreshingly free of "women hysterically needing to proclaim how good the gay life is or hanging all over other women." The theme of community building in Atlanta laid the groundwork to "generate much or nothing. On this weekend of a full moon eclipse which moved from Scorpio to Sagittarius, tremendous energy was generated, tremendous potential uncovered, tremendous possibilities realized." Conference attendees hoped to set up regional and national community networks for lesbians, and they worked under the recognition that "lesbians who are self-supporting and live outside the nuclear family present a challenge" to the oppressive system of capitalism. The *Bird* article concluded that socialism would be the best path for the lesbian movement. "This was not a weekend to party" but a weekend to do the work of lesbian activism.[86]

Charlotte's Drastic Dykes led a workshop at the Great Southeast Lesbian Conference on lesbian separatism, but even at the conference there was confusion about how to proceed and whom to include. The Dykes wanted to meet exclusively with separatists in their workshop, but according to Atlanta attendee Elizabeth Knowlton, "nonseparatists could not accept this; therefore the meeting became a movement from room to room, as the separatists attempted to separate themselves."[87] The conference's focus on the issue suggested to the *Bird* writers that "lesbian separatism is a tool for survival and for developing women's strengths." The goal put forward at this conference was to remove the need for separatism but to recognize the ideology as temporarily strategic.[88] Knowlton faced a difficult decision on where to fit in the separatist debate. She "didn't feel part of either group." When she lived in the Research Triangle of North Carolina, she was a separatist, but at the time of the conference she felt a kinship with "puzzled lesbians who wanted to discuss the issue."[89] The same turmoil experienced by Joy Justice also troubled Knowlton and the hundreds of women in Atlanta who attended the lesbian meetup. The conference concluded with a call for further examination of both separatism and racism. Black women at the conference pushed for future work on third world women. While the conference recognized that "both separatism and racism are very heavy issues," the incorrect assumption that Black women would join the movement was often the norm, rather than the decision to "expand . . . to include" the needs and desires of Black women.[90] As other scholars have noted, the lesbian-separatist rejection of the family of origin, for example, proved especially difficult for Black women who remained connected to Black communities in an alliance of necessity based on racial oppression.[91]

The Great Southeast Lesbian Conference placed Atlanta in the center of the lesbian-feminist universe of the 1970s. ALFA welcomed attendees to Atlanta with warnings to beware of curious neighbors and "roving police cars" and to avoid "obvious public displays of affection" in and around the conference host houses, in an effort to protect Atlanta's feminists from ongoing "legal challenges and future vandalism."[92] Because of the national response to the Great Southeast Lesbian Conference, several feminist newsletters covered the event, including the violent arrest of five lesbians who were dining out at an eatery recommended by conference organizers as a welcoming space for lesbians and gay men. What began as a dispute about an overcharge and at least two male diners who expressed a problem with lesbians claiming space ended in the women being called "butch bitches" by the police officer and being arrested on charges of criminal trespassing and "causing a turmoil." One of the women used the word "fuck" in reference to an officer who "threw her up against the wall and started to choke her."[93] In the end, the women were released with a fine, but the event reverberated throughout the lesbian-feminist press. All told, eighteen states were represented at the Atlanta conference, 325 women attended, and featured speakers hailed from places like Northampton, Massachusetts, and San Francisco. Women from Georgia, North Carolina, and Florida represented the largest state contingents. While Charlotte's activists made regional connections and sought to make their city a hub of feminist—and occasionally lesbian—activity, the Atlanta Lesbian Feminist Alliance made national connections through the Great Southeast Lesbian Conference, where it challenged New Left ideological boundaries with the help of the *Bird*'s coverage of the event and put Atlanta on the national feminist map— even if with negative publicity.[94]

Unless an event was specifically labeled as lesbian, like the Great Southeast Lesbian Conference a year earlier, general content of specific interest to lesbians was often sidelined in alternative papers like the *Bird* and *The Road*. In both cities, lesbians largely remained outside the category of woman—even in the alternative press of the 1970s. If lesbian content was included, the word "lesbian" was often avoided and lesbians themselves usually wrote the material. Atlanta's *Bird* celebrated International Women's Day by devoting an entire issue to women, as it had done since 1969. In the opening statement on the issue, the staff (the newspaper explicitly shunned labels such as "editors") focused on "new areas" of struggle for women, like issues of concern for lesbians. Yet the issue itself contained nothing specifically aimed at lesbians. This was also the case at the Charlotte publication the *Charlotte Free Press* (*CFP*). Like many alternative periodicals of the era, the paper attempted to reach both lesbians and gay men, but content for lesbians came primarily from women like J. C. Honeycutt, Jan Millsapps, and Harriet Desmoines—women who were central figures at the Charlotte Women's Center. Desmoines wrote a review of a lesbian anthology for the *CFP*, and occasional classified advertisements in the paper contained information on how to order *Sinister Wisdom*. The *CFP* served as a tool to bring lesbians together in both social and intellectual spaces. Supportive publishing outlets allowed women to reach new communities of women, as they advertised and promoted their existence in the paper. Like *The Road*, the *CFP* relied on women from the Charlotte Women's Center for its content, but as a queer publication it offered an additional venue for lesbians to identify potential meeting spaces outside of the bars. It is interesting to note that 1977 was the third year of production for the *CFP*. *The Road* struggled to survive and ultimately failed in 1975. The relative success of the *CFP* was probably due to its promotion of men's gay bars throughout the state of North Carolina, which meant important advertising dollars that a solely political and alternative newspaper like *The Road* could not attract or did not pursue. The *Great Speckled Bird* maintained its political focus and managed to survive, but unlike *The Road*, the *Bird* was surrounded by an activist Little Five Points neighborhood. A comparable activist neighborhood did not exist to sustain a university-based leftist publication in Charlotte.

Although there was little lesbian-specific content in the International Women's Day issue of the *Bird*, a small handwritten advertisement ran for "Charis: Books & More." The ad promoted Olivia Records, the growing record label devoted specifically to lesbian music, also labeled "women's music." Olivia musicians worked to bring lesbians together for gatherings around the country, including in Atlanta and Charlotte. A small advertisement could serve as an opportunity for an isolated or new-to-town woman seeking lesbian relationships. Olivia recordings opened up a world of lesbian music to a national, primarily white, audience. The *CFP* featured Meg Christian, one of Olivia's most popular artists, on its front cover and ran advertisements for where to buy Olivia records in the city. When Christian came to the area in 1979, the CWC newsletter promoted her visit even before its writers had full details on her concert.[95] Lesbian journalist Maida Tilchen asserted that women's music was "the most commercially successful and perhaps most spiritually unifying aspect of lesbian feminism."[96] A chance meeting over an Olivia record-shopping excursion could lead to a significant lesbian connection. Locating lesbians was often a matter of locating a place that sold Olivia recordings.

Olivia Records played a fundamental role in the early formation of a haven for lesbian-feminist community building, Charis Books and More. Located in unconventional L5P, which was "'crawling with lesbians,'" the store opened in November 1974 and quickly became part of the neighborhood. In fact, the area served as a breeding ground for store volunteers and patrons who claimed Charis as their own.[97] The owners, Barbara Borgman and Linda Bryant, imagined a store offering a radical alternative space featuring women's and children's books alongside pathbreaking readings on religion and spirituality.[98] Borgman and Bryant were accidental lesbian activists who never envisioned the long-standing role that their store would come to play as an anchor in Atlanta for feminists and lesbians. Bryant remembered Chris Carroll and Karen Gold as the first self-identified lesbians from the L5P neighborhood whom she met; Carroll was distributing Olivia records and Charis began selling women's music early on. Bryant also fondly recalled frequenting the favorite bar of the L5P lesbians, the Tower, around 1975 to hear Olivia recording artists Cris Williamson and June Millington. Even though she identified as heterosexual at the time, she was thrilled by the experience.[99] In celebrating Charis for *Pulse* magazine, a writer sketched a warm and vital woman's space: "For feminists, lesbians, and feminist-lesbians, Charis may provide an adventurous pilgrimage inward. Customers can kick back on the ratty, but comfortable, reading sofa . . . breathe freely," and experience the "ambience." According to the article, patrons could use Charis as an information point to find an electrician or locate a woman's bar; the store served as a "community resource center." The article also noted the importance of Olivia music and its availability at Charis, referring to the best-selling artists such as Meg Christian and Cris Williamson by their first names, like friends who offered the "no longer hidden music of women loving women."[100] As Chesnut and Gable have shown, Charis represented a fundamental tenet of lesbian feminism, "its construction of a new lesbian identity." This new identity meant that lesbians left behind the "realms of sickness and sin" that defined them in the first half of the twentieth century and entered a public and political arena through "the production and widespread dissemination of new and diverse representations of lesbian life and culture."[101] Enke has observed that bars were "primary locations" for the "publication of a newly defined feminist subject," yet Charis Books and More served this role in Atlanta.[102] As early as the 1970s, it offered a visibly defined space outside of the dark and hidden bar for women to congregate, communicate, and identify as a lesbian and a woman.

Often described as temporary and holding idealistic goals, 1970s separatist lesbian-feminist communities throughout the United States proclaimed their commitments to political action and revolution. Lesbian-separatist scholarship repeatedly turns to the Furies of Washington, DC, often seen as the epitome of lesbian-feminist separatism even as the group's ideological platform was divisive and arrogant. In their own writings, the Furies acknowledged their fight for survival: "In our ardor and enthusiasm for what we have discovered, lesbians may be arrogant at times. However, most 'lesbian chauvinism' is a survival reaction developed to get us through the roadblocks that straight feminists erect against our ideas and experiences."[103] Relying on the history of the Furies to understand lesbian-feminist separatism leaves a gap in our understanding of local approaches and successes born of the ideology of separatism. Understanding lesbian-feminist separatism at the regional level, in the context of the urban space that shaped its growth, allows us to see what worked and what did not for lesbians, feminists, and separatist lesbian feminists in Atlanta and Charlotte.

Charis and ALFA remained in Atlanta's vibrant L5P neighborhood beyond the 1970s, and their tenacity is an example of how lesbian feminism in Atlanta differed from that in the Queen City. While Charis and ALFA were going strong, participation in the production of *Sinister Wisdom* began to wane, which would contribute to Harriet Desmoines and Catherine Nicholson's decision to move the magazine out of North Carolina at the end of the decade.[104] Just a few years after it began publishing in a flurry of fire and dramatic passion, *Sinister Wisdom* left Charlotte for Lincoln, Nebraska, and the Drastic Dykes seemed to disappear with its exit. Meanwhile, the Charlotte Women's Center struggled to maintain a physical space, and its early commitment to lesbian visibility wavered. Charlotte women supported an energetic chapter of the National Organization for Women, and it would be a NOW meeting in Charlotte that would draw Minnie Bruce Pratt to the Queen City and facilitate her love affair with Cris South. Charlotte also attempted to maintain a Gay Liberation Front chapter and briefly formed an organization known as Charlotte Gay Alliance for Freedom. In spite of these organizations, the visibility that was necessary to sustain activism in Charlotte was too high a price for many. Socializing was the focus, not gay liberation. While gay men's bars and baths thrived, activist groups struggled against a tide of queer Charlotteans who were not willing to align themselves with the movement.[105] In a city that wrestled with its own identity, gay liberation activists and lesbian feminists mirrored this identity crisis, often preferring to remain within Charlotte's invisible demimonde. Quiet lesbian and queer writing blossomed in Charlotte's isolating neighborhoods, but a permanent visible and physical space devoted to (or at least encouraging of) lesbians was harder to achieve in Charlotte. Local sites of print-media production, like ALFA, produced homegrown feminist communities that worked to distribute feminist messages on a broad and perceptible scale. These sites were crucial to sustaining the local movement community.[106] Atlanta lesbians nurtured these spaces; Charlotte women could not. As the next chapter will reveal, public celebrations of lesbian and gay identities demonstrated the causes and consequences of these differences in the queer New South.

Bull Dyke in a Queen City:
She's a Comedienne! She's a Singer!
She's a DYYYYKE! —North Carolina Pride
newsletter

4 PRIDE

. . . .

The Drastic Dykes of 1970s Charlotte would certainly have rallied around
the visibility of queer protest and defiance, but there was no community
Gay Pride event until the 1980s. Male-dominated Pride events that eventually took place in Charlotte did not offer universal appeal to lesbians
who still valued their separate identity. Lesbians who craved separate
social space turned to women's music festivals, fleeting social groups,
and short-lived bars. They occasionally attended Pride festivals, but
few women were involved in the planning of these events. For lesbians
in Atlanta, however, the Atlanta Lesbian Feminist Alliance served as a
major presence in the early origins of Atlanta's gay rights parade—the
first in the Deep South, debuting in 1971. ALFA first participated as an
organization in June 1973, and in the years following, the group was vital
to creating activities that kept the event focused on lesbian interests, like
lesbian films shown at ALFA's open house and especially lesbian softball.[1]
Gay Pride rallies played an important role in the activism of the 1970s,
but in subsequent decades the festivals increasingly functioned as public
social events and mega-media spectacles with substantial corporate support and branding. Yet they continued to bring queer-identified people
together during the daytime in public urban spaces.

For residents of Atlanta and Charlotte, these festivals would be the
only setting in which they were forced to recognize the growing queer
populations in their cities. Historians have virtually ignored the history of Gay Pride celebrations in the New South, yet these celebrations
operated as a barometer of the environment for lesbians and gay men
in each city. Whether or not lesbians or gay men participated in—or
even attended—the events, Pride celebrations demonstrated the climate
for queer community in a city. They highlighted the businesses, politicians, public safety, and community organizations that were available
to or supportive of gay people—even if only for the potential financial

relationship. In this chapter, Gay Pride serves as a lens through which the environment for lesbian lives in Atlanta and Charlotte can be understood. Atlanta's long history of supporting Gay Pride celebrations in its queer-friendly Midtown neighborhood offers a unique comparison with Charlotte's reluctant relationship with Gay Pride and its queer citizens. The events shaped lesbian life in each city—through political players and activism, through business involvement, and through the bars. Pride celebrations evolved rapidly in the final decades of the twentieth century, and they serve as a bellwether of change in the queer and urban New South.

Most Pride event organizers recognize the history of the celebration and its origins based on police harassment and arrests of queer people at the Stonewall Inn in Greenwich Village that led to frenzied rioting on the volatile weekend of June 28, 1969. As the popularity of Pride grew, the spirit of celebration and a party atmosphere supported by corporate sponsors often obscured historical or political messages about gay oppression.[2] Pride festival organizers moved from planning events in the early 1970s that focused on the right of lesbian and gay people to be recognized as citizens, or simply to exist, to creating massive weeklong extravaganzas including performers, food, shopping, and huge corporate sponsors. During the decades since the Stonewall riots, Pride celebrations have become an institution for many cities and regions of all sizes. As of 2019, for example, there are events throughout the state of North Carolina in the Outer Banks, Raleigh, Boone, the Triad, and in western North Carolina. The city of Charlotte hosts both Charlotte Black Gay Pride and Pride Charlotte. In addition to Atlanta's Black Pride, the largest in the world, and the Atlanta Pride Festival, Georgia is home to celebrations in Athens, Savannah, and the regional South Georgia Pride.[3] Atlanta's Southern Fried Queer Pride organized in 2014 to claim space for people of color, celebrate queer southern artists, and refute the southern "narrative of stigma, statistics, and struggle" for queer people.[4]

Several factors contributed to the success of Atlanta Pride and to Charlotte's difficulties in gaining and maintaining a Pride festival. Atlanta had neighborhood, business, economic, and mayoral support. ALFA and stand-alone lesbian bars played a crucial role in making sure there were opportunities for lesbians to participate in Pride, including the city's first Dyke March, which offered an alternative to corporate and male-dominated Pride in the 1980s.[5] Mayor Maynard Jackson's early backing of Atlanta Pride in the 1970s helped secure its longevity and success. In the same era, Charlotte boasted two significant gay media publications—the lesbian-feminist journal *Sinister Wisdom* and the lesbian and gay newspaper the *Charlotte Free Press*—and with the arrival of the newspaper *Q-Notes* in 1983, Charlotteans enjoyed an impressive collection of homegrown queer media. Yet gay people in Charlotte struggled to sustain a substantial and visible queer business district, locate a publicly supportive mayor, or encourage lesbian organizations like ALFA. Lacking these structures, queer people in Charlotte faced significant challenges when trying to launch an annual Gay Pride event in the 1980s and 1990s. Charlotte maintained gay media outlets like newspapers, largely invisible forms of lesbian and gay community, whereas Atlanta boasted a level of organized visibility that made queer publications secondary—only a component of a vibrant network of lesbian and gay support in the city. Signs of a visible queer presence would serve as a beacon to attract lesbians looking to relocate and heterosexuals seeking a southern life without the traditionally expected biases against socially liberal lifestyles. Many who chose to live in the South, especially transplants who were relocating for employment, used the tolerance for and visibility of a gay community as a factor in determining where they would reside.[6] Pride celebrations were often the most palpable representation of these phenomena. As one Pride organizer in Atlanta asserted, attending a celebration was the "easiest, most significant expression of Gay political Power one can make all year."[7]

The earliest Pride festivals in Atlanta, grounded in activism and visible protest, always took place in the Midtown neighborhood near Piedmont Park. At their first gathering in 1970, Atlanta activists handed out gay-rights literature in the park to commemorate the Greenwich Village Stonewall riots a year earlier.[8] In the open-air shopping plaza Ansley Mall, just under two miles from Atlanta's Midtown gayborhood, an act of police harassment against queer people fueled this first Stonewall commemoration event in the city. In what some have labeled Atlanta's own Stonewall moment, a police raid designed to intimidate and "weed out 'known homosexuals'" at a mall theater provided the impetus for queer mobilization.[9] Police interrupted a screening of Andy Warhol's *Lonesome Cowboys* with a whistle, wielding flashlights and turning on the overhead theater lights. Audience members, including lesbians, gay men, and drag queens, were called out row by row and interrogated. Police took pictures of the patrons and requested ID, and some left in a paddy wagon facing charges of drug possession and indecent exposure. According to lesbian

Abby Drue, when police called her row she was forced to line up against a wall and show ID and then questioned about a husband. Drue attended the film with a married heterosexual couple and was dismissed after her interrogation. As she exited the building, she witnessed theater management in handcuffs.[10] Ansley Mall would come to be known as Atlanta's gay square, where the businesses created a certain comfort level for lesbian and gay people, and subsequently for the spectacle of the regular Atlanta Pride Parade that took place on Peachtree Street in the same Midtown neighborhood.[11]

Atlanta's Georgia Gay Liberation Front formed in direct response to the *Lonesome Cowboys* raid. Participants organized the 1971 Pride protest, which was Atlanta's first march. Police harangued 125 activists while they paraded on the sidewalk because they could not secure a permit.[12] Marchers wearing lavender Gay Power T-shirts, carrying a matching banner, and waving signs like "Jimmy Carter Uses Hairspray" faced Sunday churchgoers, who drove by "freaking out" as protesters chanted "TWO FOUR SIX EIGHT, GAY IS TWICE AS GOOD AS STRAIGHT." Acknowledging that their event was in solidarity with other national queer events, including in New York City and Chicago, Atlantans declared their march as "Gaysouth rising up." This was Atlanta Gayday, 1971.[13] By June 1972, the Georgia Gay Liberation Front organized a leaflet campaign targeting bars as venues for promoting the events. The group viewed the rally as a "Southeast-wide demonstration" and prepared to welcome supporters from around the region. In response to a planned visit from President Nixon that June, and continuing its alignment with other leftist groups, the Georgia Gay Liberation Front hosted a booth in the city's Grant Park at planned anti-war activities.[14] A week later, over 250 marchers rallied on "famed" Peachtree Street for Pride, where some women wore paper bags over their head and one displayed a sign stating, "If I Show My Face, I'll Lose My Job."[15] Lesbians often avoided visibility because they worked in jobs, like teaching, that put them at a greater risk of discrimination and job loss. These fears prompted lesbian desire for separate all-woman spaces.

Recognizing the need for a separate leftist group devoted to women, ALFA held its first meeting on June 23, 1972. Just two years later it was well established in Atlanta's 1974 Pride celebration, sponsoring an open house and Gay 90s Carnival. The main festival was a Saturday picnic in Piedmont Park; attendees were told to "bring a basket and share it" and to look forward to "softball and happenings."[16] The gay-friendly Metropolitan Community Church held worship services in its newly purchased

CITY OF ATLANTA
OFFICE OF THE MAYOR

WHEREAS as this nation approaches the celebration of its 200th birthday, it is appropriate that all people re-evaluate the phrase "human rights" so that it may apply to all citizens in equal fashion; and

WHEREAS all citizens deserve basic legal rights regardless of race, sex, age, religious belief, economic status, national origin or sexual preference; and

WHEREAS the Gay Pride Planning Committee is organizing the Gay Pride Week celebration to emphasize two things: solidarity among the gay community and the need for legislative change to eliminate discrimination so that, as myths and stereotypes are shattered, change can come about:

NOW, THEREFORE, I, Maynard Jackson, Mayor of the City of Atlanta, do hereby proclaim Saturday, June 26, 1976, as

GAY PRIDE DAY

in Atlanta, and urge our citizens to recognize the rights of all people.

IN WITNESS WHEREOF I have hereunto set my hand and caused the seal of the City of Atlanta to be affixed.

MAYNARD JACKSON
Mayor

Mayor Maynard Jackson's Gay Pride Proclamation, "Gay Pride Day," 1976. The full proclamation appeared with an article detailing Citizens for Decent Atlanta's attack on Jackson's support for Pride. *Great Speckled Bird* 9, no. 7 (August 1976), courtesy of the Atlanta Progressive Media Foundation and Special Collections and Archives, Georgia State University Library.

building on North Highland Avenue, just two miles from the heart of the event. In 1977, organizers labeled their celebration "Christopher Street South" and demanded "Gay Civil Rights! Repeal of Sodomy Statutes! Defend Lesbian Mothers' Child Custody Rights!" This year also featured a Black Gay Pride Night at the lesbian favorite Tower Lounge and a performance by Womansong Theatre "anticipating the future in lesbian culture." Publicizing events and activist commitments like these demonstrated the willingness of Pride organizers to embrace the diversity of their community.[17] Although the early demonstrations varied in their scope and approach, ALFA remained at the center of Pride beginning in the 1970s. And Pride remained tied to the alternative Midtown neighborhood in Atlanta, anchored by gay businesses and catering to those seeking an identifiable gayborhood.[18] Although queer neighborhoods are fleeting, in Atlanta they helped to establish queer spaces from the World War II era through the first few years of the twenty-first century. Dating back to Ginny Boyd and lesbian softball, the Midtown neighborhood hosted decades of queer action and visibility, demonstrating that queer Atlantans understood where to find others like them.[19] Even as it changed and vulnerable residents could no longer afford to live there, the Midtown anchor continued to symbolically represent queer space, leading to the 2017 installation of painted rainbow paths.[20] Still, as Timothy Stewart-Winter has shown in Chicago, marking a queer urban space usually "links gayness to whiteness," and rarely does the claim of queer space include lesbian residents, according to Jack Gieseking's examination of fleeting lesbian social space in San Francisco.[21]

The possibility of local political support fostered Pride's early success in Atlanta. When Atlanta's first Black mayor, Maynard Jackson, won his office in 1973, local gay media celebrated. Writers at the *Atlanta Barb* believed that Jackson represented a positive future for gay citizens of Atlanta. Newspaper staffers intended to hold him to his preelection promises, and Jackson did not disappoint. The mayor declared June 26, 1976, as Gay Pride Day in Atlanta, urging "citizens to recognize the rights of all people"—by official proclamation—in an effort "to emphasize two things: solidarity among the gay community and the need for legislative change to eliminate discrimination so that, as myths and stereotypes are shattered, change can come about." Jackson connected the bicentennial celebration of the United States as a new nation to an equal rights initiative for queer people in Atlanta: "As this nation approaches the celebration of its 200th birthday, it is appropriate that all people re-evaluate the phrase 'human rights' so that it may apply to all citizens in equal

ALFA *Atalanta* cover, 1977. *Atalanta* was the Atlanta Lesbian Feminist Alliance's
publication, named for a huntress in Greek mythology. This issue was in celebration of Gay Pride. It included a speech given after Pride to reinforce the "Women's
Movement" and feminism as central to ALFA's mission. *Atalanta*, 1977, accessed
from James T. Sears Papers, 1918–2008 and undated, box 116, Sallie Bingham Center
for Women's History and Culture, David M. Rubenstein Rare Book and Manuscript
Library, Duke University, Durham.

fashion." In 1976 some 300 people, including several lesbian groups
including ALFA, Atlanta Women's Union, and Dykes for the Second
American Revolution, marched on Atlanta's Peachtree Street headed for
Piedmont Park. According to the alternative paper the *Great Speckled
Bird*, "The march was a couple of blocks long and included several cars
(Atlanta's version of floats) with people atop."[22] Marching on Peachtree
was significant; it was the main thoroughfare running through the heart
of the city and offered marchers maximum visibility.[23]

In response to Jackson's declaration, a group known as Citizens for
Decent Atlanta (CDA) ran ads in several newspapers suggesting that
while they would not deny the right to free expression, they took issue

with Jackson's right "to affix our city's seal of approval to a sexual orientation which the majority of his fellow citizens believes to be against the moral law of the Judeo-Christian tradition and the institution of the home family unit."[24] Additional ads took aim at the "perverted sex" that Jackson's proclamation supposedly ordained. The CDA consisted of seven individuals who initially refused to identify themselves for fear of retaliation, but the *Great Speckled Bird* was unwilling to ignore the potential of uncovering a racist plot against Jackson. The newspaper's investigation suggested that politicians and businessmen were at the core of CDA funding. The paper named names—including "Cathy Truitt, who could not be identified," but was likely the evangelical businessman Truett Cathy, of Chik-fil-A fame.[25] The seven mystery funders paid over $6,000 for newspaper ads (equivalent to over $25,000 in the year 2020), working with several local ministers, including the Reverend Charles Stanley of First Baptist of Atlanta, who publicly "attacked the proclamation from his pulpit." The Black newspaper the *Atlanta Daily World* also carried advertising funded by the CDA. Some in the Black community were angry at Jackson over the proclamation, but only one Black pastor publicly opposed it. The fundamental problem was not that gay people existed but that they would take pride in that existence—that they would "flaunt" it. And, there was an underlying fear that Atlanta would become like San Francisco—"a city of real nuts."[26] Writers at the *Great Speckled Bird* viewed the CDA as a white moneyed attempt to oust Jackson—the group could not get away with "hollering 'n——r,'" but it would be acceptable to yell "'pervert' and 'queer.'" Going after Jackson's support of Pride in Atlanta also allowed the ministers to make a veiled racist attack against the power of Atlanta's new Black political leadership.[27] As a result of pressure from the CDA, Jackson backed away from his Gay Pride Day declaration a year later and changed the proclamation to a watered-down "Civil Liberties Days."[28]

It would be a decade before Charlotte's queer activists enjoyed similar mayoral support by electing their city's first African American mayor, Harvey Gantt, in 1983. Like Jackson, Gantt brought a palpable excitement to the queer press in Charlotte. While campaigning before a gay social group, supported by the local and fleeting Lambda Political Caucus, Gantt stated that he would support antidiscrimination legislation to protect lesbians and gays from housing or job discrimination and would appoint a recommended lesbian or gay leader to his Community Relations Council.[29] Yet unlike the CDA in Atlanta, those in Charlotte's influential religious community did not fear repercussions as a result of their vociferous and visible opposition to Gantt's efforts to work with queer constituents.

Religious leaders in Charlotte, some of whom held political aspirations, pressured Gantt to act against the sale of sexually explicit material, which they linked to lesbians and gay men. Adopting the moniker Concerned Charlotteans, the group focused on materials sold in the Charlotte Douglas Airport. Pastor Ed Adams of Charlotte's Word of Faith Church was one of many religious leaders who wrote to Gantt and rebuked him for his supposed lack of action on the issue. Gantt faced a city that was not ready for vocal mayoral support of lesbian and gay concerns. Buoyed by their powerful status, religious leaders equated homosexuality with what they deemed to be pornographic material—and saw both as similarly harmful to Charlotte. In response to Gantt's answers when questioned by Concerned Charlotteans, Adams wrote, "I hate to think that the Mayor of our city thinks that *Playboy* and *Penthouse* aren't pornographic. Also your answer to, 'do you believe homosexual acts should be legalized' concerns me. Surely you know what homosexual acts are." Adams pleaded with Gantt to "use the position that God has entrusted to you" so that "the city of Charlotte will know that its major is a man of integrity indeed."[30] The founding member of Concerned Charlotteans, Reverend Joseph Chambers, was profiled by the *Charlotte Observer* in a 1986 examination of his organization's expansion of its focus to include homosexuality, abortion, and prayer in schools. The piece opened with Chambers examining a *Rolling Stone* magazine that featured an article on his activism: "The Rev. Joseph Chambers flips through a September issue of *Rolling Stone* magazine until a picture catches his eye. 'Do you think this promotes lesbian sex?' he asks, pointing to a Bloomingdale's department store ad. Two pages later, there's a color photograph of Chambers, standing with a Bible in front of a glowing cross and a U.S. flag. The article, about North Carolina's one-year-old obscenity law, mentions Chambers and his anti-pornography group, Concerned Charlotteans."[31]

Charlotte's anti-gay activism made national news that year, but because of archconservative senator Jesse Helms, the state as a whole would also gain notoriety in this arena. Just three years after the national investigative television news show *20/20* joined *Rolling Stone* magazine in highlighting Charlotte's energetic, conservative religious movement, Vice President Dan Quayle attended the fifth annual Concerned Charlotteans conference at Helms's behest. Reverend Chambers touted the visit as an indicator of North Carolina's "'conservative renaissance' in the battle against pornography and other problems."[32] By aligning themselves with a morals-based conservative resurgence in the country as a whole, members of Concerned Charlotteans sent a message to local queer people, warning them that their presence was not welcome and their city did not want to be known as a hospitable space for sexual liberalism.

In many ways Charlotte's move to greater tolerance lagged at least a decade behind Atlanta's.[33] It was a full ten years after Maynard Jackson's election that Harvey Gantt would take office as Charlotte's first Black mayor and the first mayor to acknowledge queer activists in a marginally positive way. This decade of separation was also true for Pride. Ten years after Atlanta's first politically motivated march, a Gay Pride celebration finally came to Charlotte in 1981. The first event in Charlotte created great excitement and anticipation. The *Front Page*, a regional gay newspaper based in Raleigh, reported that during this week Charlotte would be "the gay/lesbian capital of the Mid Atlantic."[34] Local activist Don King, seemingly the one and only person behind all visible gay organizing in 1980s Charlotte, was eager for this first event to put Charlotte on the southeastern gay map. As early as 1975, King worked to unify the queer community. Any group that hoped to survive would have to collaborate with those in the gay bar community and not be perceived as a threat to their power. Bar owners, and the drag performers that supported them, were influential in the Queen City, and many lesbian and gay people preferred the anonymity of the bars to visible activism.[35] By 1981 King was "tired of people having to run off to Atlanta, Washington and other places to hear nationally known speakers and to get that ecstatic feeling of togetherness."[36] He saw the first Charlotte Pride week as an opportunity to address these concerns.

Many of the events, along with housing for out-of-town visitors, took place at the University of North Carolina at Charlotte, located an inconvenient eleven miles from one of the main Pride host bars, the Scorpio, and ten miles from Uptown. The university was the site for a film festival, an outdoor disco, a softball tournament, and workshops, including the keynote speech by Barbara Gittings, a nationally recognized activist, former editor of the first national lesbian journal, *The Ladder*, and founder of New York's first chapter of the lesbian homophile organization Daughters of Bilitis.[37] The Scorpio sponsored a softball team for the tournament, the Stinging Scorpians, again highlighting the problematic distance from the bar to the main events of the festival. In fact, events that year took place at venues scattered in different parts of the city, and in the coming years Pride in Charlotte would continue to move the entire festival to varying venues with little consistency.

The Scorpio's Winning Softballers Celebrate On Gay Pride Day. 1981

Charlotte Pride celebration, 1981, featuring host bar the Scorpio's softball team, the "Stinging Scorpians." *Q-Notes*, June 1, 1986, accessed from J. Murrey Atkins Library, Special Collections, University of North Carolina at Charlotte.

Queen City Quordinators (QCQ), the group responsible for Charlotte's first Pride event, hoped to coordinate programming and organize funding to be shared among several lesbian and gay advocacy groups, including the Gay/Lesbian Switchboard of Charlotte, the Metropolitan Community Church, the Gay/Lesbian Caucus of Charlotte, and the North Carolina Human Rights Fund. The organizations needed money and hoped to pool their resources by joining with queer bars to combine entertainment with fundraising. Like the Charlotte Women's Center, queer activist groups shared members and often found that there were not enough bodies to populate events. The Gay/Lesbian Caucus struggled to survive since its membership overlapped significantly with the QCQ leadership. Many who participated in the caucus also worked with QCQ, which led to fading energies and recycled ideas. In addition to a frustrating lack of community support for organizers' efforts, the highly anticipated Pride celebration of 1981 did not live up to the *Front Page* hype or QCQ's financial expectations. In fact, the only financial failure for the Quordinators in 1981 was the Gay Pride Week celebration in Charlotte. From the beginning, Pride in Charlotte was uncertain. It would remain troubled throughout its tumultuous incarnations.[38] But for QCQ cofounder Samis Rose, the 100-person event was magic: "I was just on a cloud the entire weekend. . . . It was like we could actually breathe there, you know?"[39]

Again in 1983, the Charlotte Pride celebration was the least profitable QCQ event, earning just over $200 (equivalent to approximately $500 in the year 2020) and trailing financially behind all other events for the year. QCQ's greatest point of success was that year's quarter-page advertisement in the *Charlotte Observer*. At a cost of almost $600, the ad promoted Pride and explained the importance of the celebration's history to the wide readership of the local paper. That same year QCQ also celebrated some positive television news coverage.[40] Due to the launch of *Q-Notes*, the Quordinators' newsletter, and a general belief that "Charlotte's gay men and lesbians" were "acting like a community," 1983 was seen as a banner year. Yet the Quordinators also noted that while local "nongays" knew that Charlotte's population included lesbians and gay men, "they think of it as a united, self-supporting segment of the city. It is, therefore, highly ironic that so very many gay men and lesbians still think that a sense of community is something reserved only for activists or elite partiers."[41] It was obvious to the QCQ leadership that Charlotte's queer citizens were divided, but the group failed to recognize that its predominantly white male leadership alienated those who did not fit that limited demographic. QCQ's frustration reeked of an inability to acknowledge the inherent cost of visible activism that many feared.

Collaborating with Oleen's, the local drag bar catering to gay men, QCQ promoted a "wimmin's winter carnival & celebration" to address the separate needs of lesbians. The event was so successful that Oleen's planned to hold regular Tuesday women's nights going forward, although it is unclear how long this commitment lasted.[42] Because there was no bar in Charlotte solely devoted to lesbians at this time, Oleen's "wimmin's nights" addressed the desire for separate lesbian socializing. According to *Q-Notes*, some lesbians felt that "the future of lesbianism in Charlotte appeared bleak" due to the lack of lesbian bars, which came and went quickly in the Queen City. "Others said that while bars may be one place to have a good time, they are hardly conducive to conversation or to establishing relationships."[43] Lacking the substantial presence of a group like the Atlanta Lesbian Feminist Alliance, a few Charlotte lesbians hoped to provide space for socialization outside of the bar.[44]

To provide alternatives to the bar scene and to the active gay men's organization Acceptance (a QCQ group open to women but attended primarily by men), two women's groups offered new opportunities for lesbian community in the 1980s. It is unclear how many lesbians participated in the Charlotte Women's Center that still operated on Lyndhurst Avenue in 1985, but the newly formed lesbian social group New Vida met there for a time. Just a year later, a woman identified only as "Linda" tried again to form a new social group for lesbians. This effort stemmed directly from her work at the Gay/Lesbian Switchboard in Charlotte, a group originally supported by QCQ. Linda took calls at the Switchboard from women looking to meet other lesbians outside of the bars or the Metropolitan Community Church. The new group, Queen City Friends, planned to hold meetings at a barbecue restaurant, the Hickory House. The restaurant was desirable because it was a window-less building owned by a male "member of the community" and had a private back room. The scheduled meetings coincided with the Scorpio's Thursday women's nights in case anyone wanted to "continue the eve-ning."[45] No matter how desperate some lesbians were for social interac-tions, they could not sustain an organized social group and were forced to rely on men's establishments like the Hickory House, Oleen's, or the Scorpio. These businesses were willing to concede a poorly attended weeknight for women's patronage. Although *Q-Notes* regularly covered women's efforts to organize, women were not visible in the reporting on QCQ actions. Because the Charlotte Women's Center newsletter dis-solved, no organized group of lesbians regularly chronicled their stories and struggles in the way that Don King did for his primarily gay male audience in Charlotte, resulting in a paucity of evidence on lesbians in 1980s Charlotte.

In comparison to nascent Pride events, large regional separatist wom-en's events held more interest and excitement for some lesbians, who created discrete social events and temporary queer spaces in the 1980s. For example, the Southern Women's Music and Comedy Festival, sim-ilar to the better-known Michigan Womyn's Music Festival, was held just eighty miles north of Atlanta in the northeast Georgia mountains.[46] Aimed at and attended by mostly white women, the festival featured a variety of primarily white comedians, musicians, and political speakers. Like the Michigan festival, participants could sign up for work exchange and select alcohol-free "clean and sober" cabin space. The festival ran for several years, hosting nationally recognized speakers like writer Rita Mae Brown, an early contributor to *Sinister Wisdom*; comedians Lea DeLaria and Kate Clinton; leaders from the National Organization for Women and the American Civil Liberties Union; Olivia recording art-ists Meg Christian, Cris Williamson, and Holly Near; and the Atlanta Feminist Women's Chorus. The event allowed women to hone skills, like plumbing, that were not available to them in male-dominated spaces, and taught them to value women's perspectives and differences, like class and race. At separatist festivals, women learned to hear their voice as the most powerful in the conversation—an opportunity that did not exist for them in any other venue.[47]

Recognizing women's music festivals as safe spaces where she could be naked and free, without being ogled by men, Samis Rose founded "Winter Woman Music" in Charlotte. She organized a three-day festival where popular lesbian recording artist Cris Williamson appeared; Rose recalled that tickets were sold out (standing-room only) for the high-school gym performance. It was important to Rose that Charlotte's women could experience these performances that were often held only in larger northern or West Coast cities. Women in the Queen City were relatively isolated in terms of the unifying spirit of women's music community. When the Williamson concert convened, Rose and organizers newspapered the glass in the lobby of the gym so that protesters, led by "Joe," a local minister, could not view or film the event.[48] Fellow Charlottean Sarrah Kelly prioritized live music, availing herself of the lesbian bar as a place to meet women but then hopefully "drag" them to hear a band. Although she sometimes attended Pride for the live music, she worried about being filmed there. She owned her own business and did not want to be known as "that lesbian on TV." Enjoying music with other women and local music lovers was her prime entertainment goal, not Pride with other queers.[49]

Three years after the first Pride celebration in Charlotte, a banner splashed across the corner of Q-Notes promoted the "Gay Pride Issue." This time the event was held in Park Road Park, a central location in contrast to the 1981 event at UNC Charlotte. Yet this move meant that Pride was now happening in white neighborhoods bordering the city's lavish Myers Park community. The festival featured a softball game and a potluck luncheon, held under an isolated shelter in a remote area of the park to ensure invisibility. During the week of Pride, QCQ held a private meeting with local clergy to clarify commonly misunderstood issues about lesbian and gay people. Despite some progress for Charlotte's Pride celebration, the excitement was tempered by Don King's decision to close his Friends of Dorothy Bookshop. After two and a half years in business, King closed the queer boutique during the same year that he would be the sole Charlottean to make the "Advocate 400," a list of 400 gay rights leaders published by the national queer magazine the Advocate. King was the face of gay Charlotte, but he was helpless to maintain the bookshop while working a full-time job. This decision exposed the limits of his capabilities to juggle many responsibilities and also his inability to find community support for the only gay shopping outlet in the city.[50] Just after Pride that year, the Odyssey bar and Lambda Political Caucus, a group of only five members, also failed. Organizations, often more than bars, struggled mightily to survive in the Queen City.[51] In 1984, members of QCQ consulted with John D'Emilio, a pioneering gay scholar and activist at the University of North Carolina at Greensboro, to help them refocus. They committed to change gears with an emphasis on social activities and outreach for the whole community because their umbrella fundraising concept was no longer working. In the city of Charlotte, an organizational name and local media coverage might suggest an engaged community, but activist groups rarely boasted more than twenty regular participants.

The ostensible flurry of activity that *Q-Notes* promoted represented only a small slice of gay Charlotte. QCQ was responsible for the print and organizational visibility of queer Charlotte in the 1980s, yet many lesbians and gay men showed up in force only at the bars and to a lesser extent at Pride gatherings. QCQ hoped to change this by promoting Pride in Charlotte through aggressive advertising, but mainstream media quashed the group's attempts. The city bus service and three local radio stations rejected QCQ's Pride advertising because it was "blatant" and "in poor taste." Local radio station WSOC's operations manager expected "a super backlash" if the station ran the sixty-second radio ad. Featuring two straight men discussing discrimination against gays in North Carolina, the radio manager stated that the ad "promoted physical contact" by suggesting that if listeners had a gay friend or relative, "how about giving 'em an extra warm hug this week."[52] Although their organization eventually folded, QCQ's *Q-Notes* publication remained, continuing to thrive in the twenty-first century by creating community through published content unavailable elsewhere.

While Charlotte's lesbian and gay organizers continued to flounder, Pride in Atlanta celebrated tremendous visible growth. The 1984 Atlanta Pride events, for example, stretched from June 21 to July 3, organized around the theme "Once More . . . with Feeling." Featuring plays, voter registration drives, church services, an ALFA open house, an AID Atlanta Health Fair, a Dyke Tour of Homes, a "Wet Jockey Contest," a forum showcasing candidates for upcoming congressional races, and the International Association of Black and White Men Together conference, the event was diverse and visible. Organizers corralled members from the Fulton and DeKalb County police departments to meet at All Saints Church for a discussion on crimes against lesbians and gay people.[53] A Pride softball tournament featured teams like the Meshugenehs and the Amazons; the Tower Tornadoes, of the long running Tower Lounge; and the Sports Page Sports, from the popular lesbian bar, and culminated in an All-Star Game featuring men from the "Hotlanta League" team. Once again marchers paraded up Peachtree Street and rallied between the area blocked off at Tenth and Eleventh Streets in Midtown Atlanta, just two blocks from Piedmont Park, where the first leaflets on gay rights were distributed fourteen years earlier. Because the goal was a large and conspicuous presence, those who were concerned about being identified in the march were encouraged to wear masks or a costume to conceal their identity. Consistency in its Pride location and the participants' insistence on queer visibility earned Atlanta national media recognition.[54]

Two years later, Atlanta's *Pride Guide* boasted fifty-four gay organizations in the greater Atlanta area. Pride 1986 welcomed the prominent speaker Kevin Berrill, the anti-violence project coordinator from the National Gay and Lesbian Task Force, a group committed to identifying and countering anti-gay violence while creating organizational resistance models for local activists to replicate.[55] Pride was Atlanta's Bastille Day, according to local activist Maria Helena Dolan. She pleaded for attendees to "please, celebrate and nurture that spirit during Pride week—and all year."[56] Participants marched on Peachtree Street headed toward the state capitol, and they rallied at Washington Street in downtown Atlanta. Central Presbyterian Church provided the restrooms for the event, a significant accommodation given the growing panic over AIDS and the general friction between southern evangelical churches and lesbian and gay people.[57] Yet, like Charlotte, Atlanta's activist groups faced divisive tensions around issues of race and activism, fighting to maintain a committed base of people who were willing to volunteer in addition to functioning as partiers for events. By the 1980s, a local newspaper columnist estimated Atlanta's queer population to be approximately 15 percent of the city's inhabitants. Although not a united or monolithic voting bloc, some activists believed they must embrace the power of the voting booth. First Tuesday (the city's first gay political action committee), Black and White Men Together, and several other queer activist groups organized a 1983 meeting, which was attended by Atlanta's future mayor Shirley Franklin. Introduced as "the mayor" when the current mayor Andrew

Young was not in town, Franklin assured the activists of Young's support for attacking race discrimination within queer Atlanta. She also addressed concerns about government support for AID Atlanta, transportation and trade, and the city council's recent approval of a "Gay/Lesbian Civil Rights Proclamation."[58] Young's and Franklin's engagement with queer constituents exemplifies the pro-queer leadership of Black Democrats in the Atlanta mayor's office, beginning with Maynard Jackson in 1974 and continuing into the twenty-first century.

Queer Atlantans embedded themselves in church groups throughout Atlanta's parishes and protested the arrival of Moral Majority leader Jerry Falwell during a 1981 visit to the city. Additionally, the Gay Atlanta Minority Association (GAMA), consisting of "Black, Hispanic, and Third World" queer people, boycotted Atlanta Pride that year in order to draw attention to racism, claiming "rampant and blatant discrimination within the gay community." GAMA identified the problem of all white-male leadership in some queer spaces, pointing to women and minorities who were "triple carded" when trying to gain entrance to a few of Atlanta's queer bars. Lesbians in ALFA and the lesbians and gay men of First Tuesday were particularly attentive to GAMA's grievances. Speakers at Atlanta Pride also took note of the GAMA boycott, giving voice to the issue of racism and inequity in their community.[59]

Queer newsletters constantly pleaded for money and volunteers. Don Weston of the all-male steering committee for the 1986 Atlanta Pride event aimed a subtle jab at those who were visibly involved but socially problematic in that year's *Pride Guide*. He recognized the importance of political and economic clout in protecting gay rights and called for wide attendance and visibility at Pride, especially by those who would be more palatable to powerful straight leaders in Atlanta.

> The vast majority of gays in metropolitan Atlanta are taking advantage of the limited features of the gay community here and are doing nothing to protect or advance those features. This has left the "battle" to a small number of dedicated individuals who have been carrying the whole load. Many of those individuals are in the forefront because of a much greater personal stake in being openly gay—drag queens, leather lovers, etc. Thank God they have been there. They represent the diversity and strength of the gay community. But they are also some of the most controversial, easy-to-criticize members of our community. It is unfair and ineffective

for the rest of the Atlanta Gay community to rely on these few brave souls for representation to the media, to the politicians, and to our own community.[60]

In Atlanta's *Pulse* magazine for lesbians and gay men, a male writer lamented the fact that the Atlanta Gay Pride parade featured people who flaunted their sexuality and crowded out those who arrived to march with a respectable and appropriately dressed contingent of protesters. "We have places (bars, parties, etc.) that we can run around in drag and leather. Hell, I love to slip on some pumps and purple taffeta and paint the town pink! But there is a time and a place for everything, and it sure would help if some of us learned where these times and places were."[61] Statements like these suggest that overworked activists failed to understand that Pride and visibility were not always a priority for queer people, and the price of visibility meant different things to different people. As much as Pride organizers and attendees longed for a united queer front and an appropriate face for lesbian and gay people, such a diverse group of people could not assume this singular identity. Neoliberal respectability permeated the messaging from the primarily white male leadership of Atlanta's queer organizers and media outlets.

Pride festivals grew in the 1980s and 1990s because of the support of queer business districts in Atlanta. Even though many gay-friendly businesses eventually faded away due to typical small business struggles and gentrification, the importance of separate business spaces that catered to a queer audience cannot be overestimated. The Atlanta Business and Professional Guild worked to beautify Peachtree Street in Midtown Atlanta by adopting its burgeoning gay business district. In 1982 the *Advocate* celebrated Atlanta's "blossoming" gay community by noting the importance of businesses with front doors brazenly facing Peachtree Street—recognizing the remarkable move toward gay business visibility in Atlanta. One such center known as "Peachtree 800" featured a whole block of gay businesses, including a florist, a gift shop, a gym, a clothing store, bars, and a video arcade.[62] When a retailer was accused of making anti-gay comments to shoppers, Selig Enterprises, the owner of the property, confronted the store owners, even offering to buy out the lease so that they would leave. When these attempts were unsuccessful, Selig compensated by offering free space for a year to the fledgling queer organization Lambda Community Center.[63] As predicted by the *Advocate*, "the gay and multinational renovation of Atlanta's midtown may have a profound effect on the future of the city's tourist and convention business. At one time Midtown was seen as a natural northern extension of the central business district. Now it appears to have taken on the role of arts and entertainment center. With the demise of underground Atlanta, Midtown is at the forefront of attractions. It is becoming the city's heart and soul."[64] Atlanta's Peachtree Street fastened the vibrant Midtown gayborhood to the most important throughway in the entire city, welcoming queer patrons with accessible shopping and visible on-street entrances, which replaced the secret back doors of queer bar spaces from earlier decades.

A visible queer business district and successful Pride marches and celebrations in Atlanta should not be read as an indicator of a united queer community in the city—or even in the Midtown neighborhood. Divisions among gay people continued to seethe below the surface, and the welcoming Midtown environment could be deceiving. Although some lesbians worked together with gay men to organize Pride celebrations and they moved in the same circles as they shopped in the visibly gay Peachtree Street Midtown district, everyday socializing and relationship building often took place in separate spaces. Just as the larger heterosexual socializations that took place in Atlanta often occurred in socially segregated neighborhoods and establishments, queer people socialized in spaces separated by race and class. For example, a 1987 issue of *Phoenix*, a publication of the Atlanta Business and Professional Guild, featured a story that considered racist behavior among gay people. Inspired by the recent overt racism featured on an episode of *Oprah*, a writer tried to explain why Forsyth County—a Georgia county made famous for its virulent hatred of Black people—was really not that different from Midtown Atlanta. In retelling the story of a party hosted by elite gay male Atlantans, where a racist slur was bandied about as entertainment, the presumably white writer struggled with his own quiet complicity in the incident: "The real danger of Forsyth County is not the hatred and the blind prejudice that unquestionably exists there. It is that those of us in luppie/guppie households in Midtown and Virginia Highlands and Buckhead and Grant Park and Ansley Park and all points in between may, because such hatred is visible OUT THERE, come tacitly to believe that it is not present, alive and well, in our neighborhoods, in our friendships, and in ourselves."[65] Social spaces segregated by race were still the norm in Atlanta—whether gay or straight.

Beyond Fulton County's queer Midtown enclave, Atlanta's suburban counties labored to cope with their burgeoning gay communities. Neighboring Cobb County's 1993 anti-gay resolution made national headlines by condemning "'the gay life style' as incompatible with community standards." Enacted in response to a local theater production of *Lips Together, Teeth Apart*, a Terrence McNally play exploring the queer world of the vacation destination Fire Island, New York, swift national backlash snowballed. The hostile response to the resolution drew national celebrity vitriol and a structured community response. Lesbian Avengers member Lisa King urged the county commissioners to vote against the suggested legislation because the city needed to address "the diversity of all residents in Cobb County appropriately."[66] The activist group Olympics Out of Cobb successfully ensured that Olympic volleyball, slated to take place in Cobb County for Atlanta's 1996 Centennial Olympic games, would not be played there.[67]

In adjoining DeKalb County, Mayor Mike Mears of the county seat, Decatur, encouraged embattled gay Cobb County residents to come to his city, where he welcomed all residents and took a "180-degree opposite view of that in Cobb."[68] Along with the city of Atlanta, DeKalb County led the way in securing rights for gay people in public employment and in offering protections through local law enforcement. Indeed, DeKalb's Decatur became a white lesbian hub (some labeled the city "Dick-hater") in the late twentieth century. Organized in 1990, the Digging Dykes of Decatur regularly marched in Pride parades with toy lawn mowers and southern belle–styled hats as the members poked fun at traditional southern garden clubs.[69] This type of predominantly white in-migration led to the destruction of historically Black neighborhoods, leaving many Black residents feeling unwelcome in their home community.[70] Ignoring the racial implications of this gentrification, Mears and DeKalb courted potential lesbian and gay residents while also advertising the importance of their business district in providing a healthy environment for the arts. Funding for the arts in Atlanta's DeKalb County, as in many places, often signaled that community's environment for lesbian and gay people. Mayor Mears hoped to land Marietta's Theatre in the Square, the theater that sparked the Cobb County resolution, for his business district. The campaign to bring the theater to Decatur focused on promoting the acceptance of both the arts and gay people. As one writer wryly observed, "Should the relocation take place, an appropriate first performance might be a stage adaptation of 'The Wizard of Oz' with a slight rewrite of one of Dorothy's most famous lines: 'Gee. Toto. Thank goodness we're not in Cobb anymore.'"[71]

While some in Atlanta encouraged gay community and neighborhoods, in spite of suburban pushback and anti-queer action, Charlotte's activists faced state legislators who worked to erase a path forward for lesbians and gay men. By 1992, thanks to Senator Helms, North Carolina struck some as the most "queer hating state." Southern lesbian feminist and original member of the *Feminary* collective Mab Segrest worked to mobilize activists across rural and urban borders in North Carolina to respond to homophobic violence perpetuated by Helms. Segrest also was a consultant to the local state organization NC Coalition for Gay and Lesbian Equality, focusing on bringing statewide campaigns together against homophobic violence. This was the only statewide effort of its kind at the time. She invited the celebrated speaker from the 1986 Atlanta Pride event, Kevin Berrill of the National Gay and Lesbian Task Force, to support her efforts toward an anti-violence alliance. Segrest recognized the challenges of their endeavor, noting that "countering these unifying efforts is a tendency towards turf issues and fragmentation into many smaller organizations. This problem is exacerbated because gay activists receive recognition in these smaller organizations that we are denied in heterosexual society." The front page of the national publication *Resist: A Call to Resist Illegitimate Authority* featured Segrest's efforts and a photo of two men at a 1992 North Carolina state Gay Pride festival held in Asheville. Decked out in camouflage, the men held (misspelled) protest signs, including one that read, "Fagits Get Out of Ashville."[72] The NC Coalition for Gay and Lesbian Equality promoted the kind of action that Queen City Quordinators used with Gantt—recommending participants for the mayor's human relations commission and advocating for anti-violence campaigns and worker protections. In response to hate-laced speech promoted by protesting churches at the North Carolina state Pride gatherings, Segrest pointed to the need to engage the churches whose congregations were willing to reach out in a more loving way to queer people. The North Carolina Council of Churches had in 1991 "passed a strong resolution condemning anti-gay violence and calling for churches to examine the ways they have contributed to the suffering of lesbians and gay men." According to Segrest, this type of church leadership on lesbian and gay issues would go a long way in a state like North Carolina, especially in rural areas and smaller towns. Because of the significant representations of churches, including the sizable Southern Baptist contingent, church repudiation of anti-gay violence was crucial.[73]

While North Carolina made national headlines for its anti-gay violence and political and religious leadership, visible mayoral cooperation was still the byword in Atlanta. In the same year that Segrest worked to organize leaders in North Carolina against homophobic violence, Atlanta's Maynard Jackson appeared publicly with queer constituents in an effort to quell frustration over his absence from the upcoming Pride celebration. Although lesbian and gay activists were often unhappy with Jackson, he continued to express open support for Pride festivals in Atlanta. In his 1991 proclamation, celebrating the upcoming June Lesbian and Gay Pride Human Rights Days, Jackson announced that he would actively seek a lesbian or gay person to serve in his administration, noting the importance of the community's contributions to Atlanta: "One of the things that bothers me is some people who want to condemn the lesbian and gay community on the one hand and on the other hand accept the help of the lesbian and gay community in all the things the city does. That is sheer hypocrisy and I'm sick and tired of it."[74]

Nowhere was this hypocrisy more evident than in the North Carolina state Pride festival hosted in Charlotte in 1994. The event was the largest state Pride ever, with an estimated attendance of 3,800, and at least half of the festival attendees surveyed were from cities outside of Charlotte. In spite of its success, however, it would be the only time that the statewide event would be held in the Queen City.[75] Charlotte's gay leaders had an opportunity to put Charlotte on the queer map but would quickly find that the necessary political and business support to sustain the event would not materialize. As the largest city in the state, Charlotte city leaders missed an opportunity to claim a foothold in state Pride celebrations. Businesspeople and boosters in the city who loved to make money (look no further than Charlotte's 1970s chamber of commerce slogan, "Charlotte—A Good Place to Make Money") were happy to take gay dollars but not to embrace those who spent them. The slogan was shameless in its celebration of the city's economic obsession, and it continued to define Charlotte in subsequent decades. But in 1994, Charlotte politicians alienated gay consumers by suggesting that civic leaders' brand of economic boosterism did not extend to the gay community in the 1990s.[76] They were guilty of the very hypocrisy that Mayor Jackson highlighted in Atlanta. The state Pride event brought $500,000 in revenue to Charlotte. This was a boon to the city's economy, but in the indignant speech of Charlotte's mayor and battles waged by the religious community over the festival's appearance in the Queen City, the economic advantage was ignored.[77]

Recognizing the importance of Charlotte as a leader in the southern financial landscape, event cochairs Sue Henry and Dan Kirsch hoped to avoid competition with other Pride events that might drive down attendance numbers and revenue. They requested the June 3–5 dates so as not to compete with Atlanta Pride on June 12, South Carolina Pride, or the Pride celebration of the twenty-fifth anniversary of the Stonewall riots in New York City. By emphasizing the "economic clout" of the Pride march, they hoped to woo Charlotte's business leaders, who then perhaps would spearhead antidiscrimination policies for their lesbian and gay employees.[78] Pride organizers were eager to "show off" and "to use the opportunity to demonstrate to Charlotte's mainstream community the power and political strength" of lesbians and gay men in Charlotte.[79]

Charlotte was the only city to submit a bid to host the 1994 state event, and even though the state Pride committee viewed Charlotte as a more conservative city than other previous hosts, like Chapel Hill, Durham, and Raleigh, it approved the Charlotte bid because it would focus attention on lesbians and gay people who were local to Charlotte.[80] The committee awarded the festival to Charlotte *because* it was conservative, and committee members expected controversy: "We chose Charlotte I would not say despite the fact that we're expecting some organized protest, but because of it in a way. . . . It's going to bring a lot of attention to the local community. I think it's going to focus attention on the fact that lesbian and gay people are not 'out there' but that they're in town."[81] Pride in Charlotte would serve as a vehicle to force the city's anti-gay factions, and the community as a whole, to see lesbian and gay citizens marching and gathering in the streets. Henry and Kirsch led the campaign to bring the event to Charlotte, which would be its one and only appearance in the Queen City: "We look at the Pride March as the chance to increase visibility of our local gay and lesbian community in a positive way."[82] Although organizers of North Carolina Pride in Charlotte viewed the weekend as a success, Charlotte's local Pride events would remain inconsistent and unpredictable. State Pride brought to Charlotte an event and a public presence that the city's gay leaders could not sustain. North Carolina Pride's 1994 success depended on the financial support from the state committee and the substantial attendance by those who lived outside of Charlotte. Absent this external support, the state Pride weekend of 1994 was an anomaly rather than the beginning of an era of successful Pride events in Charlotte.

North Carolina Pride in Charlotte faced an abysmal social and political climate. Unlike previous host cities, the city of Charlotte did not offer any legislative protection for lesbian and gay people, rejecting such an ordinance in 1992, just a year before the city was awarded the state Pride march.[83] In the debate over the legislation, which would have modified the city's anti-bias amendment to include protections against discrimination based on sexual orientation, city council member Hoyle Martin stated that he could not support an ordinance that would allow lesbians and gay men in Charlotte to publicly "flaunt" a "lifestyle" that he "couldn't explain to his grandchildren."[84] Mayor Richard Vinroot opposed the amendment, as did council member Pat McCrory, a future mayor of Charlotte and eventual governor of North Carolina. But in a continuation of his support for Charlotte's gay citizens, former mayor Harvey Gantt appealed to council members to support the amendment as an effort to build bridges within the Charlotte community.[85] Lesbians and gay men worked diligently to sway the council's opinions on the amendment. Diana Travis, a lesbian business owner, appeared before the council to argue that her tax dollars were happily accepted in Charlotte (never returned and marked "lesbian") but without the promise of protection from city leaders in return.[86]

Visibility was at the heart of Pride in Charlotte. Henry and Kirsch were eager to attract national entertainers for the event, but they were unsuccessful in securing appearances from important political leaders, like Harvey Gantt. One of the highlights of the weekend's activities was landing the nationally known lesbian comedian Lea DeLaria; the proud headline read, "Bull Dyke in a Queen City." A year earlier DeLaria became the first openly gay comic to appear on national television. She epitomized drastic dykeness, taking on late-night television when the only host to allow her appearance, Arsenio Hall, embraced DeLaria's self-proclamation in a masculine suit: "'It's great to be here because it's the 1990s, and it's hip to be queer and I'm a big dyke.'"[87] Several blocks out of Uptown, the Scorpio was the only bar to be named as an official Pride celebration spot, while the main festival dance was held Uptown at Founders Hall in the artsy and swanky Spirit Square, a venue that epitomized the chamber of commerce's obsession with pretense. Marshall Park was the site of the parade organization and the celebratory rally—a site that just a few years later would be too visible and highly problematic for the city of Charlotte.[88]

Organized around the theme "Our equality is inextricably linked to our visibility," the keynote speech given by Derek Charles Livingston, "a pro-choice, openly gay, African-American man," recognized the work of various organizations across North Carolina fighting against Jesse Helms and anti-gay attacks. Livingston acknowledged the importance of women's groups, like the Lesbian Avengers, whose "protests are creative, fun, visible, and viable," and those advocating for lesbian mothers and fighting against Helms. While noting the efforts of local churchgoers who "made a mockery of Christ's teachings" trying to stop the Pride event, he situated his speech in the heart of the Bible Belt by repeatedly turning to religious themes of Christian acceptance.[89] The event culminated in a parade, where native Charlottean Sonya Lewis celebrated the visibility of marching in Uptown Charlotte with her parents and siblings in the Pride parade.[90] In a city where lesbian Lynnsy Logue felt unsafe parking her car at the Scorpio, a parade seemed risky. She and her partner weighed the costs of participating in the 1994 parade. They decided to attend because they did not have children to protect and thought that Henry and Kirsch's capable leadership lent an air of safety. Although no one was killed, Logue remembered thinking that they believed such a scenario was possible. Sue Henry recalled that people were expecting bad things.[91] It would be almost twenty years before a Pride parade took place again in the Queen City.[92]

The thought of queer people like Lewis and Logue in the streets of Charlotte was exactly what some religious leaders and their congregations feared and abhorred. Several members and pastors of Charlotte's churches wrote letters to the city's Parade Permit Committee protesting the Pride march and the requested Sunday kickoff time. The pages of the *Charlotte Observer* were filled with letters to the editor, opinion columns, and coverage of the rancor—especially the vociferous pleadings of the First Baptist Church, located just two blocks from Marshall Park, where the march organizers would gather. First Baptist's pastor, Reverend Charles Page, a leader in the 1992 melee against the anti-bias ordinance that would have extended protections to lesbian and gay people in Charlotte, also led the battle against state Pride. Parishioners at the First Baptist Church viewed the parade portion of the Pride weekend festival as a direct provocation: by marching near the church, gay people would be expressing animosity against the church's anti-gay teachings.[93] A local political cartoon illustrated First Baptist's "proposed 'alternate' finishing point" for the Gay Pride event as a path lined in arrows leading to a barely opened closet door.[94]

Business leaders with ties to First Baptist wrote letters pleading with the Parade Permit Committee chair to deny the permit. The letter writers were clearly instructed to reference the 1993 national March on Washington for Lesbian, Gay, and Bi Equal Rights and Liberation as an example of the inappropriate nature of the event planned in Charlotte.

Protesters and parade participants at North Carolina Pride in Charlotte, 1994. (*Above*) A Pride attendee taunts Bible-carrying protesters lining the parade route. (*Below*) Parade participants ride on a float with a message to North Carolina's anti-gay senator Jesse Helms. Accessed from Sue Henry Papers, MS0478, J. Murrey Atkins Library, Special Collections, University of North Carolina at Charlotte.

The gay marches on Washington began in 1979, when a contingent of Atlanta women carrying a purple and white ALFA banner joined thousands in the nation's capital to commemorate the events of Stonewall.[95] When organizers arrived for the second march in 1987, they were overwhelmed by a somber gathering of at least 500,000 attendees, many of whom were living with AIDS. Reagan's lack of attention to the pandemic and to the organizers' drive for queer political clout in the 1988 elections politicized the 1987 march attendees, including Charlotte's Henry and the Georgia organizing committee for the march.[96]

Approximately 1 million queer people participated in the 1993 march. While the gathering would be used as a weapon by religious leaders in Charlotte, the fact that Black queer Atlantan Pat Hussain, member of the March on Washington's national executive committee, took the stage with fellow queer leaders from across the country serves as an example of how national queer visibility elevated Atlanta's queer citizens while it was used to oppress Charlotte's.[97] March attendees enjoyed support from Congress members like Nancy Pelosi, leaders in the NAACP, and President Clinton. Although he did not attend, Clinton issued a statement in support of gay civil rights. Just a few months before his "don't ask, don't tell" policy was finalized, some chanted, "Where is Bill?" in frustration, but many at the march saw Clinton as a sign of potential progress for queer people.[98] Drag entertainer RuPaul took the stage in an American flag costume proclaiming that queer voters had put Clinton in the White House and that was where she saw herself in ten years. On the same stage, Indigo Girls, Atlanta's Grammy-winning superstar white lesbians, performed, with Emily Saliers sporting a Clinton/Gore campaign T-shirt.[99]

Media coverage of the 1993 march was unprecedented. *Newsweek* magazine featured a full cover on the event, while the *New York Times* described the mood as celebratory, noting that Americans would see "conventional" and "well behaved" attendees on the evening news coverage.[100] In its feature on lesbians at the march, *Newsweek* quoted lesbian comic Kate Clinton, who dubbed 1993 the "year of the woman squared," because women who loved women were having a moment in what many march participants called the Gay '90s. The article noted Roberta Achtenberg's new position as the assistant secretary of the US Department of Housing and Urban Development, the first openly gay person to be confirmed by the Senate. Yet that visibility came at a price. North Carolina's senator Jesse Helms railed against her appointment and called Achtenberg a "damn lesbian."[101] The nonprofit cable television channel

C-SPAN ran six hours of live and unedited coverage of the march, which *Newsweek* noted as vulgar to "many liberals who . . . were offended by the spectacle of some women—albeit from the lesbian fringes—who were kissing or half naked."[102] Even though the *New York Times* deemed attendees' behavior "conventional," the C-SPAN exposure riled up First Baptist's parishioners and encouraged them to react like the aforementioned offended liberals when North Carolina state Pride came to the Queen City the following year.

Attorney Tim Sellers and other letter writers offered to share a video from the national march with the Parade Permit Committee in an effort to demonstrate the "*illegal* and horrifying activity" that a similar "gay rights march" might bring to the streets of Charlotte.[103] Harking back to a 1970s style of conservative activism, similar to the rhetoric promoted by Florida's Anita Bryant in her anti-gay "Save Our Children" campaign, several letter writers expressed concern for children's safety and the risk of exposing them to the state Pride event. Architect Graham Adams referenced his firm's work with neighborhood students who lived in a housing project just a few blocks from Marshall Park and who "must not be subjected to such a parade that would certainly be protested if it were proposed to occur in another neighborhood." Adams's suggestion that at-risk youth were being exposed to the danger of an influential gay message that would not be allowed in more affluent neighborhoods smacked of a feigned concern for the students who would "suffer emotionally and educationally" from Pride's message.[104]

To quiet the hubbub, Pride's Henry and Kirsch quickly responded to the frustrated Reverend Page and his congregation. The organizing committee offered to meet with church members, provide volunteers to direct festival attendees away from the church property, and change the start time of the parade (from noon to 1:30 P.M.) in order to reduce any interference with the Sunday worship activities. In his response, Page reiterated his opposition to the parade and declined the committee's offers to meet and to monitor festival attendees near church property. But Page gave up the church's public fight. The media made hay of this common ground between the Pride organizers and the church, even suggesting that the speedy compromise by Pride leaders demonstrated a more "Christian" approach.[105]

Two years after his opposition to the antidiscrimination amendment, Charlotte's mayor Richard Vinroot refused to be involved in North Carolina Pride, stating, "'I happened to watch on C-SPAN about two months ago what looked like a gay-Pride march. I was embarrassed by the language and the references and the public exposition of sex. It was very offensive. If that's what this is, I want no part of it.'"[106] Charlotte's lesbians and gay men heard Vinroot's message loud and clear. It was publicized in the local media during the weeks leading up to state Pride, and they knew that their visible presence was not "desirable," as the mayor stated in a letter to one of his gay constituents the following year.[107] Those in the Fellowship of Deacons for First Baptist celebrated Mayor Vinroot's complete opposition to the march and noted their delight at the mayor's efforts to keep Charlotte from becoming a "worldly" class city.[108]

Politicians and congregations were not the only Charlotteans who reacted negatively to Pride. In fact, some lesbians and gay men were not pleased with the perceived flamboyance that the event might bring to Charlotte. In a promotional mailer for the Saturday night dance, two shirtless couples were pictured in an embrace—a lesbian couple and a gay male couple—with the words "Trust Your Desire."[109] The "inappropriate" flyer generated complaints, primarily from lesbians who were upset by the blatantly sexual nature of the postcard. Linda Carmichael wrote to Pride organizers to express her embarrassment at receiving the promotion. She shared a mailbox with her landlady and viewed the mailer as disrespectful of her privacy.[110] Sheelagh Anderson went further by noting that people often go to dances to find partners, "but as far as I know, they do not go topless!" Anderson suggested that men who failed to recognize the difference between male sexuality ("sex sex sex") and female sexuality, which she believed to be relationship-focused, must have been responsible for the postcard.[111] Worried about the event as a whole, Ruth Derrow wrote to the Pride committee asking that a "smart" dress and behavior code be suggested for the weekend's events. Derrow hoped that attendees would "consider the city" where they would be marching and avoid making waves that would garner negative media attention, similar to that received by the 1993 March on Washington.[112] Some lesbians and gay men desperately hoped to garner heterosexual approval and tolerance and embraced respectability politics as the best way forward.

Steering committee member Don King also worried about the negative and lasting impact of the national March on Washington. He worked with Pride cochairs Henry and Kirsch to negotiate a balance between promoting palatable behavior for heterosexual power players and creating a welcoming environment for groups like the queer leather community and the motorcycle-riding Dykes on Bikes, fixtures at Pride parades and darlings of a media eager to show the most outrageous footage from festivals. But King made a point to clarify in media coverage leading up to

Pride that bankers and lawyers (respectable businesspeople "within the bounds of good taste") would also be at Pride and that organizers "might even issue guidelines for recommended behavior."[113] King admitted to being offended by four-letter words at the March on Washington and expressed his concerns about "good taste" and not wanting to encourage hecklers, in an effort to appease powerful religious and business leaders in Charlotte.[114] While local Pride organizers wrote in their grant proposal to the state committee that they wanted to celebrate the community's "decorative fringe," some statements in the local press suggested that they would work hard to highlight "normal everyday" gay people. As in Atlanta a decade earlier, Pride organizers in Charlotte deployed respectability politics to gain acceptance from the Queen City's conservative business community while attempting to also embrace the vast gamut of queer people.[115]

State Pride helped queer organizers in Charlotte to recognize their collective power. As a result of Henry and Kirsch's success, they spearheaded a new cultural festival that would place queer people in the public eye in a positive light, while working to avoid controversy. Henry believed that harnessing the performance art and entertainment components of the state Pride festival (without the difficulty of putting on a parade) would help to combat some anti-gay rhetoric through community education.[116] Local media labeled OutCharlotte a quiet gay festival, but it could not be quiet enough for the city's mayor: "Three years ago, I spoke out strongly against a proposed 'Gay Rights' ordinance then under consideration; last year I stated publicly (when asked) that I wished that the 'Gay Pride' parade which occurred in June would not take place here; and this week I essentially responded the same way (when asked) about the 'OutCharlotte' event which prompted your letter. I've no idea what the 'Christian Coalition' thinks about all these things, but my position has been consistent and quite public for most of my term as Mayor."[117]

A few years after the highly contested 1994 North Carolina state Pride event in Charlotte, the festival returned to Asheville, North Carolina, in 1998. Met with angry picketing just six years earlier, many of Asheville's citizens now welcomed Pride with increased excitement and a growing acceptance for lesbian and gay people. Festival attendees organized a visible and supportive response in spite of some remaining opposition. Community support for state Pride was a result of the growth of a thriving gay-friendly business district in the city of Asheville, a large lesbian population, and a heterosexual community of allies. Although a significantly smaller city, whose 1990 population stood at 64,625 in comparison with Charlotte's 395,934, Asheville, like Atlanta, possessed the necessary attributes for lesbian and gay visibility that Charlotte lacked.[118] Nationally recognized as queer-friendly, and occasionally referred to as the "San Francisco of the South," by 2000 Asheville ranked within the top fifteen cities nationally for same-sex partnerships.[119] Increasingly welcoming to lesbian and gay people in the 1990s, the culture of the city's business climate proved that even in the "queer hating state" of North Carolina, a visible queer community could thrive.

Asheville's large lesbian population supported its vibrant and eclectic downtown entertainment district, including the beatnik and lesbian hangout Malaprop's Bookstore.[120] Catering to the broad and eclectic Asheville tourist market, Malaprop's attracted a diverse clientele willing to sustain the store in the long term. Like businesses in Atlanta's Peachtree district, Asheville's lesbian and gay business owners created an energized and revitalized downtown. When Malaprop's opened in downtown Asheville in 1982, the district was all but abandoned. Charlotte's *Creative Loafing* newspaper observed that Asheville's independent businesses maintained original building structures, including the original "art deco edifices," and the city itself exhibited "all the idiosyncrasies of a truly metropolitan life—including homosexuality." It was "no wonder" then that Charlotte destroyed "every fine piece of old architecture"; according to the wry journalist, suburbanization was clearly a "right-wing conspiracy."[121] Lesbian activist and North Carolina state Pride organizer Sue Henry opened a similar store in Charlotte: Rising Moon Books. Located in the Dilworth neighborhood just a five-minute walk from the Charlotte Women's Center, Henry's store did not experience the reinforcement of a like-minded and unconventional business district that Malaprop's enjoyed. Recognized as a niche business strictly for lesbian and gay people, it was a haven for queers seeking gay-friendly reading, greeting cards, information, and sex videos. When white lesbian Lesley Brown arrived in Charlotte from Lawrence, Kansas, she searched to find her queer people. Leaving behind a big community of lesbians and gay men, she landed at Rising Moon. Seeking a seemingly hidden community, Brown recalled someone there telling her that most people in Charlotte were just there for their jobs. She knew that some groups of women were sharing potlucks, but it all seemed so factionalized.[122]

Although Henry's store was "gay Charlotte's unofficial headquarters," it closed in December 1997 due to inconsistent and insufficient sales.[123] Henry concluded that the "demise was due to the lack of support from the majority of the gay and lesbian community." In an interview with

WRITE-IN CANDIDATE

SUE HENRY for MAYOR

CHARLOTTE

An Alternative to Intolerance

In 1995, Sue Henry ran as a write-in candidate for Charlotte mayor. Accessed from Sue Henry Papers, MS0478, J. Murrey Atkins Library, Special Collections, University of North Carolina at Charlotte.

the *Charlotte Observer* on the store's closing, she aptly observed that "in pin-striped Charlotte, gays and lesbians are often as conservative as their heterosexual counterparts."[124] Lesbian and gay Charlotteans were also *Charlotteans*. They were residents of a city known for its commitment to banking, religion, and making money—for its shiny veneer of appropriateness and always operating with an eye toward attracting business. Charlotte was not a place to ruffle feathers. But Sue Henry's business ruffled feathers, and it was not the kind of business that most Charlotteans, gay or straight, were willing to support. Charlotte's queer activists were not enjoying the gay moment of the 1990s that seemed to be barreling forward in Atlanta and Washington, DC, and elsewhere.

Asheville and Atlanta offered the funky business districts necessary to maintain an energetic lesbian and gay community in the 1980s and 1990s. Pride festivals were visible manifestations and celebrations of a thriving lesbian and gay population, and this was directly related to a gay-friendly business climate and mayoral backing. Charlotte's inability to mount a Pride festival in the 1970s, maintain lesbian-feminist activism, or sustain gay business districts directly reflected the troubled political and religious climate for lesbian and gay people.[125] The foundation for consistent Pride events and a cohesive gay neighborhood did not exist. It is telling that in the early days of queer and leftist activism in Charlotte, one small business owner lamented the lack of support and an appropriate business district for his Uptown head shop, Asterisk. He felt that his location was perfect for complementary businesses, such as a leather store, coffee shop, bookstore, or theater, and he craved this camaraderie since he knew that "soon even Kmart will sell roach clips." This shop owner longed for an independent shopping district—a "strip like most big towns."[126] Cities like Asheville and Atlanta grew these districts in the late decades of the twentieth century, but the lack of artsy shopping areas would plague Charlotte's lesbian and gay community in its effort to maintain identifiable queer urban space. Atlanta's booming Midtown neighborhood, its consistency in its Pride location, and the participants' insistence on visibility created Pride spectacles that would help the city earn the *Advocate*'s coveted "Gayest City in America" title in 2010.[127] Asheville also joined the celebrated list that year as a "prime example of the new gay South," due in part to "its thriving art scene and adorable homes."[128]

The city of Asheville offers an instructive comparison because it demonstrates that a vibrant and resilient queer community is possible regardless of a city's size. Because of its celebration of eccentric community, Asheville created a queer-friendly tourist destination in the often ignored queer South. Popular media portrayed the city as hospitable to lesbians and gays, a city separate from the mythological South in many ways, but as in Atlanta and Charlotte, what works for queer people at first glance often excludes non-white experiences. Asheville's reputation as uniquely welcoming did not materialize for some Black women. Although the city possessed a thriving lesbian population, Asheville resident Stephanie remarked, "There are lesbians who are racist."[129] At the time of Asheville's second North Carolina state Pride, the white population outnumbered the Black population by almost 60 percent, which meant that for some Black women Atlanta was the safer place to be Black and queer, offering a more integrated space than Asheville.[130]

From the earliest days of claiming gay visibility, queer activists faced challenges. In the 1950s, it came at the expense of marginalizing those who did not present a heterosexually palatable persona. Drag queens, butch lesbians, Black homosexuals, and working-class queers were all viewed as problematic in the accommodationist politics of homophile activism. As Marcia Gallo has shown, "The lengths to which a lesbian would go for societal acceptance was a contested issue from the beginning," and in the 1950s, the Daughters of Bilitis "championed outward conformity to achieve integration, primarily through the provision in its Statement of Purpose that required members to adopt a 'mode of dress and behavior acceptable to society.'"[131] Decades earlier in Atlanta, historian Tera W. Hunter found that the "Black bourgeoisie lamented the shame and disgrace that befell the entire race" when Black domestic workers danced in public halls on seedy Decatur Street.[132] In the first decades of the twentieth-century South a middle-class Black elite "sought to impose its own values and standards on the masses" and "asserted its paternalism through the language of morality" directed at working-class African Americans. In the final decades of the twentieth century, so too did queer elites assert a similar authority aimed at southern Pride attendees.[133]

Decades after the midcentury homophile movement, Gay Pride in the New South was not always a celebration of the variety of ways that queer could be expressed but instead was often a chance to represent a respectable identity to the straight community. It was "Morning in America," according to Ronald Reagan's presidential reelection campaign, and with Georgians and North Carolinians giving Reagan more than 60 percent of their votes in his landslide 1984 victory and supporting George W. Bush overwhelmingly in 1988, 1950s-style conformity made good sense for the politics of Pride in the South.[134]

We are enraged; I mean we are pissed. . . .
We demand Latina space and respect for our
Latina voices. —Visible Latina Lesbians at
the National Lesbian Conference

5 INSTITUTIONS

In the final decades of the twentieth century and at the dawn of the twenty-first, Atlanta and Charlotte experienced substantial changes linked to institutions that influenced queer organizing and life for queer people. These urban institutions often controlled the popular presentations of queer life in the New South. Activist communities evolved differently in Atlanta and Charlotte but often in relation to the development of urban institutions. Local policing fueled queer perceptions of safety and protection in each city. Queer groups grappled with racism and sexism as they tried to find a middle ground between organizing social opportunities and advocating for political visibility. Universities provided sustenance and space for queer students to connect with social and political groups beyond the campus environment. Corporate support for Pride events and corporate benefits for lesbian and gay employees altered the climate for queer life in each city. The arrival of national sports teams in Charlotte resulted in new social spaces for lesbians, while the presence of the Olympic Games in Atlanta threatened the safety of lesbian social space. Religious institutions in each city shaped political decisions and national perceptions of urban identity. And when seeking a place to be out, Atlanta's gay infrastructure attracted queer people, while Charlotte's queer community garnered considerably less attention.

In the mid-1980s, the Atlanta Lesbian Feminist Alliance continued to serve as a resource for interested lesbians and as a liaison for the growing gay community, celebrating achievements and fighting for change. A 1985 survey of its *Atalanta* newsletter readers showed a membership with diverse interests including coffeehouse meetings, a police advisory committee, racial and social discrimination, and social events like movies and concerts, but interestingly the survey included nothing on Pride. During the days surrounding the annual Pride festival, ALFA continued to offer workshops and events designed for lesbians, but in the 1980s its focus on community-oriented goals that often crossed the rigid borders between lesbians and gay men linked the organization to a variety of institutions and organizations in Atlanta.

When the Atlanta Gay Center added two women and two African Americans to its board, ALFA celebrated the move in *Atalanta*, noting it as a step toward "representativeness."[1] When gay men were harassed by Atlanta police, ALFA participated in community meetings organized by the Lesbian and Gay Police Advisory Committee. Writers in the February and March 1985 issues of *Atalanta* detailed the meeting in thorough reports over several pages. Ten members of the committee met, including two women. All who attended were white, although the committee did include two Black members. Seven police officials met with the group, including Chief of Police Morris Redding and Eldrin Bell, who would be appointed chief in 1990. ALFA's newsletter regularly covered the advocacy of the Police Advisory Committee, and even though there were only two lesbians at this particular meeting, their support for the privacy concerns of their male colleagues demonstrates the organization's investment in gay men's rights. Of particular concern was the perceived solicitation in gay men's bars, where police would arrest gay men who actively sought sex. The committee argued not only that these bars had a right to exist but that a gay bar should be a safe and legitimate space to seek sex. The committee worked with the police leadership by submitting the names of currently operating bars and noting those, including the popular lesbian hangout Toolulahs, not in compliance with the posting requirements for liquor licenses.[2]

Meetings such as these resulted from the direct orders of George Napper, chief of police in 1981. Napper encouraged leaders of the gay community, specifically gay activist and clergyman Reverend Mike Piazza, to work with his department to assure that officers were "aware of and sensitized to the fact that there is a sizable gay community in the City of Atlanta with lifestyles and concerns that on occasion differ from other groups in Atlanta."[3] In a 1981 memo to his deputy chief, Napper asked for additional meetings with Reverend Piazza to ensure "meaningful interaction and dialogue" that would adequately address officers' concerns and questions with regard to gay people and their safety in Atlanta. He also requested an ongoing commitment to continued "in-service training" for the police department. The following year, Piazza occupied a prominent place in media coverage of the politically focused Atlanta Pride event. He recognized that gay people in Atlanta enjoyed a substantial level of acceptance for a southern city and that the 1982 Pride celebration was successful, in spite of "a few street preachers" along the parade route, with no substantial incidents.[4] Atlanta's police department continued its advocacy for gay concerns throughout the 1990s and into the twenty-first century by employing LGBT community liaisons, maintaining its relationship with an active LGBT Advisory Board, and supporting lesbian and gay officers who marched in the city's Pride parades.[5]

ALFA's involvement with the Police Advisory Committee was in accordance with its revised 1985 mission statement that incorporated "the entire spectrum of lesbian feminist issues," including "the liberation of women; eliminating discrimination based on sexual orientation; ending racial, anti-Semitic, and economic oppression; eliminating nuclear weapons and reducing the threat of war"; and other social justice causes.[6] By 1991, however, some leaders of ALFA recognized that while the organization once served as "the nucleus for everything from a softball team to political groups," with so many new lesbian and gay opportunities in Atlanta it was time for them to refocus.[7] They remained committed to their political goals, noting that without ALFA in Atlanta, the city lacked "an explicitly political group that tackles lesbian, feminist, and other rights issues at the same time." The group was concerned with issues that affected "lesbians not only as lesbians, but as women," and "a host of other 'isms' that marginalize and oppress many in our society."[8] Although ALFA remained decidedly political in its focus, for some lesbians in Atlanta the social arena was much more important.

Lesbians found an additional social and political option in Atlanta when the group Fourth Tuesday formed in 1982. Members hoped to "sponsor and encourage communication and networking between professional and entrepreneurial women, and to provide a social atmosphere to encourage mutual support." The organization was made up of an elite group of educated women primarily in their thirties. Over 70 percent of respondents to a membership survey had a college degree, with 41 percent holding graduate degrees and 25 percent reporting an income over $50,000 a year. The most important aspect of the organization was providing the opportunity to meet other women socially.[9] The *Fourth Tuesday Forum* newsletter regularly promoted dinners, cocktail hours, book clubs, events at local bars like the Otherside, and regional events like the Southern Women's Music and Comedy Festival and a Queen City Valentine's dance hosted by Fourth Tuesday's "sisters in Charlotte."[10] By 1990 the group had virtually doubled, boasting almost 400 members.[11]

Similar to the lesbian-feminist newsletters of the 1970s but lacking the separatist rhetoric, the monthly *Forum* offered regional and national information on social and political topics. Unlike these earlier newsletters, however, the *Forum* accepted advertising. For example, it promoted the first all-lesbian Bahamas cruise hosted by Olivia Records, a travel opportunity marketed to elite women seeking a private social escape. Fourth Tuesday and Olivia Records are examples of tenacious lesbian institutions that changed with the social landscape by reinventing themselves; as a result, both organizations remained active in the first decades of the twenty-first century. "Olivia Travel" left behind the vinyl industry and instead promoted exclusive all-lesbian vacations featuring lesbian comedians and musicians, while Fourth Tuesday became the LGBTQ Health Initiative's "social network for women," offering regular happy hours and other lesbian community events.[12]

Fourth Tuesday included lesbian-focused caucuses who regularly contributed to the newsletter with reports like "Old Lesbian Expectations" and "Racism 101 for White Women." Designed to address the power of white privilege and feelings of white guilt, the *Forum* outlined "Racism 101" as a "white people's problem," noting that white people facing presumptions about the white race as a whole was not akin to racism. "There is no such thing as reverse racism," the caucus warned. "As white women we do not have to take personally (as guilt) every single statement from women of color of their anger over racism." "Racism 201" outlined racism as an "opportunity" to form "alliances" and "friendships" with Black women in order "to think together strategically about dismantling institutional racist structures." "Racism 301" proposed an exploration of "Revolutionary Movements," and "Racism 401" imagined "Post Revolutionary Societies."[13] Efforts like these defy the stereotype of tenacious southern positions on race as these women worked to foster understanding across racial divides.

The *Forum* occasionally featured a column on Black lesbians contributed by Dr. Shirlene Holmes, a lesbian playwright and professor at Georgia State University. In her first column, Holmes introduced the group Hospitality Atlanta. Members of this African American lesbian social-networking organization considered it a sister group to Fourth Tuesday and sought collaboration, although it is hard to say how much interaction occurred. Based on its 1,000-name mailing list, Hospitality Atlanta garnered a substantial level of interest after only three years of existence. Like Fourth Tuesday, some Hospitality Atlanta members eagerly pushed the group beyond a social focus to engage in political organizing. The political arm of Fourth Tuesday joined ALFA, the Women of Color Caucus, and "Women of Wisdom" to bring the 1991 National Lesbian Conference (NLC) to Atlanta. Uniting with women in diverse groups, like LIFE (Lesbians in Fun Endeavors) and Fatdykes, the leaders of Fourth Tuesday believed that Atlanta's "80 to 100,000 lesbians" could use this as an opportunity to "work and grow together toward a common goal."[14]

The NLC emanated from the momentum of the 1987 March on Washington for Lesbian and Gay Rights. Dividing the country into regions, planners began with a focus on geography, race, culture, and the desire for a national lesbian agenda. In January 1989, approximately 125 lesbians from nine southern states convened at Emory University for the southeast regional meeting. They were stymied by this frustrating core question: Who would "we" represent in the language produced for, and radiating from, the conference? The goal was to achieve "lesbiana"—a conference representing all concerns and topics. Organizers brainstormed funding ideas, like a traveling "private kissing booth" to be set up at Pride celebrations allowing women to go in and make out for a donation to the conference planning. Observers described the "precious diversity" of the Emory attendees as "blue collar, white collar, Black, white, Chicana, Native American, moneyed, poor, variously abled, separatist, coalitionist, softball, intellectual, political, humorous, serious, musical, tonedeaf, and every other sort and variety of dyke that knew about the planning meeting."[15]

Issues of race permeated the Durham national organizing gathering, which was an attempt to bring all regions together to discuss the NLC. The women wandered into the "stormy waters of lesbian group dynamics" trying to determine how they could they reach agreement with the massive diversity in their ranks.[16] Durham attendees participated in a fishbowl discussion of racism, where white women sat on the outside of a circle of women of color and then moved to the inside to discuss their own racism and observations of racial issues at the meeting. Despite intense frustration, attendees decided that women of color should have 50 percent representation on the steering committee, a point that was heavily debated, and women with disabilities had to be involved at the structural level of planning. The *Fourth Tuesday Forum* gleefully reported the final location result as Atlanta, chosen in part because it would be a better space for the Black lesbian community in comparison to other possibilities, like Dallas and Washington, DC, which was favored by lesbians with disabilities.

Approximately 3,000 women attended the NLC in Atlanta, where they received an official welcome from Mayor Maynard Jackson read into the conference proceedings. The five-day conference tackled issues such as parenting and violence against lesbians, health care, housing, racism, and aging. White women met in support of lesbians of color with a plan to "anticipate" and "interrupt racism."[17] Entertainment included a performance by popular 1990s drastic dyke comedian Lea DeLaria, "Two Spirited Thunder People Native American dancers," and the singers Alix Dobkin and the Washington Sisters. Attendees were reminded about how to avoid news photographers, as a public address system in the host Radisson hotel repeatedly "blared a warning" so that those who did not want to be associated with the conference in the media, for fear of losing their jobs or being outed, could plan their clandestine exit strategies. Featuring a photo of diverse participants, the *New York Times* recognized the national significance of the NLC for attendees who chose to be visible, for those from small towns, and for others who recognized that this was not a lesbian caucus of a bigger queer or feminist group, not an appendage, but a meeting for lesbians only—on their own terms. Organizers insisted on "lesbian" (not gay) for visibility yet also worried about literature from the conference being spread beyond the conference doors, which they viewed as a liability.[18]

Early NLC organizing meetings focused on feminist ideas of consensus, parity, and grassroots decision-making, yet there were significant problems in figuring out long-term communications and accountability over the several years of planning. The decision-making model led to problems when the conference convened, as frustrated attendees looked for leaders whom they could hold accountable when things began to fall apart.[19] "Vibe-watchers" monitored conference presentations, which proceeded diplomatically and productively, but the conference opened with controversy.[20] Latina lesbians declared their rage, posting flyers around the hotel protesting the invisibility of women of color in the planning and final program. Women of color promoted massive agendas for the conference and beyond, but by the end of the NLC there was too much racial controversy and disagreement for a national lesbian organization or agenda. Keynote speaker Urvashi Vaid, who almost did not have time to speak because of the chaotic racial frustrations, felt "traumatized" by the racism at the conference. She encouraged the crowd to focus on the importance of being together and recognizing the problems that all lesbians faced, noting that "to be lesbian means to be invisible, to face multiple systems of oppression." Notwithstanding their substantial differences, Vaid urged attendees to value themselves as a "powerhouse of a community" performing revolutionary work.[21]

Atlanta's African American Lesbian/Gay Alliance (AALGA) fostered a "visibly involved" presence at the NLC, as members aimed "to establish a Black gay political force in Atlanta through local forums."[22] Relatively balanced between women and men, the AALGA hosted two separate caucuses for women and men, which met regularly. The group, usually about thirty to forty members, looked to increase women's involvement and visibility with substantial focus placed on issues related to Black lesbian health. Regular AALGA events centered on Black cultural representations in cooking, through recipe sharing and potlucks, and in entertainment, through a film festival, music, and a talent showcase. Additional goals for the organization's community-building initiatives included outreach to college campuses and gay bars, wellness, involvement at Atlanta Pride, and identifying a media contact to focus on Black and queer issues.[23]

In addition to planning for increased visibility at the NLC and community Pride, the AALGA coordinated efforts to host the third National Black Gay and Lesbian Leadership Forum in Atlanta in 1990 and succeeded in securing an official welcome from Atlanta City Council member Mary Davis. Further, the AALGA reached out to the Atlanta consortium of gay organizations to encourage attendance at the conference and worked with TRAXX, a primarily Black gay male bar, for fundraising and organizing meetings. During the conference, TRAXX hosted an AIDS benefit for attendees. Approximately 500 people showed up for the leadership forum, recognizing Atlanta's status as a "mecca" for Black people.[24] In keeping with the conference theme, "Celebrating Our History/Creating Our Future," the host hotel conference rooms were renamed for Black queer leaders, like Pat Parker, Bessie Smith, James Baldwin, Mabel Hampton, and Bayard Rustin, transforming the Hyatt Regency conference level into an "African American plaza."[25] The conference featured a groundbreaking new workshop, "Grand and Proud," a historical look at "cross-dressing and transvestites," and several workshops focused on building relationships between lesbians and gay men. Barbara Smith of Kitchen Table: Women of Color Press delivered a keynote speech encouraging audience members to move away from capitalism and economic status symbols and instead spend money on a Black political agenda.[26] The conference organizers identified six areas for a

Black queer agenda: health, media, politics, spirituality, history and culture, and networking. Like the NLC, the leadership forum was not without controversy. A conference wrap-up in a national feminist newsletter noted lesbians "assaulted by numerous instances of sexism and looksism," including "a male poet [who] called a lesbian a stupid bitch."[27] The divisiveness among lesbians at the NLC also existed among Black queers at their national conference, demonstrating that a unifying identity did not exist in either space as both race and gender presented significant challenges and painful behaviors.

The AALGA's leaders prioritized outreach to the heterosexual Black community. It was vital for them to have this support, whereas this type of heterosexual social relationship was not essential to white queer groups because of their racial dominance. Skin color is a visible marker, and queer people carried with them the privileges of whiteness and the oppressions of Blackness into the heterosexual community. Activists craved the political and social community fostered by their racial identity, as evidenced in their group affirmation: "As Proud of our Gayness as we are of our Blackness."[28] For example, when members of the AALGA participated in the March on Washington in 1987, they were as excited by the visibility of Black celebrities (such as Whoopi Goldberg and Jesse Jackson) as they were at being surrounded by queer people. And when group members presented their humanitarian award, they chose to meet at Paschal's Restaurant, a historic site of civil rights meetings known to welcome famous Black entertainers and leaders in Atlanta. The AALGA realized the importance of the space and the speaker, a member of Atlanta's Fulton County Board of Commissioners, in setting forth a path toward a new civil rights movement to include Black queer people. When running for his third term as mayor, Maynard Jackson (known for his wishy-washy support of Pride in the 1970s) reached out to the AALGA and secured its active backing of his campaign.[29] As promised by Jackson, he appointed an advisor on LGBT issues when he took office. That person was AALGA founder Joan Garner.[30]

The AALGA's newsletter, *Crossroads*, revealed the group's work to facilitate communication between Black lesbians and Black gay men. The organization was active in Atlanta Pride festivals, sought representation of women to achieve balance on its governing board, and focused on an appreciation of Black culture. In choosing this name for the publication, the editors noted the definition of an intersection: "(1.) a small community located at the intersection of two or more roads; (2.) a central meeting place; (3.) a crucial point especially where a decision must be made."[31] Two years before Kimberlé Crenshaw published her pathbreaking article coining the term "intersectionality," the AALGA grappled with the intersections of Blackness and queerness. While Crenshaw argued that scholars must employ both gendered and racial analysis to address the subordination of Black women, she did not directly apply the theory to queerness.[32] The AALGA embraced intersectionality in practice, recognizing Crenshaw's dictum that "the racial context in which Black women find themselves makes the creation of a political consciousness that is oppositional to Black men difficult." The AALGA brought Black women and men together under the umbrella of their queer identity. Yet it also identified the societal tendency to treat race and gender as mutually exclusive, leaving Black out of "woman" and women out of "Blacks."[33] This exclusion similarly applies to "lesbian," which rarely includes Black women or separates Black lesbians from the category of "lesbian," sending the message that this is a category reserved for white women.[34] Black culture, community, and tradition mattered in queer organizing. Lesbians were operating with gay men in the AALGA to address concerns for women and concerns for Black queer people. I am reluctant to simply compare white lesbian organizations with Black lesbian activisms and organizations; instead I find that the goals for Black women in queer activisms addressed issues that were necessarily separate from the issues of white organizations.

While historical evidence suggests that Black lesbians worked with white queer women to bring lesbian community and visibility to Atlanta, the reverse is not true. In the AALGA's women-of-color caucus notes, participants logged a commitment to join ALFA (the predominantly white lesbian-feminist group) for a "racism caucus" meeting.[35] ALFA's newsletter promoted concerns related to the AALGA's women, like the Black Women's Health Project and Charis Books and More, which promoted Black women authors and supported queer Black activisms, usually organized by lesbians in the AALGA. According to narrators in E. Patrick Johnson's oral histories, Black southern lesbians valued the "alternative spiritual community" found at Charis's literary and "community organizing" happenings.[36] The events created and funded by the AALGA did not intersect with organizations run primarily by white queer people. Black women organized separately because white women organized in ways that did not, indeed could not, represent Black women's needs.

Atlanta's Black lesbian activists craved local and national visibility and Black queer community. They built these necessities apart from white lesbian organizations. For example, the long-running and dynamic Black lesbian activist group ZAMI described its mission: "ZAMI is a collective of lesbians of color who work together to provide a positive self-image and a sense of community." Topics for ZAMI-led discussions included "relationships with your mother, substance abuse, and sexual fantasies," while social events included picnics, movies, games, and camping.[37] Additionally, the AALGA organized events connected to Black religion and spirituality, like its "Spiritual Gay Pride Service" and celebration of Kwanzaa.[38] Johnson argues that the Black church offered "refuge" for Black queer men but was more of an obligation for Black lesbians. The male-dominated church and structure of the biblical canon served as an affront to women who loved women, who often preferred their own path to a spiritual existence.[39] White queer women's groups did not focus on issues like spirituality and health because they enjoyed a broad network of white accessibility, where health care outlets prioritized their needs and spirituality was not necessary to build community with other white people. White community was a given.

The roots of 1970s lesbian and New Left activism in Atlanta can be directly traced to the surrounding and supportive college community in Atlanta's Little Five Points neighborhood. The two closest universities, Emory and Georgia State, sustained queer visibility in the neighborhood for the coming decades. In the heart of Atlanta, Georgia State University students formed the Alliance for Sexual and Gender Diversity in 1982, the oldest gay-straight association in the state.[40] Founded in 1913, Georgia State University was a newer institution compared with Emory, nearby University of Georgia, and Atlanta's Georgia Tech, but it established a unique identity by the 1950s.[41] Student members of the Alliance for Sexual and Gender Diversity led the fight to join the 1986 Martin Luther King Jr. celebration parade where, less than twenty-four hours prior to the parade, queer marchers were accepted for participation.[42] The students met with two other groups carrying a banner that read, "We oppose racism, sexism, and anti-gay bigotry. Repeal all sodomy laws." Made up of an all-white contingent, students claimed that the late-in-the-day invitation to march came too late for them to gather a "representative" contingent of participants.[43] By 1989, the Metropolitan Atlanta Council of Lesbian and Gay Organizations secured a permit for the parade and encouraged a variety of groups to march.[44] Student activists were among the first to pave the way for groups like the AALGA and improved the parade by bringing queer visibility to the King event. It is significant that even in this celebration of Black civil rights, whiteness afforded the students that initial privilege. Lesbian and gay students provided legitimacy for queer actions in Atlanta. They tied gay visibility to an academic environment, and they offered an outlet outside of the bars for social organization and interaction.

Organized queer student activism dates to 1972 at Emory University, which operated at the cutting edge of gay Atlanta in the 1980s.[45] The Emory Lesbian and Gay Organization (ELGO), active throughout the decade, served as a model to other southern universities interested in lesbian and gay student inclusion on campus. A prominent figure in Atlanta's AIDS Coalition to Unleash Power (better known as ACT UP), David Lowe, served as ELGO's vice president for political action, which linked the campus organization to the wider queer activist community in Atlanta.[46] But the structure of most community organizations, including gay ones, either did not include women or marginalized their roles. Lesbians at Emory occasionally worked separately from ELGO to discuss their role within the group and to identify like-minded organizations in Atlanta. They hoped to foster community for lesbians on campus and off. In order to address lesbian-specific concerns, women in ELGO found more fulfillment by working outside the main organization.

In January 1990, ELGO sought help from the assistant dean of campus life and other campus leaders to establish an office for lesbian and gay student needs. ELGO was one of nine lesbian, gay, and bisexual student groups on campus by 1991; their activist efforts connected the university to the larger queer Atlanta community. When Emory sought a full-time director for its Office of Lesbian, Gay, and Bisexual Life in 1992, the office was believed to be the first of its kind in the South, offering a salary of $28,000 a year to "an educator for the university and advocate for non-heterosexual life."[47] By creating the position, the university administration hoped to send a "clear signal of support," following recent campus uproar surrounding the harassment of two male students who showed physical affection in a freshman dorm.[48] After marching on campus to protest the administration's original response, Saralyn Chesnut, a doctoral candidate at Emory, became the office's first director. In her first year, Chesnut organized a variety of initiatives, including the addition of sexual orientation to the campus policy on inclusion, a campus-wide "Safe Space program, a speaker's bureau," a National Coming Out Day event, and the eventual provision of same-sex benefits.[49] The 1990s ushered in a decade of queer transition defined by the campus activism of lesbian and gay students. Emory would join an elite group of universities actively seeking better queer representation on campus, protection against violence, and even university funding for queer student groups.[50]

A student activist vision of the Southeast headed straight to Atlanta, bypassing Charlotte completely. Sustained student activism did not materialize in Charlotte because it lacked a community of established universities linked to a distinct gay enclave. At the University of North Carolina at Chapel Hill and Duke University in Durham, queer students organized in the 1970s. Yet when they planned the third annual Southeastern Gay Conference in 1977, it was designed without the Queen City in mind. The Carolina Gay Association, a student group at UNC Chapel Hill, noted the importance of moving the conference from Chapel Hill to Atlanta—a location that could provide "big city polish and scale." As suggested in the conference planning materials, "outside of places like Atlanta or Miami, gays in the Southeast are more or less isolated."[51] Like the 1970s Southeastern Gay Conferences, North Carolina's statewide Pride festival originated from the same student activist organizations, including the Carolina Gay Association and the Duke Gay Alliance in the Research Triangle. These were organizations resembling ELGO, with roots in the activism of the New Left and the university structures necessary to sustain them in the future.

Students from the historically female college Queens University in Charlotte participated in events and found lovers at the Charlotte Women's Center, but the origins of queer student engagement at this venerable university remain hidden, as does any indication of an active queer student group.[52] Although gay students tried to form an organization at UNC Charlotte in the 1980s, there is no traceable history of sustained lesbian and gay student activism there. Nascent queer student organizations have struggled for viability since the inception of the Multicultural Resource Center at the university.[53] At the historically Black school Johnson C. Smith University in Charlotte, visible gay student activism did not appear until 2002, under the leadership of the outspoken student AIDS activist Jonathan Perry. Although Perry started the first lesbian and gay student organization there, ten years later it was no longer active.[54]

The geographic separation of UNC Charlotte from a queer-friendly neighborhood or other universities led to a significant divide between the activism of groups like the Charlotte Women's Center and queer student engagement at the Queen City's largest university. Efforts to bridge this gap, like the 1970s student-run alternative newspaper, *The Road*, failed. Although the paper featured content of interest to women, such pieces were often contributed and written by the feminists at the CWC, not university students. The paper showed no evidence of queer student organizing in the 1970s.[55] Meanwhile, Atlanta's lesbian feminists in ALFA drew from students at Georgia State University and Emory University. They even maintained connections with students at the University of Georgia, almost seventy miles away in Athens. These universities had a sense of place and community. For example, a 1990 intercollegiate dance and fundraiser brought queer students together from all three schools plus Atlanta's Georgia Tech and Oglethorpe University.[56] Although the University of North Carolina at Charlotte began as a metropolitan college, built to meet the needs of returning World War II veterans in 1946, the college did not have its own campus until 1961. The lack of an established identity at the new campus location (it was ten miles from the center of Uptown Charlotte) and the limited public transportation connecting the campus to the inner city proved divisive.[57] The university's struggle to define its place, while located on the fringe of Charlotte's urban borders, served as an example of the city's lingering "identity crisis."[58] It was unclear where education fit in to Charlotte's developing persona as a corporate powerhouse of the Southeast.

Just as universities shape the urban environment, so too do corporations. For queer people, corporate might was at its most visible at Pride celebrations. The transition from the politically activist Pride festivals of the 1970s and 1980s to the corporate spectacles of the twenty-first century was an economically driven process. According to Alex T. Urquhart and Susan Craddock, corporate sponsorship at Pride festivals allowed advertisers the "opportunity to brand a vanguard of young attractive gay men and high-end fashionable lesbians. Pride celebrations are filled with the edgy sexuality and even sex that corporate America often pays unbelievable amounts of money to an ad agency to produce."[59] The temporary tattoos, bottle openers, plastic cups, highlighters, and other branded giveaways were wise and cost-effective investments when compared with a national, or even regional, advertising campaign.[60] Pride sponsors did not risk a widely visible alliance with the local queer community, given Pride's limited and targeted advertising venue. This opportunity to quietly support Pride was especially important for regional sponsors in the South. For example, North Carolina–based Food Lion grocery stores sponsored Pride in Charlotte in 2012, but because Pride sponsorship was promoted in targeted gay media outlets and through visible merchandising at the festival itself, most people who did not attend were never aware of this affiliation. In the case of Food Lion, for example, its support of Pride remained invisible on its company website and in broad-based advertising campaigns in the early years of the twenty-first century.[61] Yet for queer revelers, corporate financing of Pride brought significant popularity and visibility to the festivals and offered a false sense of acceptance in the mainstream marketplace. As Kevin Murphy has shown, the "organic and politically meaningful" roots of Pride celebrations were seemingly "co-opted by superficial and commercial interests in later years."[62] Indeed, the long history of gay visibility is tied to the marketplace and capitalism in several ways.[63] As in many urban centers, queer visibility in Atlanta and Charlotte did not occur without significant ties to the marketplace—even as corporate backing and branding in both cities increasingly undergirded Pride's continued success in the 1990s and the next few decades. Organizers of the festivals embraced commercial sponsorship of Pride just as queer people had long engaged the marketplace in other venues, like bars, bookstores, and publications. Pride sponsors also played a significant role in the urban development of queer life in each city, perhaps none more so than Bank of America in Charlotte.

The late twentieth-century merger of Charlotte's NationsBank and San Francisco's BankAmerica transformed the Queen City. It would also hold significant weight for Charlotte's lesbian and gay population. In 1991, members of Concerned Charlotteans were still shepherded by Reverend Joseph Chambers, who had led an anti-pornography fight that he linked to gay people just a few years earlier. Now Chambers's group gathered to protest a meeting of the International Federation of Parents and Friends of Lesbians and Gays hosted at Charlotte's Uptown Omni Hotel. More than two decades earlier, the Citizens for Decent Atlanta feared that the visibility of gay people would result in "a city of real nuts," like San Francisco; Chambers articulated a similar fear to the *Charlotte Observer* by declaring that he did not want Charlotte to become like San Francisco, "a homosexual mecca."[64] But with the arrival of San Francisco's BankAmerica, lesbians and gay men witnessed the symbolic merger of a "homosexual mecca" with a veritable queer desert. Journalists on the West Coast seemed to enjoy spouting perfunctory ridicule of Charlotte as too southern and therefore uncultured. As historian David Goldfield observed, "It was as if Dog Patch had conquered the Emerald City."[65] Florida's *St. Petersburg Times* had a field day. The marriage of the two cities was excellent fodder, especially since Florida's Barnett Banks were recent casualties in NationsBank's meteoric rise to power. The *Times* noted that San Francisco "never anticipated becoming a distant banking colony to some Southern-twangin' town whose streets roll up at dark and where the Billy Graham Parkway is the main route into town from the airport."[66] Rampant media comparisons of the two cities focused on Charlotte's backward and redneck identity—often linked to its unwelcoming environment for gay people.

The question of how the merger would affect lesbians and gay men, who were accustomed to the visibility of queer San Francisco and corporate benefits for same-sex couples at BankAmerica, came quickly. Hugh McColl of NationsBank in Charlotte was surprisingly blunt in his support for employees who depended on BankAmerica's domestic partnership benefits.[67] As the *St. Petersburg Times* noted, his was a one-word answer, "yes," which would have a resounding impact: "The thought of NationsBank, headquartered deep in the Bible Belt, offering such liberal benefits" indicated "a merger of cultures as well as assets between the Charlotte, N.C.–based NationsBank and the San Francisco–based BankAmerica."[68] McColl's declaration was particularly notable, given that other major corporations headquartered in urban centers, like General Electric, Eli Lilly, and Atlanta's United Parcel Service, did not offer these benefits until 2004.[69]

McColl, a South Carolinian armed with a banking degree from Chapel Hill, represented the core of the city's long-standing chamber of commerce slogan that it was a "good place to make money."[70] A fourth-generation banker, McColl began his career in the Queen City and often epitomized the chamber's commitment to growth at all cost—even when his new skyscraper for Uptown, satirized as the "Taj McColl," razed significant landmarks on the Uptown landscape.[71] McColl aspired to make Charlotte a "great city" without forsaking his love of big business.[72] His commitment was typical of city promoters who throughout the twentieth century prioritized a strong business climate. For example, when the midcentury civil rights movement crippled many southern cities, "businessmen and development leaders became the agents of peaceful desegregation" in Charlotte as they had in Atlanta.[73] City boosters hoped to avoid the volatile upheaval that brought notoriety to Little Rock and Birmingham. Even before the 1964 Civil Rights Act passed, white civic leaders in Charlotte made a visible statement by going out for lunch with their Black counterparts as an act of desegregation; "lunching rather than lynching characterized Charlotte's approach to race relations."[74] But when it came to a business-first approach for its lesbian and gay citizens, city politicians did not acquiesce, choosing instead to prioritize the anti-gay positions of local church leaders.

Charlotte landed on the national radar as a city where being gay was a liability when the Concerned Charlotteans group participated in a community protest of epic proportions. Similar to the Theatre in the Square debacle in Atlanta's suburban Cobb County, the brouhaha over the 1996 Charlotte Repertory Theater performance of Tony Kushner's controversial play *Angels in America* placed the city in the spotlight of the 1990s culture wars. The debate over the gay themes and nudity in the play garnered national media attention, engaged the local religious community, inspired local gay activism, and ultimately led Charlotte's county commissioners to cut all arts funding for the following budget cycle.[75] McColl led the business community opposition to this move because he was committed to claiming Charlotte's new place as a financial leader, and this was not the image of Charlotte that he wanted to put forward. As the *Philadelphia Inquirer* noted, Charlotte was typically a city that would rather "make money than headlines."[76] The brutal critique of Charlotte that arose during the NationsBank and BankAmerica merger was an assault based in part on the actions of Charlotte's now infamous "Gang of Five," the nickname bestowed upon the conservative Christian county commissioners who led the virulent protest against the arts and queer community in Charlotte. To some it seemed that the county commissioners did their very best to help reinforce the stereotypes that were hurled at them by the national press.

In their furor, commissioners repeatedly identified San Francisco as a den of iniquity. Commissioner Hoyle Martin, a Democrat, was determined to keep Charlotte from becoming "'the Sodom and Gomorrah capital of the East Coast, as is San Francisco on the West Coast.'"[77] It is ironic that the prospect of becoming more like San Francisco would be realized later that year at the hand of Hugh McColl. The *Washington Post* summed up the damage of the anti-gay arts funding flap in an almost prophetic statement written just two months prior to the announcement of Charlotte's 1998 banking merger:

> Whatever happens next, some damage has been done. A new
> virulence has been introduced into the city's once genteel public
> discourse; the arts community has been cowed; a segment of
> the population feels stigmatized; business leaders worry that the
> controversy is a step away from the city's progressive tradition. And
> Charlotteans, who want so desperately to be denizens of a world class
> city, have been forced to confront an embarrassing narrowness that
> has left them looking less like Atlanta and more like Cobb County,

Ga., which lost its piece of the 1996 Olympics because of similar anti-gay sentiment.[78]

This picture of Charlotte as anti-progressive and more like Cobb County than Atlanta proper was exactly the kind of scenario that McColl worked to avoid. While virulent gay hatred was apparent in Atlanta's suburban Cobb County, Charlotte's embarrassment was centered in the city's local government—smack-dab in the middle of "Uptown," the progressive nickname for Charlotte's downtown district. As he planned one of the largest corporate mergers in history with one of the queerest cities in the United States, McColl's own city was making the wrong kind of headlines with comments such as, "'If it were up to me, we'd shove these people [gays] off the face of the earth,'" which was offered by Hoyle Martin and quoted in the *Washington Post*.[79]

Prior to the 1990s, the lesbian and gay community in Charlotte could not sustain the visible activism and organization necessary to garner the support of the business community, but McColl's support was significant. Bank of America would become one of the largest employers in Charlotte and would be a top-tier sponsor of Pride, as its leaders recognized the significant growth of lesbian and gay buying power.[80] The importance of this corporate backing cannot be underestimated. In 2000, the *New York Times* called McColl a "champion of gay rights," citing both his same-sex partner benefits package at Bank of America and his efforts to bankroll campaigns to replace the "Gang of Five" with Democrats who would proceed to restore arts funding in Charlotte.[81]

At the dawn of the last decade of the twentieth century, Atlanta's major corporations affirmed the city's rightful place on the global stage, having fostered and attracted Fortune 500 companies like Coca-Cola and Lockheed Martin, both of which appeared continuously on the revered *Fortune* list since its 1955 debut. In 1991, Coca-Cola opened the World of Coke Museum, United Parcel Service moved its headquarters to Atlanta, Delta Airlines gained a new global-carrier identity with the purchase of Pan Am, and CNN earned viability as a legitimate news network through its coverage of the first Persian Gulf War—all of which helped forge international connections for the city. Atlanta was named *Fortune* magazine's number one city for business that year, but a national corporate real estate magazine ranked Charlotte ahead of Atlanta as the second-best site for "corporate facility destination" in 1991. The Queen City was sandwiched between Dallas, Texas, at number one and Atlanta at number three, and the article recognized all three cities as "top-notch" business environments.[82] The ultimate nod in global recognition, however, went to Atlanta for attracting the 1996 Olympic Games. Atlanta's place on the global stage would have a significant impact on lesbian life there in the 1990s.

Just a few months after a domestic terrorist placed a pipe bomb at Centennial Olympic Park in Atlanta, a lesbian nightclub, the Otherside, was targeted by the same perpetrator. Eric Rudolph believed homosexuality to be an "assault upon the integrity of American society," and in his confession he stated that "the attack itself was meant to send a powerful message in protest of Washington's continued tolerance and support for the homosexual political agenda."[83] The Otherside was located in Midtown's gay bar district, and its 1997 bombing sent a message to the surrounding gay businesses and queer residents that this might be the first in a string of hate-motivated attacks. National gay activist groups like the Human Rights Campaign and the New York City Gay and Lesbian Anti-Violence project stepped in, drawing attention to the bombing as anti-gay and hate-motivated.[84] The most severely injured victim was accidental activist Memrie Creswell, who was doubly victimized in the attack, "essentially outed by news media accounts of the incident." As reported by the *New York Times*, she lost her job as a result, "but with no laws prohibiting discrimination against gay men and lesbians in Georgia," she had little recourse.[85] Creswell lacked protection against workplace discrimination on the basis of her sexual orientation, and until the June 2020 Supreme Court decision *Bostock v. Clayton County, Georgia*, this protection was unavailable in the majority of southern states.[86] The Otherside bombing reignited this important conversation in Georgia, a conversation that lesbian and gay activists began to pursue in the 1980s. Based on this historic lack of legislative security, queer activists instead focused their efforts on individual corporations for workplace protections. The long-term results of their endeavors would be slow in coming but remarkable nonetheless. Because Rudolph targeted a gay gathering place, the event prompted Georgia legislator Vince Fort to escalate hate crimes legislation. When his successful legislation was declared unconstitutional in 2004, Fort used the tenth anniversary of the Otherside bombing as an occasion to reintroduce a new bill and refocus the spotlight on crimes motivated by hatred of gay people.[87]

The Atlanta Business and Professional Guild worked with the National Gay Task Force to fight for workplace protections. Members of the guild targeted top-ranking public companies in Georgia, including

Delta Airlines, Georgia Pacific, and Coca-Cola. Following the guidance of the task force, the guild proceeded gingerly, using respectful language and making clear in contact letters that the goal of outreach was "*not* to castigate, criticize or publicize a corporation's failures to maintain formal policies with regard to sexual orientation." Georgia Pacific officials "'cordially' declined to participate" in the program, stating that they assessed their employees solely on merit, but at Coca-Cola and Delta this outreach was eventually more effective.[88] By 2002, both companies offered same-sex partner benefits, and for more than a decade they, along with UPS, have consistently been ranked by the Human Rights Campaign as top-tier companies for queer employees.[89]

Although Hugh McColl led the way in the South by offering same-sex benefits to Bank of America employees in 1998, Atlanta's gay-friendly corporations overshadowed the Queen City quickly in the coming years. Bank of America's progressive policies for its queer employees have been no match for the conservative politics and religious attitudes in Charlotte. A cutting-edge corporate policy toward queer employees dovetails nicely with the various structural supports for lesbian and gay people who live in Atlanta, but in Charlotte these supports are lacking. There is undoubtedly a noticeable advantage for corporations who offer same-sex benefits and participate in Pride through visible and economically substantial sponsorships. At the festivals they have a targeted and receptive audience, most of whom are young white middle-class consumers who delight in the corporate branding often perceived as support of their imagined queer community.[90] Similar to Bank of America in Charlotte, Delta, Coca-Cola, and other Atlanta heavyweights like Home Depot serve as visible corporate sponsors of Atlanta Pride, with vibrant employee contingents from Home Depot and Delta often marching in the Midtown parade (and throwing branded giveaways to the crowd).[91]

In addition to corporate support for same-sex partner benefits, McColl secured and funded professional sports teams for the city of Charlotte, inadvertently creating substantial new opportunities in the lesbian social scene. McColl was a major player in the epic arrival of the National Football League expansion team the Carolina Panthers. The headline in the 1993 *Charlotte Observer* was "stripped across the top in Christ-returns-to-earth-size type" and professional football's arrival was celebrated by McColl and other Charlotte leaders in similar fashion.[92] The NFL in Charlotte provided critical financial sustenance to Hartigan's Pub, a longtime lesbian-owned bar. The pub fostered socialization and community for lesbians but relied on financial support from primarily heterosexual football tailgaters to meet the exorbitant rent in the Uptown stadium district. The negotiations for the successful NFL bid directly followed the 1988 arrival of a National Basketball Association franchise for Charlotte—the Charlotte Hornets, also made possible by McColl.[93] The presence of the Hornets paved the way for the 1997 arrival of one of the original Women's National Basketball Association franchises, the Charlotte Sting. Both the Sting and the Hornets served as corporate sponsors for one of the longest running LGBT organizations, the Charlotte Business Guild, one of the few organizations created and supported by both lesbians and gay men.[94] Women's professional basketball games took place "in a unique space that is different from most gatherings of lesbian and bisexual women." As one lesbian fan shared, "'It's a place, another outlet that's not a bar, you know, that's not just a once a year pride march or whatever, you know. And if you don't get out that often, it's nice to have an event that brings lesbians together.'"[95] Sting games provided a site of new community formation for many lesbians; they served as a sort of lesbian church.

For ten years Sting games offered a distinctive lesbian social space that could not be recreated. When the Sting folded in 2007, it was due in large part to poor attendance. The year before the team's demise, it ranked thirteenth in attendance out of the fourteen teams in the WNBA. In the same way that the Charlotte Women's Center struggled to maintain community involvement, Sue Henry and Dan Kirsch worked to support their queer bookstores, and Queen City Quordinators failed to identify a core of committed activists to sustain their organization, the Charlotte Sting's loyal lesbian audience was not enough to back the team financially.[96] In the fall of the Sting's failing year, the city of Atlanta secured an expansion WNBA team, the Dream. The WNBA's presence changed social opportunities for lesbians in Charlotte and Atlanta, and the story of women's professional basketball is representative of differences in the two cities generally. Lesbians in Charlotte were dependent on the city's economic support for professional sports teams as a means to find this new social space—this "lesbian church"—of the WNBA game. The Sting game as a venue for lesbian socialization would not remain in Charlotte; this had as much to do with Charlotte's metropolitan identity as it did with the size or commitment of its lesbian population.

Charlotte's troubled past with its professional sports teams, particularly in the realm of providing desirable arenas and sufficient attendance, set the stage for the Sting to be another casualty in the professional sports war. Men's professional basketball faced similar difficulties in Charlotte.

When the Charlotte Hornets joined the NBA for the 1988–89 season, some feared the city was too small to support the team. Miami, Orlando, and Minnesota also gained professional teams in the same year, but at 988,000 metro Charlotte's population trailed that of its nearest competitor, Orlando, by roughly 200,000.[97] According to the NBA, "Many doubted the Charlotte community's ability and willingness to support a professional basketball team." Beyond being small for an NBA market, Charlotte was in North Carolina, which was college basketball country, "where the fans' ardor for the amateur game had never translated into a similar affection for the NBA."[98] The difficulties of Charlotte's boosters in trying to define their city also played a part in its difficulties in maintaining a loyal audience for professional sports teams. Aside from hockey, major professional sports in Atlanta have enjoyed a long and colorful history that is intimately tied to the city and its identity. Even professional teams that relocated to Atlanta in the 1960s, like Major League Baseball's Braves and the NBA's Hawks, established deep ties to the city and boast strong attendance records.[99] But rather than a defining, identity-building presence in Charlotte, professional sports often served as a facade. The teams exemplified superficial efforts in Charlotte's "perennial search for respect."[100]

While Charlotte boosters searched for respect, the Queen City continued to earn a reputation as unwelcoming to gay people due in part to the 2003 relocation of Reverend Flip Benham's anti-abortion and anti-gay organization, Operation Save America (OSA), from Dallas to Charlotte. Benham's organization harangued the 2005 Charlotte Pride festival and worked to completely shut down the celebration. Wearing bright red shirts, OSA protesters blared loud religious music alternated with preaching and infiltrated the crowds in Uptown's centrally located Marshall Park. Many festival attendees were disheartened after the event, and later that year, partly due to organizational burnout and frustration, the future of a Charlotte Pride festival was in question. In the face of this burnout, the OSA publicly claimed "victory over Charlotte Pride."[101] In the same year, Atlanta's Gay Pride festival scored record crowds, with Georgia's own white southern lesbian folk-music icons and former Emory University students, Indigo Girls, headlining a successful three-day weekend event in sprawling Piedmont Park. Joining a long line of Atlanta's Black leaders who supported their queer citizens, Mayor Shirley Franklin welcomed Atlanta's festivalgoers. Meanwhile Charlotte's white Republican mayor, Pat McCrory, openly expressed disapproval for his city's Pride celebration and its public park venue, telling one supporter that he was "insulted" by the "visual and verbal vulgarity displays" at the festival.[102]

Pastors from Forest Hills Church, Hickory Grove Baptist, and Central Church of God wrote to McCrory in support of his disdain for the visibility of a Pride celebration in Charlotte and his refusal to formally welcome the Human Rights Campaign and its statewide dinner, held in Charlotte in 2006. McCrory told the ministers that he appreciated their prayers and attached copies of letters that he had received—"over 750 total"— in support of the Human Rights Campaign event, hoping to share with them what he was "experiencing." The tone of his letters suggested that McCrory believed he was under attack and was relying on the prayers of the ministers and their congregations to sustain him. Meanwhile some ministers in Charlotte worked to combat what they viewed as an ominous new tide of religious consensus. At Myers Park Baptist, the Reverend Steve Shoemaker took a vocal stand against the twenty-first century resegregation process occurring in the Charlotte-Mecklenburg public school system and a stand *for* tolerance of gay people.[103] James Howell, the new minister at Myers Park United Methodist in 2005, lamented the loss of "virtue" in "disagreement" and expressed frustration at the push toward sameness in Charlotte's churches—noting that churchgoers would rather find agreement with their pastor's message than be challenged to think beyond the comfort of their pew: "Twenty-five years ago . . . the highest compliment for a minister at the end of a sermon was, 'You stepped on my toes. You really made me think.' Today, the highest compliment is, 'I agree with you.' Some axis has shifted."[104]

The development of Charlotte and Atlanta as bastions of the southern Sun Belt ideal rested on economic and political decisions that were heavily informed by religious influences and a national rise in conservatism. Religious conservatives held sizable power in both cities and often challenged economic or political commitments to seemingly immoral causes. In North Carolina and Georgia, as in most of the South, "white Baptists and African-American Protestants" represented the bulk of religious affiliation, with evangelicals constituting a majority among Protestants and "white Baptists" comprising "the largest single religious group" in each state.[105] In this study, Atlanta stood out as a "burgeoning archipelago of religious diversity." At 8.5 percent, for example, Jews in Atlanta's Fulton County were in one of thirteen southern counties where they represented "more than 3 percent of adherents."[106] According to a 2010 Association of Religious Data Archives report, Atlanta's metro region was indeed diverse with four different Hindu religious bodies claiming over 20,000 adherents, while in the Queen City's metro area there were three Hindu affiliations with approximately 1,200 congregants. The same report showed that approximately 485,000 of metro Charlotte's 1.7 million residents were evangelicals, compared with 1.3 million evangelicals in Atlanta—approximately 25 percent of its metro population of 5.2 million. In both regions, Southern Baptists represented the top affiliation.[107] Evangelical Protestants defined a southern way of life, and while this was certainly true in North Carolina and Georgia, Atlanta's metropolitan region was an anomaly of religious diversity, which perhaps contributed to a more tolerant environment for queer visibility.

Although relying on census data to understand lesbian and gay populations can be problematic, the growing number of same-sex couples willing to report their status offers some usable data. Atlanta is one of three cities nationally where the number of gay couples declined in the years 2000–2006. More couples, gay and straight, left the city to move to the suburbs, where their numbers increased, suggesting a spread of tolerance beyond the borders of Atlanta. For example, at 3,481, Atlanta's Fulton County had the most reported same-sex couples in the state, as did Charlotte's Mecklenburg County at 1,777. Yet neither county had the highest percentage of gay couples in the state. Fulton ranked at number two (behind Atlanta's suburban and lesbian-friendly DeKalb), while Mecklenburg County lagged behind counties throughout North Carolina, including Durham in the Research Triangle; Buncombe, home to Asheville and a UNC campus; and Greene, part of the metropolitan statistical area that is home to East Carolina University.[108] Although these data are limited, they do support the importance of established educational institutions that often serve as anchors for a visible queer community.[109]

As lesbians faced the twenty-first century, corporate interactions with lesbian and gay employees and corporate sponsorship of gay initiatives permanently changed the queer urban social landscape. Although it is difficult to say how individual lesbians fared economically in Charlotte and Atlanta, it is worth considering the economic status of women generally in each state. These comparisons, when combined with the political, educational, corporate, and religious climates for lesbians and gay men as detailed in this chapter, serve as a marker of economic potential and personal satisfaction for lesbians. In 2004, North Carolina received a "D" in a national examination of women's employment and earnings. North Carolina's ratio of women's to men's earnings overall stood at

73.7 percent, but these numbers were significantly less for women of color, with only 62.9 percent for African American women compared with white men, and only 47.1 percent for Hispanic women.[110] By 2006 North Carolina was upgraded to a "C-," while Georgia was given a "B-."[111] Georgia ranked nationally at thirteen, with an overall ratio of women's earnings to men's at 83 percent. Again, these numbers were dismal when separated by race, however, with Black women in Georgia earning 60.8 percent and Hispanic women 49.1 percent of white men's earnings.[112] Women who owned businesses also fared better in Georgia in 2006, with the state ranked in the top third of the country, at twelfth place, while North Carolina ranked in the middle, at twenty-fifth place.[113] Women in Georgia led their North Carolina counterparts in median annual earnings: $31,700, compared with the Tar Heel State's $29,800.[114] With Georgia consistently outpacing North Carolina in a variety of economic arenas for women, lesbians in the twenty-first century would find more economic success in Atlanta than they would in Charlotte.

In a comparison of metro area wage statistics five years later, average salaries were occasionally competitive in the two regions. The number of workers in metro Atlanta, however, was almost three times that in Charlotte, which not only suggests an increased amount of job availability but is representative of its sizable population lead over Charlotte's metro area in 2011, and certainly indicates that lesbians as a group had greater buying power in Atlanta than in Charlotte—especially in higher-paying positions. In the financial sector, for example, the average salary was $68,630 in Charlotte and $73,280 in Atlanta, and in educational occupations, a key field of employment for women, Charlotte workers earned $44,160 compared with $45,550 in Atlanta. In the lower-paying food services industry, workers in Charlotte earned an average salary of $21,190, while Atlanta's workers made $20,760. In all three of these fields, the number of workers was almost tripled in the Atlanta region. Those in the protective services field, which includes law enforcement and security officers, earned an average salary of $36,140 in Charlotte, just slightly higher than Atlanta's protective service employees at $35,290, and unlike many other employment fields the number of people working in this area was slightly closer in the two cities, with approximately 24,370 workers in the Charlotte area and 53,400 in Atlanta.[115] These numbers suggest that while lesbians might have enjoyed slightly higher salaries in one city or another, the likelihood that they would have a greater economic impact in Atlanta was strong when considering the queer community-building institutions. For example, while lesbian police officer Christina Cougill might have earned a slightly higher salary in Charlotte, in Atlanta she would work with a greater number of officers in a department that demanded lesbian and gay inclusion and in a city that provided a greater level of visibility in her daily life.[116] Although there are many lesbian and gay police officers in Charlotte, there was no community liaison or an organization for lesbian or gay officers as of 2012.[117] In fact, the well-publicized 2010 resignation of six volunteer chaplains who refused to work with an invited lesbian chaplain on the force indicated the contentious nature of the department's posture toward LGBT issues.[118]

Limited data, combined with the development of urban institutions, indicate that lesbians who had the opportunity to seek a region where they would be both financially successful and personally fulfilled might have found Atlanta's infrastructure more appealing. When public policy professor and urban consultant Richard Florida spoke at the University of North Carolina at Charlotte's Urban Institute in 2003, he suggested that Charlotte needed to attract what he termed a "creative class." Recognizing Austin, Texas, as a successful magnet for this group, Florida cited "a high concentration of gay people" as an "important draw . . . because it indicates that a place has a high level of acceptance for those who live outside the norm." Florida ranked cities in a variety of categories, assessing their ability to attract and sustain a creative class. In the category of "tolerance," Florida ranked Charlotte in 69th place out of 331 regions examined.[119] His assessment confirmed the challenges that Charlotte's lesbians and gay men continued to face. In his analysis of Florida's research, historian James C. Cobb acknowledged that a "growing recognition of gay economic clout" often produced "greater tolerance" for lesbians and gay men, and that "the four southern metro areas, Atlanta, Austin, Dallas and Houston, that ranked within the top fifteen nationally in concentrations of high-tech industry also ranked in the top twenty-one in gay representation in the population."[120] Charlotte might have held solid ground between Dallas and Atlanta when it received its 1991 recognition as a "top-notch" business environment for corporate site location, but it lacked the "tolerance" that Florida deemed necessary to attract and maintain high-tech industry.[121] In a city known for its obsession with a New South identity (Charlotte is home to the Museum of the New South) and its proud-as-punch success in wooing the NASCAR Hall of Fame, it seemed that Charlotte's city leaders often desired to mimic and even bypass Atlanta. But this desire for growth and prestige did not generate sufficient pressures for more than a marginally tolerant embrace for its queer citizens. Lesbians and gay men were not a part of these visions for growth.

Metropolitan Atlanta's population surged past 3,000,000, and city leaders continued to embellish its economic and corporate credentials in the late twentieth century. As a result of the roots of activist organizing in the 1970s, Atlanta's Pride festival enjoyed support from booming corporate growth in the twenty-first century, as did lesbian and gay employees of these corporations. The powers at the top, especially corporations, eventually responded to queer wrangling at the bottom. In addition to corporate recognition, queer organizations in Atlanta worked to build community buoyed by a cooperative police department and engaged college-age activists.

Both Atlanta and Charlotte gained national attention in the 1990s that dramatically altered lesbian lives in the New South. The recent history of lesbians in these two cities has been shaped by the role of local police communities, queer social groups, universities, the corporate climate, professional sports, and religion—all competing to form a cohesive metropolitan identity. The composition of these institutions influenced opportunities for queer people. It is hard to say how they affected particular individuals, but what is clear is that when seeking a place to call home at the end of the twentieth century, lesbians found an unmistakable consistency in Atlanta's queer environs that did not exist in Charlotte.

EPILOGUE

In May 2012, North Carolinians approved an amendment to the state constitution mandating that only marriages between one man and one woman would be legally recognized. The amendment also excluded domestic partnerships and civil unions from legal recognition. Charlotte's own iconic evangelist Billy Graham paid for a full-page advertisement in fourteen newspapers and recorded a televised video in the final hours before the election to urge voters to support the amendment, which he believed upheld God's definition of marriage.[1] The fight over the amendment brought national attention to the state, especially when President Obama declared his personal support for legal same-sex marriage on national television just a day after the North Carolina vote.[2] Same-sex marriage was already illegal in North Carolina, and it was the last southern state to approve such an amendment, in spite of the growing national support for marriage equality. Legal marriage for gay people was also illegal in Georgia, where voters approved a similar amendment almost a decade earlier in 2004.[3] Seven of the eight counties that voted *against* the amendment also boasted major universities, meaning that these counties included heavy concentrations of young and educated voters. Charlotte's Mecklenburg County was among the eight, with 54 percent voting against the amendment, and in Orange County (home to the University of North Carolina at Chapel Hill) a whopping 79 percent voted to reject the amendment.[4] Perhaps the most remarkable support for same-sex marriage came from former Charlotte mayors Richard Vinroot (a Republican) and Harvey Gantt (a Democrat) to encourage North Carolinians to "Vote Against." During their time in office, both men faced challenges dealing with the politics of sexuality, with Vinroot memorably refusing to welcome or participate in the 1994 state Pride festival in Charlotte. But in 2012 they appeared together on a widely shared Internet video describing the amendment as "unnecessary," arguing that it would "write discrimination" into the state constitution and might discourage businesses from relocating to North Carolina.[5] Several months before the video and the subsequent May 2012 vote, the *Charlotte Observer* printed an opinion piece questioning the apathy of big businesses in North Carolina—many of whom remained silent on the issue. The article accused Republican legislators who authored the amendment of "a transparent attempt to rile up the state's most socially conservative voters for the 2012 election."[6]

In a city conspicuous for both its relative moderation in race relations and its virulently anti-gay political and religious stances, twenty-first-century Charlotteans continued their bumpy path toward change for lesbian and gay citizens in the turmoil of the Amendment One fight. The city faced a growing public relations challenge as the controversial amendment roiled voters in the face of the impending Democratic National Convention, scheduled for September 2012. Like Maynard Jackson in Atlanta and Gantt in Charlotte, Mayor Anthony Foxx acknowledged the importance of queer Charlotteans politically. But Foxx went further. Making public appearances at the LGBT Community Center and the Uptown Pride festival, Foxx promoted a business-first stand against Amendment One. While speaking at the 2012 Human Rights Campaign Gala, Foxx noted his opposition to the amendment because it would deter business relocation and harm job growth in the Queen City.[7] That same year, LaWana Mayfield, a Black lesbian, became the first openly gay person to be elected to Charlotte's city council. Mayfield represented a predominantly Black district in which, just a few months after electing her, many of her constituents, despite majority opposition in the county at large, voted to approve the anti-gay marriage amendment by a two-to-one margin.[8] The pastor of a large Black congregation in Mayfield's district celebrated the statewide approval of Amendment One by noting that "the voters of North Carolina have chosen to protect the soul of the state and the nation; that is marriage and family."[9] Mayfield's lesbian identity did not deter voters from supporting her on the city council, yet she represented a district that would not support her right to marry.

These sentiments notwithstanding, some of the political and religious reactions surrounding the contentious vote in Charlotte seemed to bode well for lesbians and gay men. The North Carolina NAACP waged a campaign to defeat Amendment One, and the national leadership of the organization announced its support for gay marriage just a few days after President Obama made his public announcement of support. As an increasing number of African American ministers took a stand in 2012 for gay rights as indistinguishable from civil rights, the large number of African American churches in Charlotte, and especially Atlanta, positioned themselves to play a critical role in making their cities more hospitable for queer citizens. As one suburban Black minister in a district of conservative Black churches noted in 2004, when Georgians faced their own gay marriage amendment battle, "I'm a pastor and I don't support gay marriage, but I resent people playing political football with our religious beliefs."[10] The history of Black mayors in Atlanta and Charlotte and Black political leadership on the issue of gay marriage refute the myth that Black leaders and churches are universally anti-queer. Atlanta's citizens consistently elected Black Democratic mayors and boasted one of the largest Black queer populations in the twenty-first century South. In both Atlanta and Charlotte, from Mayors Jackson and Gantt to Franklin and Foxx, Black leadership improved queer livability.

The early twenty-first-century growth of hip churches, like Elevation in Charlotte, harks back to the days of popular evangelists Jim and Tammy Faye Bakker, whose PTL (Praise the Lord) ministries, based just a few miles from Uptown Charlotte, later became the subject of federal investigation and a media feeding frenzy in the 1980s. Jay Bakker, their tattooed and pierced son, led a movement of edgy churches in the mid-1990s that was a forerunner of popular and trendy nondenominational churches across the country. While the younger Bakker's church, Revolution, found a successful home in Atlanta and later in New York City, his efforts to sustain a branch of the church in Charlotte were less successful. Yet metro Charlotte's Elevation Church is one of the fastest-growing Protestant churches in the country, boasting almost 10,000 worshippers in its first few years of existence.[11] It is hard to say how much youth-oriented churches like Elevation will matter to lesbians and gay men who are seeking a church affiliation in Charlotte or Atlanta. Elevation Church is not overtly gay-friendly; in fact, its leader pronounced homosexuality a sin in 2009 while awkwardly attempting to assert his church's love for the sinner so as not to alienate his queer followers. On the issue of Amendment One, however, Elevation and Charlotte's other nondenominational megachurches remained largely silent.[12] Meanwhile, Bakker's Revolution Church operated primarily in Brooklyn and on the Internet with little reference to the branch congregations in Atlanta and Charlotte, although it celebrated Gay Pride with a special message posted on the church's Facebook page in 2012.

For many less politically engaged lesbians and gay men in Atlanta and Charlotte, the rumored demise of the twenty-first-century queer bar scene probably had a greater impact on their daily lives than any church or vote on same-sex marriage. With the arrival of the Internet generation and the survival and significance of gay bar spaces in doubt, *Entrepreneur* magazine confirmed what many feared as it added the gay bar to its 2007 list of endangered businesses.[13] The popular lesbian-owned bar Hartigan's, which remained in business for over a decade in Charlotte, met this fate in 2014 due to declining sales and support. Standing in the shadow of Bank of America Stadium, home to the NFL's Carolina Panthers, Hartigan's Irish Pub functioned as both a restaurant and a nightclub welcoming a mix of patrons across many traditional barriers, including class, race, and gender. It regularly featured country line-dancing lessons, Latin dance nights for women, and fundraisers for the fledgling gay community center and often hosted Sunday drag brunches—including a 2012 Democratic National Committee kickoff brunch: "Pledge your Drag Allegiance"—and weekday business lunches. It was voted the best tailgating location for football game days by *Charlotte* magazine, and because of its famous pudding wrestling, it was named by ESPN's magazine as one of the top sports bars in the country.[14] In 2012 the bar owners hosted a results party on the night of the Amendment One vote. The next day Hartigan's patrons appeared on the front page of the *New York Times* observing televised coverage of President Obama's fresh declaration in support of gay marriage.[15] When the pub closed in 2014, its loyal clientele flooded the establishment's Facebook page with laments about its demise and memories of their time there. Hundreds of supporters flocked to the bar in its final days, providing a boost of financial and moral support to help cover the overwhelming final debts faced by the pub's owners.[16]

Lesbians in Atlanta continued to face a relatively slender selection of lesbian bars, despite their substantial metro population.[17] In an article titled "Why Can't Atlanta Sustain Lesbian Bars?," a writer for a local queer paper expressed frustration over the disparity in the number of lesbian bars in comparison to gay men's establishments, noting that "it's unlikely that gay men outnumber lesbians by the same ratio that gay bars currently outnumber lesbian bars in Atlanta, which is roughly 24 to 1."[18] It is possible that a generally higher level of comfort for both lesbians and gay men in Atlanta may have reduced their need for separate spaces. But as chapter 2 of this book demonstrates, economic inequality impedes women's ability to support separate spaces for socializing. Because women generally earn less than men and are more likely to have family obligations to aging parents, children, or both, lesbian bars are the first casualties in the twenty-first-century demise of queer bar spaces.[19]

Only one dedicated lesbian bar remained in Atlanta in 2021.[20] Moving several times since its opening in 1996, My Sister's Room welcomed patrons in its first location in Midtown Atlanta near Piedmont Park, the site of Ginny Boyd's hangout, the Tick Tock Grill. The bar moved temporarily to lesbian-friendly Decatur, slightly northeast of Atlanta, but returned to Midtown again, where it is located just four miles from ALFA's neighborhood of Little Five Points and the original site of Charis Books.[21] The arrival of the popular but short-lived bar L4 marked a queer space in Charlotte's eclectic and diverse Eastside neighborhood, attracting a mixed crowd including Latine and Asian queer women, a direct outgrowth of a massive immigrant population surge in Charlotte in the last two decades.[22] Hattie's neighborhood bar opened nearby in 2014, and although many lesbians claimed it as their own, the owners eschewed a gay bar label.[23]

In both Atlanta and Charlotte, twenty-first-century activists worked to sustain gay community centers but faced a variety of funding and attendance struggles. As one Atlanta organizer noted, the bulk of the financial support aimed at defeating the constitutional amendment banning gay marriage in Georgia came from the straight community, and as a result she was concerned about the necessary queer financial commitment to a community center. In addition, the all-white activists at a 2010 organizational meeting recognized the need to attract a racially and socioeconomically diverse group of queer Atlantans, grappling with how to bring about such a collaborative effort. This would prove particularly difficult since Atlanta already had the Phillip Rush Center, which supported office and meeting space for the LGBT community. Some saw an additional community center as vital because it was Atlanta's obligation to lead the queer South by making a "splash" with the substantial monies available to support a new physical structure.[24] Atlanta's queer leaders often viewed their role as ostentatious representatives of the entire queer South, while Charlotte's gay activists frequently absorbed the mindset of city boosters in their hope to build up a queer scene equal to Atlanta's but respectable enough to gain support or tolerance from business and religious leaders. Organizers in Charlotte moved the location of their community center three times in ten years due to financial struggles. In 2014, after eleven years in operation and as a result of infighting among members of its board over financial issues, the center closed its physical location. The center's closure highlights the Charlotte activist community's ongoing struggle to maintain familiar spaces in identifiable queer neighborhoods and business districts.

In a June 2012 *Forbes* magazine list of the finest cities for business and careers, Charlotte bested Atlanta's twenty-first position by coming in at number eighteen. But the Queen City was itself bested by neighboring Asheville at seventeen, Durham at fourteen, and Raleigh at number two.[25] Asheville, Raleigh, and Durham boast rich lesbian histories and continue to nurture vibrant lesbian communities. These rankings might hold some weight for lesbians who enjoy the privileged opportunity to choose a gay-friendly city in which to pursue their careers in the Tar Heel State. But most people land in a particular city for a variety of complicated reasons that may have little to do with personal preference. Some lesbians in Charlotte and Atlanta will care less than others about the neighborhoods, institutions, or politics that define queer life in their home cities. It is likely, in fact, that not all lesbians even voted on North Carolina's Amendment One or Georgia's amendment banning same-sex marriage. While surely disturbing to some activists, the diverse priorities of queer women often hinder the organization of a united community. Activist women, whether suffragists, ERA fighters, Black Lives Matter organizers, or lesbian rights leaders, have had to work as a coalition from the margins while they chafed at the resulting discord of attempting to unite women under a catchall category. In many cases, lesbians have prioritized comfortable and satisfying environments in which to establish personal and private relationships with other lesbians, rather than focusing on political leverage and recognition at the group level.

That some lesbians in Atlanta sustained activist and social groups like ALFA and Fourth Tuesday, supported the bookstore Charis and its surrounding neighborhood, and now heavily populate the lesbian-friendly community of Decatur suggests that they made considerably more headway socially in the years after World War II compared with their sisters in Charlotte. Perhaps even more telling is the history of nondiscrimination ordinances in each city. Local government support mattered most to some, like Sue Henry, who valued workplace protections far more than the right to marry her partner.[26] Atlanta added language to its nondiscrimination city code to include sexual orientation in 2000 and gender identity in 2013.[27] But in a contentious 2015 battle, Charlotte's city council voted down an LGBT protection ordinance, with council member LaWana Mayfield voting no on the final revised proposal because it removed the controversial language allowing transgender people access to the bathroom of their choosing.[28]

When the Supreme Court ruled in favor of same-sex marriage in 2015, the marriage equality fight achieved success, but the ruling did not address discrimination (most notably in the workplace) against LGBTQ people. A year later, when Charlotte's city council attempted to address this through yet another local antidiscrimination ordinance, its actions sparked a firestorm over the anti-transgender House Bill 2 (HB2), confirming what lesbian writer and activist Mab Segrest asserted more than two decades prior: North Carolina was indeed the "most queer hating state in the U.S."[29] In spite of his reputation as a moderate Republican, enjoying over twenty years of consistent endorsements by the *Charlotte Observer* and an unprecedented seven terms as mayor buoyed by Democratic voters, Pat McCrory now governed the state. Having waged a long-running campaign against the LGBTQ community beginning in the 1990s as a Charlotte City Council member, McCrory now wielded his anti-queer hatred at the state level. A year after Mayfield's no vote, McCrory made national headlines by signing the most restrictive and discriminatory anti-transgender legislation in the country: HB2. It eliminated "municipal nondiscrimination ordinances" and required "transgender people to use the bathroom of the gender listed on their birth certificates."[30] McCrory quickly became the face of the anti-LGBTQ movement, while major media outlets decried his actions and labeled the state of North Carolina as an actor in defining discrimination.[31]

The week I revised this coda for *Drastic Dykes and Accidental Activists* was also the week of the Supreme Court decision *Bostock v. Clayton County, Georgia*, which granted nationwide protection to queer people in the workplace.[32] Many news sources and social media outlets quickly filled with comments throughout the decision day, noting that for many queer people this decision was of far greater importance than marriage equality. For lesbians in the Deep South, where statewide workplace protections did not exist before *Bostock*, the decision immediately altered their daily lives. As many in the media noted, queer people no longer feared getting married on a Sunday and being fired on a Monday.

Throughout the latter half of the twentieth century, Atlanta's queer enclaves offered community to its queer citizens in a way that Charlotte's neighborhoods did not. Yet Charlotte's less visible forms of queer community, like the locally owned and operated newspaper *Q-Notes* and the Charlotte Business Guild, are examples of quiet tenacity in the Queen City.[33] During the early years of the twenty-first century, state-by-state decisions on queer rights should not be read as a complete indicator of the climate for lesbian and gay life in cities, or even as a priority for all queer people who live there. With the second decade of the twenty-first century ushering in federally mandated marriage equality and workplace protections, stable gay-friendly neighborhoods continued to provide support for queer people in the South, offering a growing variety of social outlets beyond the bar or private house party. Historical and contemporary evidence demonstrates that while drastic dykes work to establish or advance political or interest-group identities in each city, accidental activists, in search of places to find personal fulfillment consistent with their individual lesbian identities, will also continue to alter and challenge the urban spaces of the U.S. South.

POSITIONALITY STATEMENT

As I am a white lesbian who is often assumed to be Black because of my first name, the purpose of this statement is to address race as both a personal identity and as a subject in my research. Although it is not news to me that my name carries certain racial expectations, the more I have immersed myself in the study of history (and taught African American studies and students) the more I ponder the weight of this expectation. Historians generally avoid reflexivity statements in their work, but I believe it is vital for *Drastic Dykes and Accidental Activists*.

Many of the women and the social worlds I explore in this book are white, and their whiteness necessarily informs the daily organization of their lives. The same is true for me. While I have not avoided Black women in this project—indeed, I sought them out—I want to acknowledge that the handful of Black lesbian voices and experiences in *Drastic Dykes and Accidental Activists* does not represent a full history of southern Black lesbians.[1]

My whiteness both informs and limits the sources I have accessed in my research. For example, for many years the women of ZAMI, a Black lesbian community organization in Atlanta, actively limited access to their records, making them available only to Black lesbians. I first encountered this organization and its policy when I was researching a paper for a graduate seminar. In the years since I have thought deeply about the issue of race and access in my work, discussing the problem with leading scholars in the field of Black queer research, notably Jennifer D. Jones and E. Patrick Johnson.[2] I am inspired by Johnson's discussion of the "skeptic's copout" in the field of ethnography and appreciate that he urged me to move forward.[3] Johnson introduced me to Mary Anne Adams, the founding executive director of the newly named ZAMI NOBLA and the leader of a reorganization that now focuses solely on Black lesbian elders. Based on our conversation and on various exchanges with scholars, I understand the group's reluctance to turn Black histories over to white researchers. It is a position that I value.[4]

Lesbian and gay historical studies typically focus on white actors while using all-encompassing language such as "lesbian history" or "queer history." In fact, Black queer historical studies are often presented as separate, implying that blanket identities such as "lesbian" do not include women of color. Yet these are separate histories; to forcibly integrate them is problematic. Social lives of Black and white people were generally separate in the twentieth century, and this is also true of lesbians. The category of lesbian is not a unifier.

I accessed some Black stories for this book through white sources and white collections. This limits the fullness of the story I can tell and shapes the story told in the source. Black lesbians were there, but they came to life through a white social structure or a white research project. The spaces and social worlds organized by Black women exist separately and deserve a complete and stand-alone history, as the stories in E. Patrick Johnson's *Black. Queer. Southern. Women.* demonstrate.[5] Some of the sources I relied on are held at the Auburn Avenue Research Library on African American Culture and History in Atlanta. A small ZAMI collection opened there in 2019, and the institution is actively collecting in Black queer history. Unfortunately, some of the richest collections were unavailable when I conducted the majority of my research. In the end, I was not comfortable with simply adding a "Black chapter" or dropping in some extra content and erroneously imposing a false sense of Black and white lesbian community where one did not exist. What I learned when reviewing the most current collections at Auburn Avenue Research Library was that Black and white life remained mostly separate. For example, white lesbians, at least in their rhetoric, intended to reach out to Black women. This often meant inviting them to their white groups, like the Atlanta Lesbian Feminist Alliance. When Black groups like the African American Lesbian/Gay Alliance formed, an organization that eventually resulted in ZAMI, I did not find evidence of white women seeking these groups out or contacting them to offer support. Likewise, there was no evidence of AALGA seeking out white involvement. Black culture, community, and tradition mattered to the organization, as lesbians operated with gay men to address concerns for women and concerns for Black queer people. In *Drastic Dykes and Accidental Activists*, I avoid simple comparisons between white lesbian organizations and Black lesbian activism. Black queer women's organizations necessarily prioritized issues that were not valued in white queer groups.

As I write in the wake of an increased visibility for Black Lives Matter and in response to George Floyd's murder, Rayshard Brooks's murder, Breonna Taylor's murder, and the murder of so many other Black women at the hands of law enforcement, I expect that scholarly research on Black lives will indeed change in the coming years. Most of all, I am hopeful that as we peruse the stacks of our university libraries, seeking books on queer studies and particularly the queer South, we will find more histories researched by Black *tenured* scholars who include some white stories—not the other way around.

NOTES

Abbreviations

AHC   Atlanta History Center, Kenan Research Center

ALFA-DU   Atlanta Lesbian Feminist Alliance Periodicals, David M. Rubenstein Rare Book and Manuscript Library, Sallie Bingham Center for Women's History and Culture, Duke University, Durham

AUP-AHC   Atlanta's Unspoken Past Oral History Project, Atlanta History Center, Kenan Research Center

DK-DU   Dan Kirsch Papers, David M. Rubenstein Rare Book and Manuscript Library, Sallie Bingham Center for Women's History and Culture, Duke University, Durham

ES-EU   Ed W. Stansell Papers, Manuscripts, Archives, and Rare Books Library, Emory University, Atlanta

FP-DU   *Front Page* Records, David M. Rubenstein Rare Book and Manuscript Library, Sallie Bingham Center for Women's History and Culture, Duke University, Durham

HK-EU   Mary E. Hutchinson and Dorothy King Papers, Manuscripts, Archives, and Rare Books Library, Emory University, Atlanta

JS-DU   James T. Sears Papers, Southern States Research Files, David M. Rubenstein Rare Book and Manuscript Library, Sallie Bingham Center for Women's History and Culture, Duke University, Durham

LGA-LHA   Geographic Files, Lesbians in GA, Lesbian Herstory Archives, Brooklyn

UNCC   J. Murrey Atkins Library, Special Collections, University of North Carolina at Charlotte

Introduction

1. Eisenbach, *Lesbianism Made Easy*; Bechdel, *Dykes to Watch Out For*.

2. See, for example, Brown-Saracino, *How Places Make Us*.

3. On the importance of lesbian scholarship devoted to geographically specific experiences, as opposed to assuming a national narrative of queer histories or lesbian-feminist histories, see Freeman, "Lesbian Nation."

4. On the intertwined categories of race, region, gender, sexuality, and class, see Farnham, *Women of the American South*; Hicks, *Talk with You Like a Woman*; Hunter, *To 'Joy My Freedom*; and the University of Georgia Press's series Southern Women: Their Lives and Times (2003–18).

5. Finn Enke demonstrates this point in urban settings outside the U.S. South in *Finding the Movement*.

6. A note on word choice: I use "queer" when I mean to include the variety of identities, gender variations, and sexually marginalized people who may or may

not identify with neatly defined categories of lesbian, gay, or straight. It is meant to suggest behaviors or spaces that existed outside of heteronormative gender and sexual categories. I use "lesbian" to refer to women who chose this word as appropriate for their own self-definition. As is common in some primary sources, especially oral histories, I occasionally use the word "gay" to include lesbians, gay men, and queer people as a general group. Siobhan B. Somerville's overview of the word "queer," and the necessity of a "queer of color critique" to challenge whiteness ingrained in heteronormativity, offers a useful analysis of the problematic nature of this word choice. Somerville, "Queer."

7. Hanchett, *Sorting Out*, 14.

8. Ambrose, "Atlanta."

9. Hanchett, *Sorting Out*, 14.

10. In spite of Charlotte's seventy-year lead, by 1900 county population numbers served as evidence of the marked difference in size, with Charlotte's Mecklenburg County weighing in at 55,268 and Atlanta's Fulton County at 117,363. U.S. Bureau of the Census, *Population of Counties by Decennial Census: 1900 to 1990: Georgia*, and *Population of Counties by Decennial Census: 1900 to 1990: North Carolina*.

11. Two notable monographs on Charlotte's past are Hanchett, *Sorting Out*, and Lassiter, *Silent Majority*. There is a small literature devoted to the history of the lesbian South, including Harker, *Lesbian South*; E. Johnson, *Black. Queer. Southern. Women*; Buring, *Lesbian and Gay Memphis*; and Holloway, "Searching for Southern Lesbian History." Also see these works, which include southern lesbian histories: Pope, "Living in the Struggle"; Schultz, "Carolina Gay Association"; and Cole, "'I Wanted to Be.'"

12. Lassiter, "Searching for Respect"; S. Smith, "Development and the Politics of School Desegregation and Resegregation."

13. Furuseth, "Globalizing Crossroads," 284.

14. Atlanta's postwar 1950 population stood at 331,000, compared with Charlotte's 134,000. Real Estate Center at Texas A&M University, "Population MSA: Charlotte-Gastonia-Concord," and "Population MSA: Atlanta–Sandy Springs–Marietta, GA." As of April 29, 2022, the Texas Real Estate Research Center at Texas A&M University lists historic population data from 1970 to the present, with Sandy Springs and Alpharetta as part of the Atlanta MSA (not Marietta), https://www.recenter.tamu.edu/data/population#!/msa /Atlanta-Sandy_Springs-Alpharetta%2C_GA.

15. Harvey Gantt, interview by Lynn Haessly, January 6, 1986, interview C-0008, Southern Oral History Program Collection (#4007). Full transcript located at Harvey B. Gantt Papers, UNCC.

16. Lassiter, "Searching for Respect," 33–34.

17. In one of the most accessible considerations of this topic, James C. Cobb bewailed the scholarly obsession with identity—and the painstaking analysis of its varied meanings and definitions. But after grappling with a "theoretical thicket of literature," Cobb emerged with a useful analysis of southern identity that is equally applicable to both urban and lesbian identity, arguing that all identity

making is formed in response to "perceived oppositional identities." Cobb, *Away Down South*, 6.

18. Hanchett, *Sorting Out*, 1–2.

19. Ken Friedlein and Polly Paddock, "Charlotte's Emerging Social Scene," *Charlotte Observer*, April 27, 1981.

20. "Charlotte May Get Huge New Gay Bar by Easter," *Q-Notes* (Charlotte), February 1984, 1999–0421, box 51, *FP*-DU.

21. Pamela Shaw, "Firebirds SouthPark: Polished Casual Dining," *Charlotte Food and Wine*, December/January 2008-9, 7; "Buckhead, Georgia"; "Buckhead-Atlanta."

22. Goldfield, "Place to Come To," 17.

23. Lassiter, *Silent Majority*, 53.

24. Lassiter, 184; "Available City Population Data."

25. Lassiter, *Silent Majority*, 210. For further discussion on this point, see pp. 99, 209–12; Cobb, *Industrialization and Southern Society*, 112; and Cobb, *Selling of the South*, 122–50.

26. C. Smith, "Desegregation and Resegregation." Also see Mickelson, Smith, and Nelson, *Yesterday, Today, and Tomorrow*.

27. Lassiter, *Silent Majority*, 218–21.

28. Lassiter, 213–15.

29. Goldfield, "Place to Come To," 15–16.

30. On Stonewall and the gay liberation movement in the immediate aftermath of the riots, see D'Emilio, *Sexual Politics*, 231–39.

31. "Gay Buying Power: Expo 93 to Showcase Businesses," *Atlanta Journal-Constitution*, July 16, 1993.

32. Atlanta Gay and Lesbian Chamber of Commerce, "AGLCC History."

33. Applebome, *Dixie Rising*, 154.

34. Wright, "'How Could Love Be Wrong?'"

35. On Charlotte's struggles over Gay Pride and public park usage, see Karen Shugart, "Charlotte Pride Is Delayed, Not Dead: They're Here, They're Going to Have a Festival, Get Used to It," *Creative Loafing* (Atlanta and Charlotte), April 26, 2006.

36. I discuss lesbians, softball, and Piedmont Park in chapter 2.

37. Laura Douglas-Brown, "Atlanta Pride Celebrates 40 Years," *Georgia Voice*, October 1, 2010, http://www.thegavoice.com/index.php/community/atlanta -Pride/1228-atlanta-Pride-celebrates-40-years; Cannick, "Celebrating Black Gay Pride"; "Pride" (exhibit).

38. Cobb, *Selling of the South*, 128.

39. Dan Chapman, "Rivalry to Be Economic King of South Heats Up," *Atlanta Journal-Constitution*, May 10, 2009.

40. Galloway, "Charlotte Who?"

41. Glock, "Southern Women."

42. For a critique of *The Help*, see Rivas, "Association of Black Women Historians."

43. Hale, *Making Whiteness*.

44. Though southern Black women's identity has many layers, it cannot be swept into a monolithic narrative of southern lesbian history—just as we should avoid labeling any women who might have actively eschewed the identity of lesbian, dyke, or southerner. These identities are historically produced and, in many cases, products of self-identification that defy blanket statements because they would not reflect the experiences or desires of the women examined.

45. Eaves, "Outside Forces," 155–56; Thorpe, "'House Where Queers Go.'"

46. Somerville, *Queering the Color Line.*

47. Oral history is a segregated process, and oral histories of Black and white southern lesbians are often conducted as separate projects using separate methods. For example, in E. Patrick Johnson's *Black. Queer. Southern. Women,* he "allows women whose identities and/or sexual desires have positioned them on the margins of society to have a platform to speak on their own terms about what it means to be black, southern, and expressive of same-sex desire," 5. Also see the predominantly (but not at all exclusively) white Lesbian Feminist Activist Oral Herstory Project in *Sinister Wisdom,* issues 93, 98, and 104.

48. On Black lesbian life, see E. Johnson, *Black. Queer. Southern. Women*; Hamilton, "'I Thought I Found Home'"; and Ashley Coleman Taylor's work in progress on queer Atlanta as described in Virginia Prescott and Elena Rivera, "New Oral History Project Captures Black LGBTQ Life In Atlanta," Georgia Public Radio, October 10, 2018, updated August 13, 2020, https://www.gpb.org /news/2018/10/10/new-oral-history-project-captures-black-lgbtq-life-in-atlanta.

49. My thoughts on identity are influenced by Judith Bennett's methodological suggestion of "lesbian-like" rather than a static and named identity employed across space and time. Martha Vicinus echoed Bennett's frustrations when formulating her approach to lesbians in history: "To paraphrase Judith Bennett, I am not making a case for lesbian history, but for the central place of lesbians in history." Vicinus further observed that "lesbian history has always been characterized by a 'not knowing,'" and this leaves historians the task of finding and identifying a history that we know exists but has often been denied. Bennett, "'Lesbian-Like,'" 10; Vicinus, "Lesbian History," 67, 57.

50. Cobb, *Away Down South,* 6–7.

51. On historical identity, labels, and naming, see Kennedy and Davis, *Boots of Leather*; D'Emilio, *Sexual Politics*; Faderman, *Odd Girls*; Freedman, "'Burning of Letters Continues'"; Rupp, "'Imagine My Surprise'"; Gladney, "Personalizing the Political"; Knowlton, "'Only a Woman Like Yourself'"; Enke, *Finding the Movement*; N. Boyd, *Wide Open Town,* introduction; and Manion, *Female Husbands,* introduction.

52. In a roundtable at the Berkshire Conference of Women Historians, Nan Alamilla Boyd suggested that lesbian history should be understood as the history of an idea rather than a history of a defined group or people. This provides a useful approach for the research presented in *Drastic Dykes,* especially when we consider how sexual identity gained meaning in different places and spaces or that it had little—or possibly no—meaning for others. Meyer, "Roundtable." Arlene Stein's consideration of butch identity, the category of "lesbian," and transmen explores the need for "a more complex understanding of identities" when

engaging categories that are constantly in flux. Stein, "The Incredible Shrinking Lesbian World," 30. Jen Manion further explores the question of the butch lesbian and transgender identity in "The Performance of Transgender Inclusion."

53. Gieseking, *Queer New York*.

54. On the challenges of historicizing "erotic behavior," see D'Emilio, *Sexual Politics*, 9. Also see Kunzel's discussion of lesbian history in "Power of Queer History"; Garber, "Where in the World Are the Lesbians?"; Holloway, "Searching for Southern Lesbian History"; and E. Johnson, *Black. Queer. Southern. Women*, introduction.

55. On the importance of individual southern stories, see Inscoe, *Writing the South*. For a brief statement on the theoretical use of glimpses through "windows," see Marshall and Anderson, "Rethinking the Public and Private Spheres," 169.

56. As the anthropologist Allesandro Portelli considered the methodology behind oral history, he reminded scholars, "What is really important is that memory is not a passive depository of facts, but an active process of creation of meanings. Thus, the specific utility of oral sources for the historian lies, not so much in their ability to preserve the past, as in the very changes wrought by memory." Memory shapes the retelling of history, and the stories produced are created through combining archival scraps with the "changes wrought" by the memories of narrators. Archival sources produce an additional difficulty, however, because the privileges of whiteness, education, gender, and class are replicated in the archives. *Drastic Dykes* is a narrative of specific people, places, and memories, and it is also a story inspired by specific archival materials. This necessarily means that a vast sea of materials and experiences is not included here, and often such exclusions are based on socioeconomic class, gender, education, and race. Southern lesbian stories are found in gay men's print culture, educated white women's journals and letters, and queer newsletters. The result offers some clarity while obscuring other realities. Portelli, *Death of Luigi Trastulli*, 52. On the particularities of queer oral history, see Murphy, Pierce, and Ruiz, "What Makes Queer Oral History Different." Of note is their finding that queer oral history is often centered on a personal and shared relationship of queerness and queer desire, 12.

57. See, for example, Chenault, "Unspoken Past." Many of the narrators who are profiled in *Drastic Dykes* participated in a project titled Atlanta's Unspoken Past, under the direction of the Kenan Research Center at the Atlanta History Center. This effort was inspired by the 1990s nonprofit group the Atlanta Lesbian and Gay History Thing. Oral history practice often centers on the retelling of actions based on a specific theme. As a result, narrators adopt the language of the research inquiry. Narrators in the Atlanta Lesbian and Gay History Thing define themselves through the terminology of the project, using markers like "lesbian," "gay," or "queer," when it is possible that they would not have employed these labels at the time of the actual events.

58. D'Emilio, *Sexual Politics*, 75.

59. Kate Mullen, interview by author, Charlotte, NC, May 19, 2003; Donna Smith, "Same Difference"; and Dawn (Niki) Heard, interview by author, Charlotte, NC, June 1, 2003.

60. Clement et al., "Southern Dykes."

Chapter 1

1. Als, "Unhappy Endings."

2. Als, "Unhappy Endings"; Schulman, "Grappling with Carson McCullers."

3. Als, "Unhappy Endings"; Whitt, "Living and Writing in the Margins," 102; Carr, *Lonely Hunter*, 136–37.

4. Als, "Unhappy Endings."

5. Although McCullers lived briefly in Charlotte when her husband, Reeves McCullers, took her to Charlotte, where he was a debt collector, she moved to Nyack, New York, in 1945, as did her mother after selling the family's Georgia home. Als, "Unhappy Endings."

6. Halberstam, *Female Masculinity*, 189.

7. Shapland, *My Autobiography*, 23. For a valuable analysis of a queer comrade in the U.S. South, the story of North Carolinian Pauli Murray is instructive: Winner, "Pauli Murray."

8. On the potential joy of "private lesbianism" and the difficulty in finding lesbian lives, see Kennedy, "'But We Would Never Talk about It.'"

9. McCullers has been understood and imagined as a trans individual, under twenty-first-century terms, similar to her contemporary the Black legal scholar Pauli Murray. On McCullers and trans identity, see Schulman, "Grappling with Carson McCullers." On Pauli Murray and trans identity, see Cooper, "Queering Jane Crow."

10. D'Emilio and Freedman, *Intimate Matters*, 225–26.

11. H. Ellis, *Sexual Inversion*, 195–97.

12. H. Ellis, 204.

13. Schulman, "Grappling with Carson McCullers."

14. On the origins and nature of McCullers's relationship with David Diamond, see Carr, *Lonely Hunter*, 146–85.

15. Diamond would later share an intimate relationship with McCullers's husband, Reeves. McCullers wrote *The Ballad of the Sad Café* for Diamond.

16. On McCullers's initial reactions to meeting Schwarzenbach, see Carr, *Lonely Hunter*, 100–107. Also see Shapland, *My Autobiography*.

17. Carson McCullers to David Diamond, July 19, 1941, Carson McCullers Collection, Manuscripts, Archives, and Rare Books Library, Emory University, Atlanta.

18. Als, "Unhappy Endings."

19. Carr, *Lonely Hunter*, 145–46. On Schwarzenbach's affinity for women, see 103–5.

20. Carr, 221–23.

21. Als, "Unhappy Endings."

22. For more on McCullers and her time at Yaddo, see Carr, *Lonely Hunter*, 153–70, 212–23; on McCullers in Charlotte, see 74–81. On artistic circles as spaces of protection and cover for lesbians, see Kennedy, "'But We Would Never Talk about It,'" 38.

23. McCullers to Diamond, July 1941, at Yaddo, Carson McCullers Collection. In 1941 Carson and Reeves divorced but were remarried in 1945. In 1953 Reeves killed himself.

24. Kennedy, "'But We Would Never Talk about It,'" 19.

25. Kenschaft, "Homoerotics," 227.

26. Kenschaft, 227.

27. Gladney, *How Am I to Be Heard?*

28. Shapland, *My Autobiography*, 19, 23.

29. Shapland, 12–15.

30. Willa Gray Martin, "Mary Hutchinson of Atlanta, Whose Paintings Have Won Numerous Prizes, Failed in Art Course at College," *Spartanburg (SC) Herald-Journal*, March 24, 1940, https://news.google.com /newspapers?nid=SFOYbPikdlgC&dat=19400324&printsec=frontpage&hl=en.

31. Turner, "Hutchinson, Intelligibility," 381.

32. Turner, 401. Also see Turner, "Mary E. Hutchinson (1906–1970)."

33. Turner, "Hutchinson, Intelligibility," 378–79.

34. Turner, 375–414.

35. A collection of letters details the relationship between Mary Hutchinson and Dorothy King, HK-EU.

36. Ruth Layton to Hutchinson, March 21, 1946, HK-EU.

37. Ruth (Layton) Petersen to Geraldine Andrews, July 19, 1970, HK-EU.

38. Layton to Hutchinson, "Friday, but mailed on Monday," November 5, 1945, HK-EU.

39. Turner, "Hutchinson, Intelligibility."

40. Hutchinson to King, n.d., HK-EU.

41. Hutchinson to King, June 9, 1953, HK-EU.

42. Hutchinson to King, n.d., HK-EU. It is hard to determine from the context of the letter what "all wet" was meant to represent, but it does not follow the traditional meanings of being "all wrong." In a conversation with Jae Turner, the scholar who discovered Hutchinson and King's papers, Turner agreed that based on the entire collection (not all of which was donated), a sexual innuendo was probable here.

43. Hutchinson to King, n.d., HK-EU.

44. General letters file, HK-EU.

45. Hutchinson to King, n.d., HK-EU.

46. Martin, "Mary Hutchinson of Atlanta."

47. Martin, "Mary Hutchinson of Atlanta."

48. See Kennedy, "'But We Would Never Talk about It,'" 23 and 28, on pants as nonnormative and masculine. Also see Meyer, *Creating G.I. Jane*, 155.

49. Kennedy and Davis, *Boots of Leather*, 39.

50. Kennedy and Davis, 39.

51. On this point, see Meyer, *Creating G.I. Jane*, 9, 151–52.

52. Nell Stansell, AUP-AHC.

53. Faderman, *Odd Girls*, 128–29.

54. Faderman, 128–29.

55. On the Cold War as an era of heightened gender conformity and consensus, see May, *Homeward Bound*.

56. May, 130–38.

57. Kennedy, "'But We Would Never Talk about It,'" 16.

58. Dorothy King to herself, July 30, 1970, HK-EU. See Freedman's "'Burning of Letters Continues.'" Freedman addresses the issue of restraint and management of passions in midcentury white middle- and upper-class lesbian relationships.

59. Smith-Rosenberg, "Female World of Love and Ritual," 13.

60. Kennedy, "'But We Would Never Talk about It,'" 18–19.

61. Kennedy, 18, 33–34.

62. Smith-Rosenberg, "Female World of Love and Ritual," 14.

63. Hutchinson to King, June 19, 1957, HK-EU.

64. My assumption on the "purposefulness" of these letters being saved is based on the fact that King survived Hutchinson by many years, and because many of King's letters are not included in the collection, it is probable that she made some choices about which letters would be preserved. Burning or destroying personal and romantic letters between women was seen as a necessary evil—especially among women of higher social classes who worried about their reputations being ruined if the letters were discovered or remained after death. After Hutchinson's death, Dorothy King received a letter from Geraldine Andrews asking King to destroy Andrews's letters to Hutchinson. Geraldine Andrews to Dorothy King, July 24, 1970, HK-EU. Also see Freedman, "'Burning of Letters Continues'"; Daniel, *Lost Revolutions*, 156; and Gladney, "Personalizing the Political," 100–101. My use of "kinship networks" is based on the work of Turner, "Hutchinson, Intelligibility," 375–76.

65. King to Hutchinson, January 1954, HK-EU.

66. On this point, see Chenault, "An Unspoken Past." He argues that transportation is "intimately" tied to Atlanta's history and to lesbians and gay men's ability to forge relationships with one another. On the importance of the automobile's impact on Atlanta, Chenault draws from Goldfield and Brownell, *Urban America*, 345.

67. Howard, "Library, the Park, and the Pervert," 114.

68. Howard, *Carryin' On*, 118.

69. On this particular point, and on class in general, see Kennedy and Davis, *Boots of Leather*, 43–44.

70. Kennedy, "'But We Would Never Talk about It,'" 39.

71. See various letters, HK-EU.

72. Kennedy and Davis, *Boots of Leather*, 65.

73. *Atlanta Daily World*, April 5, 1951; February 28, 1952. On libraries and segregation in Atlanta, see "A History of U.S. Public Libraries, Case Study: Atlanta," Digital Public Library of America, accessed February 10, 2022, https://dp.la/exhibitions/history-us-public-libraries/segregated-libraries/case-study-atlanta.

74. *Atlanta Daily World*, December 5, 1945, December 12, 1945, August 9, 1959.

75. *Atlanta Daily World*, April 30, 1950.

76. Halberstam, *Female Masculinity*, 190.

77. Ginny Boyd, AUP-AHC.

78. G. Boyd, AUP-AHC.

79. G. Boyd, AUP-AHC.

80. G. Boyd, AUP-AHC.

81. Kuhn, *Living Atlanta*, 362; T. Scott, "Bell Bomber."

82. Kuhn, *Living Atlanta*, 353, 364.

83. T. Scott, "Bell Bomber."

84. Meyer, *Creating G.I. Jane*, 90. See also Canaday, "'Finding a Home in the Army.'"

85. G. Boyd, AUP-AHC.

86. G. Boyd, AUP-AHC.

87. Meyer, *Creating G.I. Jane*, 168.

88. Bérubé, *Coming Out under Fire*, 59.

89. Meyer, *Creating G.I. Jane*, 66–67.

90. Meyer, 61. Also see Hegarty, "Other War," 182.

91. Bérubé, *Coming Out under Fire*, 100.

92. Bérubé, 103–4.

93. G. Boyd, AUP-AHC.

94. Meyer, *Creating G.I. Jane*, 9.

95. Bérubé, *Coming Out under Fire*, 107–8.

96. Bérubé, 105–7. On violence against Black women at Fort Benning, Georgia, see Meyer, *Creating G.I. Jane*, 140.

97. Meyer, *Creating G.I. Jane*, 90–95.

98. D'Emilio, *Sexual Politics*, 23–24; Bérubé, *Coming Out under Fire*, 6–7, 98–127.

99. Bérubé, *Coming Out under Fire*, 59. See also 304n99.

100. Kennedy and Davis, *Boots of Leather*, 64.

101. Kennedy and Davis, 64. See 398–99n11 for pertinent references to D'Emilio's and Bérubé's research on gay social life and World War II.

102. G. Boyd, AUP-AHC. Boyd used the word "gay" while at Fort Des Moines, not "lesbian."

103. Nancy MacLennan, "Wives—but without Husbands," *New York Times*, April 26, 1942.

104. Malvina Lindsay, "Women vs. Men," *Washington Post*, July 18, 1945.

105. G. Boyd, AUP-AHC.

106. G. Boyd, AUP-AHC. Address and dates of operation for the Tick Tock were obtained from the Atlanta City Directory, accessed at the University of Georgia's Hargrett Rare Book and Manuscript Library, Georgia Room.

107. When Boyd's memory failed, there were public spaces that were potentially lost forever as sites of lesbian connection. Without Boyd's identification of the Tick Tock Grill as a place for gay people to gather, we would operate under the assumption that the Tick Tock Grill was just another southern diner, losing an important slice of an elusive southern queer history.

108. On this point, see Bernhard et al., *Hidden Histories*, 1; and Duberman, Vicinus, and Chauncey, *Hidden from History*. These pioneering works on southern women and lesbians and gay men both focused on rescuing lost voices,

demonstrating that the histories of women in the U.S. South and lesbians and gay men nationally were both understood as "hidden" in the 1990s.

109. G. Boyd, AUP-AHC.

110. G. Boyd, AUP-AHC.

111. Chenault, "Unspoken Past," 77–78.

112. G. Boyd, AUP-AHC.

113. Thorpe, "'House Where Queers Go,'" 49.

114. Kennedy and Davis, *Boots of Leather*, 43.

115. Ambrose, "Atlanta."

116. U.S. Bureau of the Census, *Georgia—Race and Hispanic Origin* and *New York—Race and Hispanic Origin*. In 1940, Atlanta's Black population was approximately 34 percent (104,533) of the city's population, in comparison with approximately 3 percent (17,694) of Buffalo's population. The Black population of Buffalo more than doubled (36,745) by 1950, whereas Atlanta's Black population remained sizable (121,285) with modest growth. This Black population boom in Buffalo probably explains the 1950s integration in Buffalo's gay bars. Additionally, it suggests that a large enough Black populace existed in Atlanta in 1940 to allow for Black lesbian anonymity.

117. Thorpe, "'House Where Queers Go.'"

118. Thorpe, 60–61.

119. Thorpe, 49.

120. Kennedy and Davis, *Boots of Leather*, 43.

121. K. Ferguson, *Black Politics*, 3. On the politics of respectability, see Higginbotham, *Righteous Discontent*.

122. K. Ferguson, *Black Politics*, 8.

123. Kennedy and Davis, *Boots of Leather*, 43.

124. Kennedy and Davis, on class, 43–44.

125. G. Boyd, AUP-AHC.

126. Kennedy and Davis, *Boots of Leather*, 65.

Chapter 2

1. Jack Strouss Jr., AUP-AHC.

2. On the role of anonymity in urban bar communities, see Kennedy and Davis, *Boots of Leather*, 42–43. On bars as preferable to activism, see Filene, review of *Sexual Politics*.

3. J. Sears, *Rebels, Rubyfruit, and Rhinestones*, 158.

4. Enke, *Finding the Movement*, 254.

5. D'Emilio, *Sexual Politics*, 99.

6. Kennedy and Davis, *Boots of Leather*, 29.

7. D'Emilio, *Sexual Politics*, 98–99.

8. Kennedy and Davis, *Boots of Leather*, 114–15, and 114n6; Lorde, *Zami*, 176–256. Also see Buring, *Lesbian and Gay Memphis*.

9. Kennedy and Davis, *Boots of Leather*, 123–31; Enke, *Finding the Movement*, 30–37; Thorpe, "'House Where Queers Go.'"

10. Enke, *Finding the Movement*, 28–37.

11. Thorpe, "'House Where Queers Go,'" 41–42.

12. Historians have made a mistake in looking to bars for Black lesbians, Rochella (Roey) Thorpe has argued. This has frustrated attempts, including mine, to locate the "semi-public" social lives of Black lesbians. Thorpe's assertion requires historians to open separate paths of inquiry to locate Black lesbians in their created communities. Thorpe, "'House Where Queers Go,'" 41–42.

13. Lorde, *Zami*, 179.

14. Kennedy and Davis, *Boots of Leather*, 122.

15. Kennedy and Davis, 122.

16. Lorde, *Zami*, 179–81.

17. Lorde, 203.

18. Lorde, 205.

19. Scotti Hooper, AUP-AHC; Chu, "Revival of Atlanta Area"; Chenault, "Unspoken Past"; Combs, "Ties That Bind," 55.

20. Combs, "Ties That Bind," 55. The Old Fourth Ward neighborhood was approximately 78 percent Black, according to 1970 census data referenced by Combs. Some of Hooper's fear of being at Dupree's was probably due to her discomfort as a white woman in a Black neighborhood.

21. D'Emilio, *Sexual Politics*, 98.

22. Kennedy and Davis, *Boots of Leather*, 69.

23. Hooper, AUP-AHC; Kennedy and Davis, *Boots of Leather*, 122–23.

24. Hooper, Nell Stansell, AUP-AHC. Hooper's oral history gives a negative view of butch lesbian identity, and this shapes her recollections of Dupree's and Mrs. P's. Dupree's name changed—as did several bar names—from "Grill" to "Tavern" or "Lounge." It remained in operation from 1957 through the 1970s. In the 1977 Atlanta City Directory, the listing reads "Dupree's Lounge" and locates the bar at 715 Ponce de Leon. Address information from Atlanta City Directory, accessed at AHC. This same information is confirmed in the *Falcon World Gay Guide, 1977* and *International Guild Guide, 1969: Gay Listings*, MSS 773, Atlanta Lesbian and Gay History Thing Collection, AHC.

25. For more on the queer history of the Old Fourth Ward, see Chenault, Ditzler, and Orr, "Discursive Memorials."

26. "The Lorelei Ladies: Their 30th Year as an Organized Team," MSS 733, Atlanta Lesbian and Gay History Thing Collection.

27. Stansell, Barbara Vogel, AUP-AHC.

28. Shelby Jewell, "Sports Page Sports Softball," *Pulse*, June 28, 1984, 17, ALFA-DU.

29. Faderman, *Odd Girls*, 162. For more on softball, lesbians, and the South, see Buring, *Lesbian and Gay Memphis*, 139–42.

30. Stansell, Vogel, AUP-AHC; Hanhardt, *Safe Space*, 23. Also see Enke, *Finding the Movement*, 7; and Gelfand, "'Come Out Slugging!,'" 96–98.

31. Boyd remembered, with great humor, Mrs. P telling customers that "Ginny is responsible for my first Cadillac." Ginny Boyd, AUP-AHC. It is interesting to note that the Atlanta Tomboys 17th Anniversary Program (Atlanta Lesbian and Gay History Thing Collection, AHC) has an entry for a "Mr. and Mrs. H. E.

Phillips" as boosters for the softball team, but I have yet to make a connection between the Phillipses who owned Piedmont Tavern and those who were boosters for the Tomboys. Buring, *Lesbian and Gay Memphis*, 137–42. Buring notes the importance of softball to Memphis lesbians and also confirms that lesbians in Memphis would frequent bars that were mixed (straight and gay clientele). To document the actual change made by lesbians from Piedmont Tavern to "Mrs. P's"—a successful gay bar that thrived throughout the 1970s—is remarkable.

32. Howard, *Carryin' On*, 118–20.

33. Stansell, AUP-AHC.

34. Boyd, Vogel, AUP-AHC.

35. Sismondo, *America Walks into a Bar*, xiii.

36. Stansell, AUP-AHC.

37. Kennedy and Davis, *Boots of Leather*, 151–54.

38. Strouss, AUP-AHC.

39. Combs, "Ties That Bind," 54–55, 100. By 2000, due to gentrification, the Old Fourth Ward neighborhood experienced significant growth in its white population. According to sociologist Barbara Harris Combs, as of 2010, the neighborhood was home to many lesbian and gay couples.

40. Kennedy and Davis, *Boots of Leather*, 139.

41. G. Boyd, AUP-AHC. Boyd remembered that their club was near Atlanta's Buford Highway before it "exploded." This was a particularly interesting choice for Boyd, who admitted spending time in a remote Black nightclub and feeling welcome there. See chapter 1 for Boyd's recollection of this time.

42. Charlene McLemore and Barbara Vogel (interviewed together), AUP-AHC.

43. Jewell, "Sports Page Sports Softball."

44. Enke, *Finding the Movement*, 29.

45. Enke, 30.

46. Hooper, AUP-AHC.

47. J. Sears, *Rebels, Rubyfruit, and Rhinestones*, 159.

48. On this point, see Chesnut and Gable, "'Women Ran It,'" 278–79n42.

49. *Cruise*, September 2–9, 1976, vol. 1, 4, 12, in Billy Jones Papers, MSS 1106, AHC.

50. Mellor and Stamas, "Usual Weekly Earnings," 17.

51. Mellor and Stamas, 16.

52. Mellor, "Investigating the Differences," 17–18.

53. *Cruise*, September 2–9, 1976, in Billy Jones Papers, MSS 1106, AHC. According to this issue of *Cruise*, Ms. Garbo's was previously located in "King's Kastle" for three and a half years prior to the 1976 opening under new management.

54. *Cruise*, September 2–9, 1976, in Billy Jones Papers; Charlene McLemore, AUP-AHC.

55. Strouss, AUP-AHC.

56. Ann McKain, AUP-AHC. It is not clear when McKain began frequenting Ms. Garbo's, but she remembered the establishment as significant because she could dine out alone with another woman—something she felt that was not acceptable in the 1960s. This comfort was probably due in part to McKain's personal acceptance of her own sexuality. It is also possible that McKain's memories

relate to frequent Ms. Garbo's visits when it was still a private club for women only—prior to 1976.

57. Vogel, AUP-AHC.

58. McKain, Vogel, AUP-AHC.

59. *Falcon World Gay Guide, 1977*, 8, 40–41.

60. *Whatever*, August 1979, private collection.

61. Hobson, *Black Mecca*.

62. *Falcon World Gay Guide, 1977*.

63. *Falcon World Gay Guide, 1977*. This Denny's location was noted for being gay-friendly after bars closed for the night.

64. Strouss, McKain, AUP-AHC. It is interesting that the *Falcon Guide* does not list Gene & Gabe's as a "G&G" establishment—meaning that it catered to women and men—but McKain recalled this meeting place as pivotal for bringing gay women and men together.

65. Darrell Sifford, "A Tour of Our Gay Nightlife," *Charlotte News*, December 15, 1973.

66. *International Guild Guide*, box 252, JS-DU.

67. Population and growth data from Real Estate Center at Texas A&M University, "Population MSA: Charlotte-Gastonia-Concord, NC-SC," and "Population MSA: Atlanta–Sandy Springs–Marietta, GA."

68. Meeker, *Contacts Desired*, 12.

69. In looking at various volumes of the newspapers and newsletters mentioned in this chapter, no more than five images of Black people appear, and they are predominantly entertainers booked for a onetime performance.

70. *Atlanta Barb*, "Prototype Edition," n.d., ALFA-DU. Although I discovered the *Barb* in the Atlanta Lesbian Feminist Alliance's archives, the paper has since been digitized by the Atlanta History Center, https://album.atlantahistorycenter .com/digital/collection/p17222coll17. This prototype edition, however, is not in the Atlanta History Center's collection.

71. D'Emilio, *Sexual Politics*, 98. Although D'Emilio makes these assertions primarily in reference to the 1950s, my research suggests that these conditions remained for women in Charlotte and Atlanta in the 1970s.

72. For more on Atlanta's MCC church, see chapter 4.

73. When African American candidate Maynard Jackson won his highly contentious mayoral bid in 1973, the *Barb* celebrated the victory noting this as a "step in the right direction toward equality for all." *Atlanta Barb*, "Prototype Edition," n.d., ALFA-DU.

74. McLemore and Vogel, AUP-AHC.

75. *Atlanta Barb*, ALFA-DU; McLemore and Vogel, AUP-AHC.

76. J. Sears, *Rebels, Rubyfruit, and Rhinestones*, 159. See 153–54 for information on the Sweet Gum Head show bar.

77. J. Sears, 137–38.

78. *Charlotte Free Press*, May 17, 1976, private collection. Oleen's remained in operation until 2000.

79. "We Lost the Mother of Gay Charlotte," *Q-Notes*, May 10, 2003, private collection.

80. "Gay History—Gay Pride," *Q-Notes*, June/July 1988, 6, private collection.

81. "We Lost the Mother of Gay Charlotte."

82. *Whatever*, issue 72, private collection. Oleen's was located at 1831 South Boulevard primarily, but I found an advertisement referencing Oleen's Lounge at 3511 Wilkinson Boulevard in 1975. This was right next to the 3513 address of the Brass Rail—a bar that Oleen's managed in the 1960s. It appears that there was a disco called Oleen's Too, advertised in 1981, open at the South Boulevard location for a period of time. Address information located in various issues of *Whatever* and *Q-Notes*, private collection. The 1831 South Boulevard location is now a Dunkin' Donuts, housed in the original Oleen's building. Information on country night from advertisement in *Q-Notes*, [1987?], private collection.

83. *Charlotte Free Press*, December 1, 1975, and August 11, 1975; *Whatever*, issue 17; *Q-Notes*, March 1987, June 1987, all accessed through a private collection.

84. "Examples of Charlotte Bars for Your Research," anonymous email message to author, April 10, 2007.

85. Sarrah Kelly, interview by author, Charlotte, NC, May 12, 2003.

86. *Charlotte Free Press*, April 5, 1976, 12, private collection.

87. *Charlotte Free Press*, March 22, 1976, 11, private collection.

88. These efforts are discussed in detail in chapter 3.

89. "Charlotte Group Plans Lesbian Center," *Charlotte Free Press*, April 5, 1976, 9, private collection. See J. Sears, *Rebels, Rubyfruit, and Rhinestones*, 248–53, for information on lesbian separatist activism in Charlotte. Coverage of Ms. Garbo's opening in *Cruise* was written by "Mother 'S,'" probably a drag queen. There is no byline for the article on a lesbian center in Charlotte in the *Charlotte Free Press*. Although the editors were both men, John Freese and Robert Freese Jr., the lesbian content was most likely contributed by lesbians who were originally involved with the Charlotte Women's Center but in 1975 separated themselves and operated under the name Charlotte's Drastic Dykes. This story is detailed in chapter 3.

90. *Charlotte Free Press*, April 19, 1976, and May 30, 1977, private collection. Finding the history of Charlotte's lesbian bar community is difficult. A focus on gay men's bars is the only option to find lesbians in gay bar spaces. Unlike in Atlanta, there was no archive actively collecting lesbian and gay materials or oral histories until UNC Charlotte's J. Murrey Atkins Library opened the King-Henry-Brockington Archive in 2013. And prior to the gay publications of the 1970s, there is no way to assess the pulse of the bar community in Charlotte without oral history connections.

91. The Greenhouse was located at 119 South Brevard in Uptown Charlotte. Unfortunately, without an oral history to document this bar, its story is lost as a site of 1970s southern lesbian community. *Charlotte Free Press*, October 4, 1976, private collection.

92. *Charlotte Free Press*, April 19, 1976, 6, private collection. The Neptune Lounge was probably one of the first gay bars in Charlotte, and some lesbians did spend time there. According to the writer James T. Sears, an African American lesbian identified by the pseudonym "Karla Brown" discovered her lesbian

identity in 1970 at the Neptune, a white men's bar, in Charlotte. J. Sears, *Rebels, Rubyfruit, and Rhinestones*, 137–38.

93. Sifford, "Tour of Our Gay Nightlife"; "Carolina Bars Celebrate," *Charlotte Free Press*, June 2, 1975, 1–2, private collection. Address information from the Charlotte City Directory and the Charlotte phone book, both accessed at Charlotte Mecklenburg Library, Main, Robinson-Spangler Carolina Room. Like other bars referenced in this paper, the Scorpio, originally located at 2209 South Boulevard, has used several names during its existence, such as Scorpio Lounge and Scorpio Disco, increasing the difficulty of tracing its physical location. As of 2019, the Scorpio dates its opening to 1968: see the Scorpio website, accessed February 9, 2022, https://www.thescorpio.com/.

94. Martin, "Wesley Heights' Decline Halted."

95. *Little David*, September 15, 1974, 54, Billy Jones Papers; *Charlotte Free Press*, December 1, 1975, 16, private collection; "PRIDE WEEK!" *Q-Notes*, June 1986, private collection.

96. Ken Friedlein and Polly Paddock, "Charlotte's Emerging Social Scene," *Charlotte Observer*, April 27, 1981. This article was part of an *Observer* series on gay life in Charlotte, beginning on April 27, 1981. There was an "Odyssey 1" located at Morehead and Tryon Streets in 1979, but the Odyssey referenced here was located at the Plaza and Eastway Drive, and it opened in 1980.

97. "Examples of Charlotte Bars for Your Research."

98. Friedlein and Paddock, "Charlotte's Emerging Social Scene."

99. *Whatever*, issue 81, December 1980, issue 87, 1981, and issue 76, probably 1980, private collection.

100. For more on Queen City Quordinators, see chapter 4.

101. *Q-Notes: A Monthly Newsletter*, August 1984, private collection. This ad was from the first version of *Q-Notes*, published in a newsletter format and organized by Queen City Quordinators.

102. "The Soft Spot," *Q-Notes*, February 1988, 4, private collection.

103. "Gay Café/Bar Opens March 13," *Q-Notes*, March 1987, 1, private collection. Steven's was located at 316 Rensselaer Avenue in Charlotte.

104. "Liaisons Open for Business," *Q-Notes*, August 1989, private collection.

105. Beth Rabena Carr, ed., *Damron Women's Traveller* (San Francisco: Damron Co, Inc., 1994), 309, MS 773, Atlanta Lesbian and Gay History Thing Collection.

106. Liaisons routinely entertained lesbians and gay men in the same space, and after its closing new owners removed the pink paint and reopened a new gay bar space in Charlotte. To mark the grand opening, the bar's owners recognized the importance of the public space as historically queer: "Like many people in our community, we are a group of friends that met having drinks at the bar in this location several years ago. We know that many people over the years have developed special friendships and built long-term relationships at this bar. We developed our partnership to re-invent the bar so that this historic icon in our community would continue beyond the 20 years it has served us." This quote taken from the defunct website for the "Bar at 316" (accessed February 15, 2012).

107. "On Homosexuality," *Charlotte Free Press*, August 25, 1975, 10, private collection; "Happy Birthday Free Press!," *Charlotte Free Press*, April 5, 1976, 12, private collection. According to *Q-Notes* staff, the *Charlotte Free Press* was North Carolina's first gay newspaper. Matt Comer, "Timeless Pride," *Q-Notes*, June 27, 2009, http://goqnotes.com/2902/timeless-pride/.

108. On the activist aftermath of Stonewall, see D'Emilio, *Sexual Politics*, 233–39. On the growth of gay people as a target market, see Chasin, *Selling Out*.

109. It is not until the 1970s that a queer bar landscape becomes archivally visible in Charlotte, although active LGBTQ collecting and oral history work in the South will likely change this knowledge in coming years.

110. *Gazette*, January 22–28, 1981, and January 29–February 4, 1981, MSS 733, Atlanta Lesbian and Gay History Thing Collection. Arney's was located at 2345 Cheshire Bridge Road.

111. Carr, *Damron Women's Traveller*, 166.

112. J. Sears, *Rebels, Rubyfruit, and Rhinestones*, 319.

113. I discuss political and corporate support for lesbians and gay men at length in chapters 4 and 5.

114. Hooper, AUP-AHC.

Chapter 3

1. Joy Justice, "Vision," *Sinister Wisdom*, no. 4 (Fall 1977): 66–71, 68, ALFA-DU.

2. Joy/Callie Justice, email message to author, October 10, 2013.

3. For another example of successful southern lesbian-feminist organizing, see K. Williams, "Louisville's Lesbian Feminist Union." On feminism in southern U.S. communities, see Gilmore, *Groundswell* and "Dynamics of Second-Wave Feminist Activism."

4. In the early issues of *Sinister Wisdom*, founders Harriet Desmoines and Catherine Nicholson referred to their publication as a "magazine." Currently, *Sinister Wisdom* is "a multicultural lesbian literary & art journal." "About," *Sinister Wisdom*, accessed April 28, 2022, http://www.sinisterwisdom.org/node/8. On the transformative possibilities of lesbian feminism, see Taylor and Rupp, "Women's Culture."

5. On lesbian feminism, see Del Rio, "'That Women Could Matter'"; Estes Blair, "'Dynamic Force'"; Valk, "Living a Feminist Lifestyle"; and Gilmore and Kaminski, "Part and Apart."

6. Justice, "Vision," 71, ALFA-DU.

7. For more on the "lavender menace," see Jay, *Tales of the Lavender Menace*; Gilmore and Kaminski, "Part and Apart"; and Warner, *Acts of Gaiety*.

8. Radicalesbians, "Woman-Identified Woman."

9. Echols, *Daring to Be Bad*, 220; Gilmore and Kaminski, "Part and Apart," 105.

10. Mathews and De Hart, *Sex, Gender, and the Politics of ERA*, 87, 192, 202–3.

11. Vicki Gabriner to Jackie Frost, April 7, 1974, box 1, 94–040, administrative files, Atlanta Lesbian Feminist Alliance Archives, David M. Rubenstein Rare

Book and Manuscript Library, Sallie Bingham Center for Women's History and Culture, Duke University, Durham.

12. Shockley, "Southern Women in the Scrums"; De Hart, "Second Wave Feminism(s)."

13. See, for example, L. Smith, *Killers of the Dream*; A. Scott, *Southern Lady*; and Clinton, *Plantation Mistress*.

14. L. Smith, *Killers of the Dream*, 140–41.

15. Gilmore, "Dynamics of Second-Wave Feminist Activism," 103.

16. Estes Blair, "'Dynamic Force,'" 39. Also see Mathews and De Hart, *Sex, Gender, and the Politics of ERA*, 111–18.

17. Harriet Desmoines, "Notes for a Magazine," *Sinister Wisdom* 1, no. 1 (July 1976): 3–4, ALFA-DU.

18. Pratt, "Out in the South." In her remarks Pratt identified the important role that Charlotte feminists played in the national lesbian-feminist movement.

19. *Charlotte Women's Center Newsletter*, ALFA-DU. In a conversation with the author on August 22, 2011, a group of white Dilworth neighbors (Kathy Sparrow, Sara and Joe Spencer, and John and Lorena Cochran) remembered several houses where groups of individuals lived together during this time.

20. *Charlotte Women's Center Newsletter*, April 1975, December 1978, ALFA-DU.

21. *Charlotte Women's Center Newsletter*, April 1975, ALFA-DU.

22. Angela Davis, "Joan Little: The Dialectics of Rape (1975)," *Ms. Magazine*, Spring 2002.

23. Hanhardt, *Safe Space*, 149.

24. *Workers World*, July 11, 1975, quoted in *Workers World*, March 9, 2006, story by Minnie Bruce Pratt.

25. "Comments on Conference: Women Speak Out," *Great Speckled Bird*, July 24, 1975, 9.

26. "Trials: Joan Little's Story," *Time*, August 25, 1975, 16.

27. On this point, see Hanhardt, *Safe Space*, 150.

28. *Charlotte Women's Center Newsletter*, ALFA-DU.

29. "Feminary (Newsletter)." See also Echols, *Daring to Be Bad*, 20–22.

30. "Feminary (Newsletter)." See also Atwell, "*Feminary*"; and Gilbert, "*Feminary* of Durham–Chapel Hill."

31. Although Pratt recalled time at the Scorpio, nowhere in the *Charlotte Women's Center Newsletter* editions is there a mention of bars—lesbian or otherwise. The center held dances and social activities, and occasionally it promoted some social events that were exclusively for lesbians.

32. Minnie Bruce Pratt, email message to author, January 23, 2012. I am grateful to Pratt for allowing me to quote from this informal email exchange.

33. Quoted in J. Sears, *Rebels, Rubyfruit, and Rhinestones*, 248.

34. For more on the origins of *Sinister Wisdom* and on Nicholson's exit from UNC Charlotte, see J. Sears, 248–53. See also Catherine Nicholson, "How Rage Mothered My Third Birth," *Sinister Wisdom* 1, no. 1 (July 1976): 35–45, quote at 39, ALFA-DU.

35. Justice, "Vision," 68, ALFA-DU.

36. Justice, 69.

37. Justice, 69.

38. *Charlotte Women's Center Newsletter*, August 1975, ALFA-DU.

39. "Kristin," *Charlotte Women's Center Newsletter*, September 1975, ALFA-DU.

40. Jan Millsapps, email message to author, November 4, 2012.

41. *Charlotte Women's Center Newsletter*, various issues, 1975, ALFA-DU. The members of the Drastic Dykes were specifically inspired by Myron and Bunch, *Lesbianism and the Women's Movement*, and looked to this national publication for direction. They noted in their exit statement that the book was available locally at Crazy Horse Bookstore on 110 E. Kings Drive in Charlotte.

42. Enke, *Finding the Movement*, 100–101.

43. Diana Press's 1975 printing of this collection of Furies writings has an image of Black and white women on the front cover, yet Furies members admitted that at the group's founding, they were all white—and all other photographs in this edition are of white women. Myron and Bunch, *Lesbianism and the Women's Movement*.

44. "Concetta," *Charlotte Women's Center Newsletter*, September 1975, ALFA-DU.

45. Minnie Bruce Pratt, email message to author, January 23, 2012.

46. Desmoines, "Notes for a Magazine," 3–4, ALFA-DU.

47. J. Sears, *Rebels, Rubyfruit, and Rhinestones*, 246–48, 263–64, 34–40, 107–18. Harriet Desmoines and Catherine Nicholson formed an early connection with Julia Penelope (Stanley) at a Gay Academic Union conference in 1975 in New York City. Penelope had a colorful history as a lesbian professor at the University of Georgia before she landed in Lincoln, Nebraska, and it would be Penelope who encouraged Desmoines and Nicholson to move *Sinister Wisdom* to Lincoln. As of 2021, the journal is edited by Julie R. Enszer. In a telephone conversation with the author on June 15, 2012, Enszer noted that although the journal has often been associated with academics, like Penelope, Enszer, and Adrienne Rich, the journal has never had university funding. This is particularly interesting given that the University of Nebraska–Lincoln now claims the journal as a "spectacular cultural complement" to its women's studies program: M. Ferguson, "History of Women's Studies at UNL."

48. Clement et al., "Southern Dykes," 5.

49. Charlotte had an active Klan presence, with an exceptionally high concentration of members (approximately 5,000 in the late 1960s). For more on this, see "Brief History."

50. Harriet Ellenburger (formerly Desmoines), email message to author, January 31, 2014.

51. Desmoines, "Notes For a Magazine," 3–4.

52. Like the other publications, this newsletter was produced in a Charlotte home on East Shade Valley Road.

53. Jennifer Justice was probably Joy Justice's heterosexual sister, whom she referred to when struggling with her own lesbian separatism.

54. *Lesbian Center Journal*, n.d., Charlotte, NC, ALFA-DU.

55. *Lesbian Center Journal*, n.d.

56. *Lesbian Center Journal*, n.d.

57. Hanhardt, *Safe Space*, 154.

58. Justice, "Vision," 66–71, ALFA-DU.

59. *Charlotte Women's Center Newsletter*, 1978, ALFA-DU; U.S. Bureau of the Census, *Population of the Largest 75 Cities*. Between 1960 and 1980, Charlotte's population grew by over 112,000, reaching 314,447 in 1980.

60. *Charlotte Women's Center Newsletter*, April 1975.

61. On the importance of a "print-centered" movement, see Chesnut and Gable, "'Women Ran It,'" 257.

62. *Charlotte Women's Center Newsletter*, August 1975.

63. *The Road*, September 1975, Alternative Press Collection, UNCC.

64. *Charlotte Women's Center Newsletter*, September 1978, ALFA-DU. This financial concern was prevalent in most women's centers across the country. See, for example, Freeman, "Lesbian Nation," 156–58. I am grateful to Julie Enszer for a productive discussion on lesbian labor, which helped me frame my thoughts as presented here.

65. *Charlotte Women's Center Newsletter*, March 1978.

66. *Charlotte Women's Center Newsletter*, March 1978.

67. *Charlotte Women's Center Newsletter*, June 1979. For more on CETA, see Liu, "Trained to Fail"; Richard Nixon, Statement; and Ronald Smothers, "CETA Cutbacks Leaving Thousands Unemployed; The Budget Targets Last of Eight Articles on Key Programs the President Wants to Cut," *New York Times*, April 11, 1981, https://www.nytimes.com/1981/04/11/us/ceta-cutbacks-leaving-thousands-unemployed-budget-targets-last-eight-articles.html.

68. *Charlotte Women's Center Newsletter*, various issues, 1979.

69. Chesnut and Gable, "'Women Ran It,'" 253–54. For a detailed look at the formation of ALFA and the direct connections to the Venceremos Brigades, see 252–57. For more on ties between the Gay Liberation Front and the Brigades, see J. Sears, *Rebels, Rubyfruit, and Rhinestones*, 86–95, 108–10. For more on ALFA, see Gelfand, "'Come Out Slugging!'"

70. Chesnut and Gable, "'Women Ran It,'" 252–53. See also Wilson, "Meet the Generation of Atlantans"; and Thomas Wheatley, "Neighborhoods—How Did Little Five Points Get Weird?," *Creative Loafing*, March 24, 2016, https://creativeloafing.com/content-232303-neighborhoods—how-did-little-five-points-get.

71. J. Sears, *Rebels, Rubyfruit, and Rhinestones*, 110. Feminists in the movement often named their houses and referred to them with the pronouns "she" or "her."

72. J. Sears, 110.

73. J. Sears, 110.

74. Quoted in J. Sears, 110.

75. Gabriner and Lorrain Fontana, quoted in J. Sears, 110.

76. Chesnut and Gable, "'Women Ran It,'" 254–55.

77. Administrative files, box 1, Atlanta Lesbian Feminist Alliance Archives, David M. Rubenstein Rare Book and Manuscript Library, Sallie Bingham Center for Women's History and Culture, Duke University, Durham.

78. Chesnut and Gable, "'Women Ran It,'" 257. The substantial collection of newsletters included in the ALFA Periodicals Collection at Duke University's Sallie Bingham Center for Women's History and Culture is evidence of the vitally important role that this organization occupied in the movement. The collection includes over 800 newsletters and journals (forty-seven boxes of materials) in addition to organizational records for many other radical women's groups: "Inventory of the Atlanta Lesbian Feminist Alliance."

79. G. Johnson, "Intermetropolitan Wage Differentials." I am grateful to James C. Cobb for locating and analyzing this data.

80. U.S. Small Business Administration Office of Advocacy, *Women in Business*. As of 2012, Georgia had maintained its position as a leader in woman-owned businesses since 1987.

81. J. Sears, *Rebels, Rubyfruit, and Rhinestones*, 137–38. Brown did attend a "white women's college near Charlotte," according to Sears, but it is unclear whether she graduated. Although Brown uses the word "most" to describe her observations of the ALFA women's class status, it is hard to say whether Brown's perceptions are representative of a large or small group of the members.

82. Rita Leda, "Celebrating a Woman's Space," *Pulse*, September 6, 1984, ALFA-DU. As noted elsewhere in this chapter, when women's content was included in predominantly male publications like *Pulse*, it was often contributed by women (like Leda).

83. "History of the Great Speckled Bird," Georgia State University Library, accessed April 28, 2022, https://research.library.gsu.edu/GSB.

84. There was a move in 1971 to increase the *Bird* coverage of gay issues, and according to James T. Sears, this culminated in a 1973 walkout by heterosexual staff members. J. Sears, *Rebels, Rubyfruit, and Rhinestones*, 89.

85. Jack Spalding to Vicki Gabriner, March 14, 1973, box 2, administrative files, ALFA-DU.

86. Sharon Evans and Kathy Ellison, "Coming Together at ALFA Conference," *Great Speckled Bird*, June 5, 1975.

87. Elizabeth Knowlton, quoted in J. Sears, *Rebels, Rubyfruit, and Rhinestones*, 185.

88. Evans and Ellison, "Coming Together."

89. Knowlton, quoted in J. Sears, *Rebels, Rubyfruit, and Rhinestones*, 185.

90. Evans and Ellison, "Coming Together."

91. See, for example, Stewart-Winter, *Queer Clout*, 140.

92. Great SE Lesbian Conference, folder 1.9, ALFA-DU.

93. Trova, "Woman's Space and Male Marauders," 24–25; "Atlanta," *Lavender Woman* 4, no. 4 (1975): 14, Archives of Sexuality and Gender, https://www.gale.com/primary-sources/archives-of-sexuality-and-gender.

94. The women who were arrested became known as the "Atlanta Five" or "Durham Five"; the label varies by source. See coverage of the turmoil in "News from the Sisterland," 14; and Trova, "Woman's Space and Male Marauders," 24–25. Also see J. Sears, *Rebels, Rubyfruit, and Rhinestones*, 185–86.

95. *Charlotte Women's Center Newsletter*, 1979.

96. Tilchen, "Lesbians and Women's Music," 287. See Tilden's biographical statement in "The Contributers," xviii, Darty and Potter.

97. Chesnut and Gable, "'Women Ran It,'" 241-44, 254.

98. Chesnut, Gable, and Anderson, "Atlanta's Charis Books and More."

99. Chesnut and Gable, "'Women Ran It,'" 262.

100. Patton, "Women's Creativity a Priority at Charis." This intimate portrait of Charis is exactly the service that ALFA hoped to provide with its commitment to archival preservation. ALFA archived periodicals like *Pulse* and as a result captured the essence of Charis in Atlanta's Little Five Points.

101. Chesnut and Gable, "'Women Ran It,'" 246-47.

102. Enke, *Finding the Movement*, 29.

103. Myron and Bunch, *Lesbianism and the Women's Movement*, 11.

104. Minnie Bruce Pratt, email message to author, January 23, 2012.

105. On this point, see J. Sears, *Rebels, Rubyfruit, and Rhinestones*, 157-58.

106. Enke, *Finding the Movement*, 64.

Chapter 4

1. *Atlanta Barb*, 1974, ALFA-DU.

2. Kevin P. Murphy examines the nostalgic view of early Pride celebrations as pure and politically motivated versus the disdain that some felt for the corporate takeover of Pride beginning in the 1980s in his essay "Gay Was Good," 313.

3. Levs, "Black Gays and Lesbians." There is a great deal of history yet to be written on variations of Pride celebrations and remembrances in the South. For more on Atlanta's Black Pride, see Mims, "Gay Pride in the Urban New South."

4. "Our Purpose, Mission and Vision."

5. Dyana Bagby, "Celebrating 44 Years of Atlanta Pride and Who We Are," *Georgia Voice*, October 10, 2014, https://thegavoice.com/news/georgia/timeline-celebrating-44-years-atlanta-pride/.

6. My initial thoughts on this point were based on anecdotal evidence, but sociologist and economist Richard Florida asserts that queer community can be a draw for urban economic growth. Florida, *Rise of the Creative Class*; Gates and Florida, "Technology and Tolerance."

7. Don Weston, "Power in Pride," *Pride Guide*, 1986, box 53, *FP-DU*.

8. "Pride History."

9. Waters, "Stonewall of the South."

10. Waters, "Stonewall of the South"; Chenault, Ditzler, and Orr, "Discursive Memorials."

11. "Ansley Square Mall/Cheshire Bridge."

12. Saunders, "'It's a Raid!'"; Waters, "Stonewall of the South." Also see Brock and Prescott, "South of Stonewall."

13. *Carolina Plain Dealer*, no. 11, box 132, JS-DU. See also J. Sears, *Rebels, Rubyfruit, and Rhinestones*, 67.

14. Tom Coffin, "Nixon Out of Atlanta," *Creative Loafing*, June 26, 1972, 2-4. Citing last-minute security concerns, Nixon sent his vice president, Spiro Agnew, in his place. Anti-war organizers in Atlanta claimed this move as a victory.

15. "First for Famed Peachtree Street."

16. *Atlanta Barb*, 1974, ALFA-DU.

17. "Gay Pride Week 1977," Atlanta Lesbian Feminist Alliance Archives, ca. 1972–1994, LGBTQ History and Culture, Part II: Subject Files, box 15, folder 28, Archives of Sexuality and Gender, https://www.gale.com/primary-sources /archives-of-sexuality-and-gender.

18. "Midtown Alliance"; "Midtown Local Historic District."

19. For more on Midtown as Atlanta's hip and queer neighborhood, see Marini, "'Looking for a City,'" 27–28, 47, 56–57, 60–70; and Huff, "New Way of Living Together," 205–9.

20. A casual Google search for "gayborhood" in Atlanta turns up several twenty-first-century references to Midtown, while a search for "gayborhood" in Charlotte turns up nothing. Hanhardt, *Safe Space*; Stewart-Winter, *Queer Clout*; Rotenstein, "Decatur Plan"; Gieseking, "Last Lesbian Bar" and *Queer New York*; Rosenthal, "Make Roanoke Queer Again"; Ghaziani, "There Goes the Gayborhood?"

21. Stewart-Winter, *Queer Clout*, 221; Gieseking, "Last Lesbian Bar."

22. Margo George and David Massey, "Gay Pride vs. Citizens for Decent Atlanta: The March," *Great Speckled Bird*, 1976, ALFA-DU.

23. Laura Douglas-Brown, "Atlanta Pride Celebrates 40 Years," *Georgia Voice*, October 1, 2010, http://www.thegavoice.com/index.php/community /pride/1228-atlanta-pride-celebrates-40-years. Just twenty years later this number would multiply by a thousand to equal 300,000 in attendance for Gay Pride in Atlanta.

24. George and Massey, "Gay Pride vs. Citizens for Decent Atlanta."

25. Cathy's anti-gay activism continued in the twenty-first century. See, for example, Kim Severson, "Chick-fil-A Thrust Back into Spotlight on Gay Rights," *New York Times*, July 25, 2012, http://www.nytimes.com/2012/07/26/us /gay-rights-uproar-over-chick-fil-a-widens.html?_r=0.

26. George and Massey, "Gay Pride vs. Citizens for Decent Atlanta." For more on the fear of San Francisco as a "city of nuts" because of its queer reputation, see chapter 5. Stanley was the pastor who Donna Jo Smith-Perry mooned at Pride in Atlanta, as detailed in the introduction.

27. George and Massey, "Gay Pride vs. Citizens for Decent Atlanta."

28. Chenault and Braukman, *Gay and Lesbian Atlanta*, 79; Dolan, "You Can't Be a People." There are minor discrepancies between these two accounts, but both recognize that Jackson backed down because of CDA pressure. George and Massey, "Gay Pride vs. Citizens for Decent Atlanta"; Chenault, "Unspoken Past," 168. According to the *Atlanta Journal* newspaper, Jackson was willing to declare a "human rights proclamation." Greg McDonald, "Gays Blast Jackson at March," newspaper clipping, n.d., LGT Pride, folder 20.38, box 16, 94–040, 1980 Proclamation, Subject Files, Atlanta Lesbian Feminist Archives.

29. "Candidates Gantt, Soukup Make Promises to Gays," *Q-Notes*, October 1983, *FP*-DU. The meeting was held by "Acceptance," a gay social group consisting mostly of white men who met at the relatively tolerant Park Road Baptist Church in Charlotte. The group was supported by the umbrella organization

Queen City Quordinators, also led by gay white men, who worked with the bars and the politicians to gain a place at the Queen City's table.

30. Ed Adams to Mayor Harvey Gantt, October 22, 1987, Harvey B. Gantt Papers, UNCC.

31. Jeri Fischer, "A Hard-Core Crusade against Porn—Preacher Now Tackling Other Issues," *Charlotte Observer*, October 11, 1986.

32. Bill Arthur, "Quayle Visiting Charlotte—Stops Include Banquet, School," *Charlotte Observer*, April 17, 1989.

33. In this instance, Charlotte's political and religious marriage remained several decades beyond Atlanta's, where John Howard uncovered a "religious-political power structure" in 1950s Atlanta. See Howard, "Library, the Park, and the Pervert," 122–25.

34. "Gay Pride Covers Carolina," *Front Page*, June 1981, box 130, JS-DU.

35. J. Sears, *Rebels, Rubyfruit, and Rhinestones*, 351n15.

36. "Gay Pride Covers Carolina."

37. For more on Gittings and the Daughters of Bilitis, see Gallo, *Different Daughters*, 40–43.

38. Don King, "Seriously Speaking," *Our South*, no. 3, box 51, *FP*-DU; "N.C. Celebrates Gay Pride 1981!," *Front Page*, July 1981, box 130, JS-DU.

39. De la Canal, "FAQ City."

40. "QCQ Helps Community Flex Muscles during '83," *Q-Notes*, December 1983, box 51, *FP*-DU.

41. "QCQ Helps Community."

42. *Our South*, box 51, *FP*-DU.

43. "Two New Lesbian Groups Thriving," *Q-Notes*, March 1984, box 51, *FP*-DU.

44. "Two New Lesbian Groups Thriving."

45. *Q-Notes*, October 1986, private collection.

46. "1st Annual Southern Women's Music & Comedy Festival," advertisement, box 51, *FP*-DU.

47. Crone, "Women's Music Festivals."

48. Samis Rose interview by Ann Hooper, April 10, 2018, Charlotte Queer Oral History Project, UNCC.

49. Sarrah Kelly, interview by author, Charlotte, NC, May 12, 2003. Kelly's comfort with Pride changed over the years, but our interview took place at the height of the anti-Pride backlash in Charlotte discussed in the next chapter.

50. *Q-Notes*, 1984, box 51, *FP*-DU.

51. *Q-Notes*, July 1984, box 51, *FP*-DU.

52. "Gay Pride Ad Rejected," *Gaze* 5, no. 8 (1984): 11, Atlanta Lesbian Feminist Alliance Archives, ca. 1972–1994; Bathhouses, Bars, Tourism, and Sex Laws, Discrimination Housing, Accommodation, Job, court cases clippings, October 4, 1977–1985; MS The Allan Bérubé Papers, Series IV: Research Subject Files, box 131, folder 12. Gay, Lesbian, Bisexual, and Transgender Historical Society, Archives of Sexuality and Gender, https://www.gale.com/primary-sources /archives-of-sexuality-and-gender.

53. 1984 Atlanta Pride Flyer, LGA-LHA.

54. For consistent coverage of Atlanta's Pride events throughout the twentieth century and beyond, see *Advocate*.

55. Hanhardt, *Safe Space*, 160–76.

56. Maria Helena Dolan, "Before Stonewall/After Stonewall," *Pride Guide*, 1986, box 53, *FP*-DU.

57. The relationship between churches and lesbian and gay populations will be discussed further in chapter 5.

58. *Cruise News* 1, no. 8, June 23, 1983. First Tuesday was founded in 1977 as Atlanta's first gay political action committee. In 1982, queer women in Atlanta founded the group Fourth Tuesday (discussed elsewhere in this book), which was primarily a social networking group.

59. Marcia Darien Elvidge, "Out of the Closet, into the Voting Booth," *Creative Loafing*, July 11, 1981. Also see Chenault, "Atlanta since Stonewall."

60. Don Weston, "Power in Pride," *Pride Guide*, 1986, box 53, *FP*-DU.

61. Guest editorial, *Pulse*, 1984, ALFA-DU.

62. Ken Bond, "Southern Exposure: Atlanta and Its Blossoming Gay Community," *Advocate*, December 9, 1982, LGA-LHA.

63. Don Johnston, "Lambda May Have a Home," *Etc.*, November 26, 1993, ES-EU.

64. Bond, "Southern Exposure."

65. "Thoughts on Forsyth and Other Counties: 'N-r Go Home?,'" *Phoenix Flyer*, March 1987, ALFA-DU.

66. H. Matthews Konlgsmark, "Rallies," *Marietta (GA) Daily Journal*, August 23, 1993.

67. Peter Applebome, "A Suburban Eden Where the Right Rules," *New York Times*, August 1, 1994; "Olympic Protest in Anti-gay Suburb," *Workers World*, June 2, 1994, LGA-LHA.

68. "A Haven for Cobb County Outcasts," editorial, *Atlanta Journal-Constitution*, September 6, 1993.

69. Laura Davis, text message to author, August 14, 2021. Davis shared the name "Dick-hater" and "Dyke-hater," which she remembered hearing when she moved there in 2002. She also recalled the well-known "Digging Dykes of Decatur," which had been in the community for several years before she arrived. Also see Chenault and Braukman, *Gay and Lesbian Atlanta*, 111; and Andrews, "Digging Dykes of Decatur."

70. Rotenstein, "Decatur Plan." On Decatur as a gay neighborhood, see Suzy Khimm, "America's Gayest Zip Codes, in Two Tables," *Washington Post*, June 15, 2012, https://www.washingtonpost.com/blogs/ezra-klein/post/americas-gayest -neighborhoods-in-two-charts/2012/06/15/gJQAv4pVfV_blog.html; and R. Ellis, "Avondale One of 'Gayest Zip Codes.'"

71. "Haven for Cobb County Outcasts."

72. Mab Segrest, "Fueled by Fury—Fighting Homophobia in North Carolina," *Resist: A Call to Resist Illegitimate Authority*, July/August 1992, 1, Geographic Files, Lesbians in NC, Lesbian Herstory Archives, Brooklyn.

73. Segrest, "Fueled by Fury," 9.

74. Holly Morris, "Gay Pride Days Hailed by Jackson," *Atlanta Journal-Constitution*, June 13, 1991. The city of Chicago offers a counterpoint to Atlanta's relationship with its pro-gay mayor. See Stewart-Winter, *Queer Clout*, 158–67.

75. North Carolina Lesbian & Gay Pride, Inc., 1994 newsletter, box 21, DK-DU.

76. On Charlotte's chamber of commerce slogan, see Applebome, *Dixie Rising*, 154.

77. "Gay Pride Event Pumps $500,000 into Economy," North Carolina Lesbian & Gay Pride, Inc., 1994 press release, box 21, DK-DU.

78. "Parade Is, for Some, a Way Home," *Charlotte Observer*, June 3, 1994.

79. Dan Kirsch and Susan Henry to Jim Duley, July 9, 1993, box 21, DK-DU.

80. Ricki Morell, "Charlotte to Host N.C. Gay-Rights March," *Charlotte Observer*, August 11, 1993, box 21, DK-DU.

81. Morell, "Charlotte to Host N.C. Gay-Rights March."

82. Kirsch and Henry to Duley, July 9, 1993.

83. Jean Marie Brown, "Anti-bias Amendment Rejected, Mayor: Measure Just a Symbol," *Charlotte Observer*, November 24, 1992.

84. Brown, "Anti-bias Amendment Rejected."

85. Brown, "Anti-bias Amendment Rejected."

86. *Charlotte Observer*, November 17, 1992.

87. "Power and the Pride."

88. For more on Charlotte and its troubled efforts to host Pride events in Marshall Park, see chapter 5.

89. Derek Charles Livingston, "Do Not Hide Your Face," *Front Page* 15, no. 11 (June 10, 1994): 35, LGBTQ Newspapers and Periodicals Collection, Lesbian Herstory Archives, Archives of Sexuality and Gender, https://www.gale.com/primary-sources/archives-of-sexuality-and-gender.

90. North Carolina Lesbian & Gay Pride, Inc., 1994 newsletter, box 21, DK-DU.

91. Lynnsy Logue, interview 1 by Joshua D. Burford, December 28, 2017, interview 2 by Joshua D. Burford, January 11, 2018; Sue Henry, interview 1 by Joshua D. Burford, July 30, 2016, Charlotte Queer Oral History Project, UNCC.

92. The Charlotte Pride organization hosted a parade in 2013.

93. William E. Poe to Kay Colpitts and other members of the parade permit committee, January 27, 1994, box 21, DK-DU.

94. Jim Hunt, "First Baptist Church's Proposed 'Alternate' Finishing Point for Gay Rights Parade," *Creative Loafing*, February 12, 1994, box 21, DK-DU.

95. Administrative files, box 1, Atlanta Lesbian Feminist Alliance Archives, David M. Rubenstein Rare Book and Manuscript Library, Sallie Bingham Center for Women's History and Culture, Duke University, Durham.

96. Despite numerous calls to action based on modeling of the civil rights movement at midcentury (calling the march "our Selma"), the gay magazine the *Advocate* noted the substantial difference between white and Black attendees, the latter of whom represented only a small portion of the march. Freiberg, "March on Washington"; Henry interview 1, Charlotte Queer Oral History Project; Southeastern Arts, Media & Education Project, 1987 March on Washington materials. This collection was unprocessed at the time of my research fellowship, 2012.

97. E. Johnson, *Black. Queer. Southern. Women*, 51–55, 380. See Pat Hussain joining the executive committee in the C-SPAN coverage here: "Gay and Lesbian March on Washington."

98. Richard L. Berke, "Milestone for Gay Rights: March for Gay Rights; Washington Rally Puts Faces with Issues, but Probably Won't Create Rapid Change," *New York Times*, April 26, 1993.

99. "User Clip."

100. Berke, "Milestone for Gay Rights."

101. "Power and the Pride."

102. "Power and the Pride."

103. Debbie Blanzie to Kay Colpitts, January 27, 1994, box 21, DK-DU.

104. W. Graham Adams to Kay Colpitts, January 27, 1994, box 21, DK-DU; "Anita Bryant's Crusade," *New York Times*, June 7, 1977, https://www.nytimes.com/1977/06/07/archives/anita-bryants-crusade.html.

105. Charles D. Page to Susan Henry, Dan Kirsch, Don King, and Mike Larson, February 2, 1994, and Ken Garfield, "Rally Time Changed to Mollify Church," *Charlotte Observer*, February 2, 1994, box 21, DK-DU.

106. Morell, "Charlotte to Host N.C. Gay-Rights March."

107. Vinroot to Robert Barret, December 4, 1995, Richard Vinroot Papers, UNCC.

108. Rod M. Alexander to Kay Colpitts, February 1, 1994, box 21, DK-DU. Charlotte's city leaders often promoted the idea of obtaining "world class" status in the 1990s.

109. "Trust Your Desire," N.C. Pride mailer, box 21, DK-DU.

110. Handwritten note signed by Linda Carmichael, May 26, 1994, box 21, DK-DU.

111. Sheelagh M. Anderson to "To Whom It May Concern," July 9, 1994, box 21, DK-DU.

112. Ruth Derrow to "To Whom It May Concern," n.d., box 21, DK-DU.

113. Ken Garfield, "First Baptist Opposes June Gay Rights March to Park Near Church," *Charlotte Observer*, February 1, 1994; Don King, "Gay Parade Welcomes Bankers, Not Just Bikers," February 4, 1994, box 21, DK-DU.

114. Vance Cariaga, "Heavenly Powers," *Creative Loafing*, February 12, 1994, box 21, DK-DU.

115. N.C. Lesbian and Gay Pride, Inc., Charlotte Local Organizing Community, grant proposal to Fund for Southern Communities, 1993, box 21, DK-DU; Morell, "Charlotte to Host N.C. Gay-Rights March."

116. Dean Smith, "Charlotte's Quietly Gay Festival—OutCharlotte Kicks Off Today with a Family Album Exhibit," *Charlotte Observer*, October 2, 1998; Henry interview, Charlotte Queer Oral History Project.

117. Richard Vinroot to Charles Friar, October 16, 1995, Richard Vinroot Papers, UNCC. "OutCharlotte" was another short-lived attempt to organize a consistent gay happening in the Queen City.

118. "Population—Regional Reports"; U.S. Bureau of the Census, *1980 and 1990 Census Counts for Cities with 1990 Population Greater than 100,000*. In

this census report, Charlotte is ranked 35th—ahead of Atlanta's 36th place, with a population of 394,017.

119. Gay Jervey, "A Southern City Rolls Out Its Welcome," *New York Times*, August 28, 2005, http://www.nytimes.com/2005/08/28/realestate/28nati.html?pagewanted=all&_r=2&.

120. Timothy Roberts, "'A Vigil, a March and a Marriage'—Gay North Carolinians Congregate as Fundamentalists Fulminate," *Creative Loafing*, June 10, 1998, accessed March 8, 2012, http://www.ncpride.org/pride/library/articles/1998-Timothy-Roberts.pdf.

121. Roberts, "'Vigil, a March.'"

122. Lesley Brown, interview by author, May 1, 2003.

123. "Southern Discomfort," *Advocate*, March 17, 1998.

124. Timothy Roberts, "Activist to Close Gay Gathering Place," *Charlotte Observer*, December 14, 1997.

125. On the history of Malaprop's Bookstore, see B'Racz, "History of Malaprop's Bookstore/Café."

126. *Carolina Plain Dealer*, no. 10, Summer Solstice issue, JS-DU.

127. Mike Albo, "Gayest Cities in America," *Advocate*, February 2010, http://www.advocate.com/travel/2010/01/13/gayest-cities-america?page=full.

128. Albo, "Gayest Cities in America."

129. Eaves, "Outside Forces," 152.

130. Asheville white population = 79%; Black population = 19.8%, U.S. Bureau of the Census, *1990 Census of Population*, table 6, p. 27; Eaves, "Outside Forces," 154.

131. Gallo, *Different Daughters*, 24.

132. Hunter, *To 'Joy My Freedom*, 179.

133. Hunter, 186.

134. Ladd and Guthrie, *Statistics of the Presidential and Congressional Election of November 6, 1984*.

Chapter 5

1. *Atalanta*, March 1985, LGA-LHA.

2. *Atalanta*, February 1985, LGA-LHA; "AIDS and Politics."

3. Chief George Napper to Deputy Chief J. Hill, October 20, 1981, box 1, ES-EU. Reverend Piazza remains active in the Atlanta religious and gay communities. At the time of these events, Piazza was a pastor at the Metropolitan Community Church in Atlanta. Currently he pastors the Virginia Highland Church in Atlanta.

4. Napper to Hill, ES-EU.

5. "Atlanta Police March in Pride Parade," *Project Q Atlanta*, October 14, 2011, www.projectq.us/atlanta-police-march-in-pride-parade-photos/.

6. "ALFA: Where We've Been, Where We're Going," box 1, 94–040, administrative files, Atlanta Lesbian Feminist Alliance Archives, David M. Rubenstein Rare Book and Manuscript Library, Sallie Bingham Center for Women's History and Culture, Duke University, Durham.

7. "ALFA: Where We've Been."

8. "ALFA: Where We've Been."

9. Jan Suchomski, "Membership Survey Results," *Fourth Tuesday Forum*, February 1989, ALFA-DU. The survey was mailed to approximately 200 members, and this information is based on 51 responses.

10. *Fourth Tuesday Forum*, 1988 or 1989, ALFA-DU.

11. For more on Fourth Tuesday and its relationship to other lesbian groups in Atlanta, see Cragin, "Post-Lesbian-Feminism," 320–24.

12. *Fourth Tuesday Forum*, ALFA-DU; "Fourth Tuesday/The Heath Initiative." For more on the beginnings of Olivia Records, see chapter 3.

13. "Caucus Reports," *Fourth Tuesday Forum*, March 1989, ALFA-DU.

14. *Fourth Tuesday Forum*, ALFA-DU.

15. *Off Our Backs*, April 1989.

16. *Off Our Backs*, May 1989.

17. Sharon, Elliott, and Latham, "Conference Issue," 18.

18. Ronald Smothers, "3,000 Lesbians Meet in Atlanta to Set Own Agenda," *New York Times*, April 28, 1991, http://www.nytimes.com/1991/04/28/us /3000-lesbians-meet-in-atlanta-to-set-own-agenda.html; Sharon, Elliott, and Latham, "Conference Issue."

19. Sharon, Elliott, and Latham, "Conference Issue."

20. Smothers, "3,000 Lesbians Meet in Atlanta to Set Own Agenda"; Sharon, Elliott, and Latham, "Conference Issue."

21. Sharon, Elliott, and Latham, "Conference Issue," 19.

22. AALGA—Notes, Carolyn Mobley Papers, box 2, folder 12, Auburn Avenue Research Library, Atlanta.

23. The AALGA looked to Alma Hill at the *Atlanta Journal-Constitution* as its media committee contact, recognizing the importance of combating negative reporting on both Black and queer as separate and potentially unified identities.

24. On the point of Atlanta as a mecca, see Hobson, *Black Mecca*. AALGA— Notes, Carolyn Mobley Papers, box 2, folder 13.

25. "National Black Gay and Lesbian Leadership Forum: A Conference Report," *Off Our Backs*, April 1990.

26. "National Black Gay and Lesbian Leadership Forum."

27. "National Black Gay and Lesbian Leadership Forum."

28. AALGA—Notes, Carolyn Mobley Papers, December 1988.

29. 1989 AALGA Minutes, Auburn Avenue Research Library, Atlanta.

30. For more on Garner, see her obituary, "Joan Garner, 65: LGBT, Civic Activist Put Passions in Public Service," *Atlanta Journal-Constitution*, April 25, 2017. Also see C. Stephens, "Maynard Jackson and the Black Gay Mecca," 34.

31. AALGA, *Crossroads*, April 1987, Carolyn Mobley Papers.

32. Crenshaw, "Demarginalizing the Intersection of Race and Sex." Crenshaw does note in footnote 59 on pages 161–62 that race is the leading identity in self-definition for Black women, just as "lesbian" is a leading identity marker for women who are "open" and willing to define themselves against the other of heterosexuality.

33. Crenshaw, 154.

34. Somerville, *Queering the Color Line.*

35. AALGA—Notes, Carolyn Mobley Papers, 1988, box 1, folder 3.

36. E. Johnson, *Black. Queer. Southern. Women,* 166.

37. ZAMI flyer, Series XI: Leaflets, 98–008, Auburn Avenue Research Library, Atlanta.

38. AALGA—Notes, Carolyn Mobley Papers, 1987.

39. E. Johnson, *Black. Queer. Southern. Women,* 16, 165–67.

40. Laura Apperson, "A Night of Fierce Drag," *Signal* (George State University), March 20, 2012, http://www.gsusignal.com/a-night-of-fierce-drag-1.2717584# .T56mQtnCaSo.

41. "Georgia State University History."

42. Coretta Scott King was outspoken in her support of gay rights during the final decades of the twentieth century. See, for example, Stewart-Winter, *Queer Clout,* 215–17; and "Coretta Scott King Memorial."

43. "Lesbian/Gay Groups Cheered, Jeered at MLK Parade," *Etc.,* box 1, ES-EU.

44. *Crossroads,* January 1989, ALFA-DU.

45. Laura Douglas-Brown, "Emory University Celebrates 20 Years of LGBT Activism, Inclusion," *Georgia Voice,* March 3, 2012, http://www.thegavoice.com /news/atlanta-news/4271-emory-university-celebrates-20-years-of-lgbt -activism-inclusion.

46. Arrested while protesting Georgia's sodomy laws with ACT UP at the state capitol, Lowe also protested at the Centers for Disease Control in Atlanta and aggressively disrupted a CNN news studio as part of ACT UP. For more on this, see "AIDS Protestors Disrupt Studio," *Lawrence (KS) Journal-World,* July 27, 1991. Lowe's papers are archived at Manuscript, Archives, and Rare Book Library, EU.

47. "Emory Seeks Director for Gay-Life Office," *Atlanta Journal-Constitution,* August 3, 1992, box 3, ES-EU.

48. "Gay Students Demanding Equality on College Campuses," *U. The National College Newspaper,* April 1990, box 3, ES-EU.

49. Urquhart, "LGBT Leader Linked." Chesnut conducted an oral history of Charis Books and More and coauthored the article "'Women Ran It,'" referenced in chapter 4 of this manuscript.

50. "Gay Students Demanding Equality on College Campuses."

51. *Lambda: The Newsletter of the Carolina Gay Association,* November 1977, and March–April 1977, Lee Mullis Papers, box 42, *FP*-DU.

52. Concetta Hinceman, conversation with author, June 12, 2012; "About Queens." There are some online indications of LGBT student groups, but no currently active group was visible or supported by the Office of Diversity and Inclusion at Queens in 2012.

53. The Multicultural Resource Center was founded at UNC Charlotte in 1996; see "History."

54. For more on Perry's activism, see E. Johnson, "Southern (Dis)comfort."

55. For more on the relationship between the Charlotte Women's Center and *The Road,* see chapter 3.

56. "Inter-Collegiate Party" flyer, November 17, 1990, box 3, ES-EU.

57. As noted in the last chapter, this separation would prove problematic during Charlotte's first Pride celebration held on campus in 1981—ten miles away from one of the host bars. On the history of UNC Charlotte, see "University History"; and Sanford, *Charlotte and UNC Charlotte.*

58. Lassiter, "Searching for Respect," 39. To address this issue, and to better connect with the business community in uptown Charlotte, a "center city" satellite campus opened in 2011.

59. Urquhart and Craddock, "Private Cures," 279.

60. Urquhart and Craddock, 279.

61. "Sponsorships."

62. Murphy, "Gay Was Good," 313.

63. Murphy, 313. Murphy offers a useful discussion on the corporate growth of Pride and the direct link between an emerging visible gay culture and capitalism. In addition to Murphy's analysis, see D'Emilio, *Sexual Politics,* 11–13; and D'Emilio and Freedman, *Intimate Matters,* 226–29. There is a large literature linking capitalism and LGBTQ history. See, for example, Joseph, *Against the Romance of Community*; Walters, *All the Rage*; Jacobsen and Zeller, *Queer Economics*; Gluckman and Reed, *Homo Economics*; A. Sears, "Queer Anticapitalism"; Drucker, *Warped*; Maynard, "'Without Working?'"; Vider, "Consumerism"; Chasin, *Selling Out*; Duggan, "New Homonormativity."; N. Boyd, "Sex and Tourism"; Enke, *Finding the Movement*; and Howard, *Men Like That.*

64. Ted Mellnik, "Hotel Pressured to Block Meeting of Parents of Gays," *Charlotte Observer,* July 2, 1991. See chapter 4 for more on the Citizens for Decent Atlanta.

65. Goldfield, *Still Fighting the Civil War,* 8.

66. Robert Trigaux, "A Tale of Two Cities: Style vs. Down Home," *St. Petersburg (FL) Times,* April 26, 1998.

67. Yockey, *McColl,* 576.

68. Teresa Burney, "NationsBank Offers Benefits to Wider Family," *St. Petersburg Times,* April 17, 1998.

69. Ebeling, "Married or Not, Gays Gain Partner Coverage."

70. Applebome, *Dixie Rising,* 154.

71. Yockey, *McColl,* 6.

72. Yockey, 159–61, 165, 169.

73. Cobb, *Industrialization and Southern Society,* 112.

74. Goldfield, "Place to Come To," 15. Atlanta also took a business-first approach to desegregation prior to the Civil Rights Act. See, for example, Goldfield, *Black, White, and Southern,* 133.

75. See, for example, Bickley, "Southern Discomfort"; and Willa J. Conrad and Jim Morrill, "One Option: Zero Public Money for Arts," *Charlotte Observer,* April 3, 1997.

76. Jeff Gammage, "Furor Grips Charlotte as Five Commissioners Target Gay Life," *Philadelphia Inquirer,* June 23, 1997.

77. Randall Bloomquist, "A 'Most Livable' City—as Long as Your Art Passes Muster," *Washington Post,* February 15, 1998.

78. Bloomquist, "'Most Livable' City."

79. Bloomquist, "'Most Livable' City."

80. "Charlotte Area Largest Employers."

81. Dean Smith, "A Powerful Banker's Other Hat," *New York Times*, May 21, 2000.

82. Venable, "Hottest Metro Areas for Facility Investments"; "Atlanta," Columbia Fun Maps, LGA-LHA.

83. "Full Text of Eric Rudolph's Confession."

84. "Another Atlanta Bomb Raises Fear of Terrorist," *St. Petersburg Times*, February 23, 1997.

85. Andrew Jacobs, "For Bomb Victims, a Sense of Relief after Years of Anxiety," *New York Times*, June 1, 2003.

86. "State Employment Laws and Policies Map."

87. Max Pizarro, "New Hate-Crimes Bill Introduced," *Creative Loafing* (Atlanta), February 28, 2007.

88. Patrick McCrary to Don Mixon, March 31, 1985, box 3, ES-EU.

89. Human Rights Campaign Corporate Equality Index, accessed May 2020, https://www.hrc.org/campaigns/corporate-equality-index?_ga=2.155035832 .188652452.1589752541-768791487.1589752541.

90. This concept of an "imagined community" is drawn from Benedict Anderson's definition suggesting that "the members of even the smallest nation will never know most of their fellow-members, meet them, or even hear of them, yet in the minds of each lives the image of their communion." Anderson, *Imagined Communities*, 6.

91. "Atlanta Companies Falter in Ranking of LGBT Love"; "More Companies Offering Same-Sex-Partner Benefits," *New York Times*, September 26, 2000, http://www.nytimes.com/2000/09/26/business/more-companies-offering -same-sex-partner-benefits.html.

92. Applebome, *Dixie Rising*, 151.

93. On McColl's involvement in the arrival of the NBA and the NFL in Charlotte, see Yockey, *McColl*, 466–82.

94. Organized in 1992 and operating as part of the Carolinas LGBT+ Chamber of Commerce in 2022, the Charlotte Business Guild focuses on the success of LGBT business professionals in the region: Charlotte Business Guild, "About Us & History." On the issue of team sponsorship, see "LGBT Business Guilds in the Carolinas Going Strong," *Q-Notes*, February 25, 2005.

95. Dolance, "'Whole Stadium Full,'" 81.

96. Mike Cranston, "WNBA Franchise Charlotte Sting Folds," *Washington Post*, January 3, 2007, http://www.washingtonpost.com/wp-dyn/content/article /2007/01/03/AR2007010301203.html.

97. U.S. Bureau of the Census, *Florida Quick Links*; Chris Baker, "A Look at Expansion in the NBA: $32.5-Million Price Tag Doesn't Scare Off Prospective Buyers," *Los Angeles Times*, April 19, 1987, www.latimes.com/archives/la-xpm -1987-04-19-sp-2064-story.html.

98. "Hornets History." On the history of the NBA in Charlotte and a recent resurgence of interest in the now defunct Charlotte Hornets name and merchandise, see Andrew Dunn, "Charlotte Hornets Gear Is Back," *Charlotte Observer*,

April 24, 2012, http://www.charlotteobserver.com/2012/04/24/3192963/charlotte
-hornets-gear-is-back.html.

99. Atlanta has not been able to keep a professional hockey team, having lost both the Flames and most recently the Thrashers.

100. Lassiter, "Searching for Respect," 24.

101. "News Reports from the Christians on the Streets of Charlotte."

102. Pat McCrory to Sandra Shoemaker, February 25, 2005, box 13, Gay Pride folder, Pat McCrory Papers, UNCC.

103. Gaillard, *With Music and Justice for All*, 97.

104. Quoted in Gaillard, 97–98.

105. Ownby, "Evangelical but Differentiated," 44–45.

106. Ownby, 46, 60.

107. "Metro-Area Membership Report."

108. Gates, "Geographic Trends among Same-Sex Couples"; Gates et al., "Census Snapshot: Georgia" and "Census Snapshot: North Carolina." In Fulton County, same-sex couples represented 1.08 percent of county households, while Mecklenburg County gay couples represented only 0.65 percent of county households.

109. Charlotte's UNC branch campus was established in 1946; East Carolina University was founded in 1907.

110. Caiazza and Shaw, "Status of Women in North Carolina."

111. Hartmann et al., "Best and Worst State Economies."

112. Caiazza and Shaw, "Status of Women in Georgia."

113. Hartmann et al., "Best and Worst State Economies."

114. Hartmann et al., "Best and Worst State Economies."

115. U.S. Bureau of Labor Statistics, "May 2011 Metropolitan and Nonmetropolitan Area," Occupational Statistics: Atlanta, and "May 2011 Metropolitan and Nonmetropolitan Area," Occupational Statistics: Charlotte.

116. U.S. Bureau of Labor Statistics, "May 2011 Metropolitan and Nonmetropolitan Area," Occupational Statistics: Atlanta and Charlotte. According to this 2011 data, patrol officers in metro Charlotte earn an average salary of $46,760 compared with their counterparts in Atlanta at $44,450.

117. Christina Cougill, personal Facebook message to author, May 15, 2012.

118. Ordoñez, "Six Volunteer CMPD Police Chaplains"; "Charlotte Chaplains Resign Over Gay Clergy Member."

119. "Make Charlotte Weird: Richard Florida Takes Message to the Masses," *Creative Loafing*, April 30–May 6, 2003.

120. Cobb, *South and America since World War II*, 370–71.

121. Gates and Florida, "Technology and Tolerance."

Epilogue

1. Campbell Robertson, "In North Carolina, Beliefs Clash on Marriage Law," *New York Times*, May 11, 2012, http://www.nytimes.com/2012/05/12/us /in-north-carolina-gay-rights-not-a-simple-issue.html?pagewanted=all.

2. Bowers, "President Barack Obama's Shifting Stance."

3. Polling numbers from 2012 to 2015 demonstrate this increasing support, with a majority in support of marriage equality in both Georgia (2013) and North Carolina (2014). "Polling Tracks Growing and Increasingly Diverse Support for the Freedom to Marry."

4. Mecklenburg County Board of Elections, "Official Results"; Summers, "Amendment One"; "Interactive Results Map"; Lynne Bonner and Jay Price, "N.C. to Add Marriage Amendment to Its Constitution," *News and Observer* (Raleigh), May 9, 2012.

5. "Video: Gantt, Vinroot Speak Out against Amendment One," *Charlotte Observer*, April 10, 2012. Unlike Graham's advertised support for the amendment, the Vinroot/Gantt video did not appear on television, instead gaining only online traction.

6. "Our View: The Missing Voice in Gay Marriage Debate," *Charlotte Observer*, September 10, 2011.

7. "Mayor Anthony Foxx Speaks Out against Amendment One." Foxx's declaration at the Human Rights Campaign Gala was significant, given Mayor Pat McCrory's refusal to acknowledge or formally welcome the event in previous years.

8. Xenotype, "Hornet's Nest"; Michael Gordon, "Amendment One: NC Voters Approve Measure to Block Same-Sex Marriage," *Charlotte Observer*, May 9, 2012.

9. Gordon, "Amendment One." On the Black church and Amendment One, see Eaves, "Outside Forces," 155. On the Black church and same-sex marriage, see Stewart-Winter, *Queer Clout*, 214.

10. Andrew Jacobs, "Black Legislators Stall Marriage Amendment in Georgia," *New York Times*, March 3, 2004.

11. Elevation Church, "History: Where We've Been, Where We're Going." ElevationChurch.org, accessed July 1, 2012, http://www.elevationchurch.org /history. This information on church history was removed by April 30, 2022; "Top 5 Largest and Fastest-Growing Churches in America."

12. Graf and Rumsey, "Gay Marriage Amendment"; Matt Comer, "Disgraced Pastor Ted Haggard and Wife Speak at Popular Charlotte Church," *Q-Notes*, May 2, 2009, http://goqnotes.com/2333/ted-haggard-to-speak-at-charlotte-church /; Matt Comer, "Concerns Raised as Anti-gay Elevation Church Makes Inroads at Local Schools," *Q-Notes*, December 21, 2012, https://qnotescarolinas.com /concerns-raised-as-anti-gay-elevation-church-makes-inroads-at-local -schools/.

13. See, for example, Stiffler, "Gay Nightlife's Identity Crisis"; Weinstein, "Gay Bars, Gay History"; and G. Williams, "Ten Businesses Facing Extinction in 10 Years."

14. "2008 Best of the Best."

15. "Obama Endorses Same-Sex Marriage, Taking Stand on Charged Social Issue," *New York Times*, May 10, 2012.

16. Jill Phillips, conversation with author, March 22, 2015. Phillips owned and managed the bar with her partner, Bethany McDonald.

17. Atlanta's 2011 metro population reached 5.3 million, in comparison with metro Charlotte's 1.8 million.

18. Laura Douglas-Brown, "Why Can't Atlanta Sustain Lesbian Bars?," *Georgia Voice*, January 12, 2012, http://www.thegavoice.com/blog/culture /4014-why-cant-atlanta-sustain-lesbian-bars. The full quote is instructive here:

> The Census doesn't count lesbians and gay men, although same-sex couples can be counted (by looking at the sex of the partners who mark that they live with a "spouse" or "unmarried" partner). The 2010 Census counted 15,271 female couples and 14,573 male couples in Georgia. Nationally, 332,887 female couples and 313,587 male couples were tallied. Even if you assume that lesbians may be more likely to be in couples than gay men, meaning there are more single gay men to add to the totals than single lesbians, it's unlikely that gay men outnumber lesbians by the same ratio that gay bars currently outnumber lesbian bars in Atlanta, which is roughly 24 to 1.

19. On this point see Gieseking, "Last Lesbian Bar."

20. Gieseking, "Last Lesbian Bar."

21. Geoff Williams, "Gay and Lesbian Friendly Neighborhoods in the South," *Front Door*, November 3, 2010, accessed July 1, 2012, http://www.frontdoor .com/buy/gay-and-lesbian-friendly-neighborhoods-in-the-south/56062/p6 (site discontinued). In this list of six notable gayborhoods in the South, Atlanta's East Lake neighborhood, just outside of gay-friendly Decatur, made the cut, along with Houston, Memphis, and Carrboro, North Carolina, only a mile away from the equally gay-friendly Chapel Hill, where voters handily defeated Amendment One.

22. The Latino population in Mecklenburg County has skyrocketed since 1990, when Latinos were 1.3 percent (6,693) of the county's population; by 2005 they represented 9.2 percent (71,904) of that population. Weeks, Weeks, and Weeks, "Latino Immigration in the U.S. South," 51; Hanchett, "Salad-Bowl Suburbs," 255. According to Hanchett, a Brookings Institution report ranked Charlotte as the second fastest-growing Latino city in the United States during 2000–5. Hanchett also notes that Mexicans were the largest immigrant group and Vietnamese second.

23. Kristen Kornbluth, "Hattie's Tap & Tavern Is a Charlotte Fixture That Welcomes All—If You're Not a Jerk," *Charlotte Observer*, July 13, 2021, https:// www.charlotteobserver.com/charlottefive/c5-food-drink/article252511718 .html#storylink=cpy.

24. Dyana Bagby, "Should Atlanta Spend Millions on an LGBT Community Center?," *Georgia Voice*, April 30, 2010, http://www.thegavoice.com/index.php /news/atlanta-news/262-should-atlanta-spend-millions-on-an-lgbt-community -center?showall=1.

25. Badenhausen, "Best Places for Business and Careers."

26. Sue Henry, telephone conversation with author, February 17, 2015.

27. Max Blau, "City Expands Non-discrimination Laws to Include 'Gen-der Identity,'" *Creative Loafing* (Atlanta), July 16, 2013, https://creativeloafing .com/content-217218-City-expands-non-discrimination-laws-to-include-'gender -identity'.

28. Ely Portillo and Mark Price, "Charlotte LGBT Ordinance Fails 6–5 in Contentious Meeting," *Charlotte Observer*, March 2, 2015, http://www .charlotteobserver.com/news/local/article11908907.html.

29. 1992 activist publication, *Resist Newsletter*, Lesbian Herstory Archives, Brooklyn.

30. Dana Milbank, "One Governor's Defeat Could Be a Watershed Moment for Gay Rights," *Washington Post*, October 7, 2016, https://www.washingtonpost .com/opinions/one-governors-defeat-could-be-a-watershed-moment-for -gay-rights/2016/10/07/fec4250e-8ca3-11e6-bff0-d53f592f176e_story .html?utm_term=.629b02256b82.

31. David A. Grahm, "North Carolina's Nearly Meaningless Executive Order on Discrimination," *Atlantic*, April 12, 2016, https://www.theatlantic.com /politics/archive/2016/04/pat-mccrory-north-carolina-hb2/477936/.

32. Bostock v. Clayton County, Georgia, decided June 15, 2020, https://www .supremecourt.gov/opinions/19pdf/17–1618_hfci.pdf.

33. The Charlotte Business Guild became known as the Charlotte LGBT Chamber of Commerce in 2015, Carolinas LGBT+ Chamber of Commerce, "Our Story," https://www.clgbtcc.org/our-story/.

Positionality Statement

1. As John Howard noted in his 1997 introduction to *Carryin' On in the Lesbian and Gay South*, Black scholars often have "better access" to materials on Black subjects for "complex reasons." Howard, *Carryin' On*, 11n10.

2. Jennifer D. Jones's manuscript in progress is titled "Queering an American Dilemma: Sexuality, Gender and the Politics of Discretion." E. Johnson, *Black. Queer. Southern. Women* and *Honeypot*.

3. E. Patrick Johnson, telephone conversation with author, August 10, 2017. On the "skeptic's copout," see E. Johnson, *Black. Queer. Southern. Women*, 13.

4. I am particularly grateful for helpful comments from the attendees at the University of Kansas's Gender Symposium, where I discussed this issue in a presentation titled "Race-ing Queer: Balancing Race and Labeling in Queer Histories," December 2, 2021.

5. E. Johnson, *Black. Queer. Southern. Women*.

BIBLIOGRAPHY

Primary Sources

ORAL HISTORIES CONDUCTED BY AUTHOR
Lesley Brown
Joe Campos
Dawn (Niki) Heard
Sarrah Kelly
Kate Mullen
Katherine Stephenson

LIBRARIES, ARCHIVES, AND COLLECTIONS
Athens, GA
    University of Georgia Hargrett Rare Book and Manuscript Library
        Georgia Room
            Atlanta City Directory
Atlanta, GA
    Atlanta History Center, Kenan Research Center
        Atlanta Lesbian and Gay History Thing Collection
        Atlanta's Unspoken Past Oral History Project
            Ginny Boyd
            Scotti Hooper
            Billy Jones
            Ann McKain
            Charlene McLemore
            Nell Stansell
            Jack Strouss Jr.
            Barbara Vogel
        Lesbian, Gay, Bisexual, and Transgender Serial Collection
        Maria Helena Dolan Collection
        Billy Jones Papers
    Auburn Avenue Research Library
        African American Lesbian and Gay Print Culture Collection
        Carolyn Mobley Papers
    Stuart A. Rose Manuscript, Archives, and Rare Book Library, Emory University
        Black and White Men Together, Atlanta Records
        Carson McCullers Collection
        David A. Lowe Papers
        Ed W. Stansell Papers
        Mary E. Hutchinson and Dorothy King Papers
        Network Q Records
        Southeastern Arts, Media, and Education Project Records, 1984–1996

Brooklyn, NY
    Lesbian Herstory Archives, Brooklyn
        Geographic Files, Lesbians in GA
        Geographic Files, Lesbians in NC
Chapel Hill, NC
    Louis Round Wilson Special Collections Library, University of North
          Carolina at Chapel Hill
        Southern Historical Collection
           Southern Oral History Program Collection
Charlotte, NC
    J. Murrey Atkins Library, Special Collections, University of North Carolina
          at Charlotte
        Alternative Press Collection
        Charlotte Queer Oral History Project
           Sue Henry
           Lynnsy Logue
           Samis Rose
        Harvey B. Gantt Papers
        King-Henry-Brockington LGBTQ Archive
        Pat McCrory Papers
        Richard Vinroot Papers
    Charlotte Mecklenburg Library, Robinson-Spangler Carolina Room
Durham, NC
    David M. Rubenstein Rare Book and Manuscript Library, Sallie Bingham
          Center for Women's History and Culture, Duke University
        Atlanta Lesbian Feminist Alliance Archives, 1972–1994
        Atlanta Lesbian Feminist Alliance Periodicals Collection, 1962–1994
        Catherine Nicholson Papers
        Charis Books and More and Charis Circle Records
        Dan Kirsch Papers
        Front Page Records
        James T. Sears Papers, 1918–2011 and undated
        Minnie Bruce Pratt Papers
Hattiesburg, MS
    University of Southern Mississippi, Center for Oral History and Cultural
          Heritage
        Gay and Lesbian Life

MAGAZINES

Advocate	*Ms. Magazine*
Atlantic	*Newsweek*
Charlotte	*New Yorker*
Charlotte Food and Wine	*Off Our Backs*
Entrepreneur	*Site Selection*
Forbes	*Smithsonian Magazine*
Garden and Gun	*Time*

NEWSPAPERS AND OTHER PUBLICATIONS

Atlanta Daily World
Atlanta Journal-Constitution
Charlotte Free Press
Charlotte News
Charlotte Observer
Creative Loafing (Atlanta and Charlotte)
Front Page (Raleigh)
Gaze (Memphis)
Georgia Voice
Great Speckled Bird (Atlanta)
Lavender Woman (Chicago)
Lawrence (KS) Journal-World

Lesbian Voices (San Jose, CA)
Los Angeles Times
Marietta (GA) Daily Journal
News and Observer (Raleigh)
New York Times
Philadelphia Inquirer
Q-Notes (Charlotte)
Signal (Georgia State University)
Spartanburg (SC) Herald-Journal
St. Petersburg (FL) Times
Washington Post
Workers World

INTERNET RESOURCES

"2008 Best of the Best." *Charlotte*, May 2008. http://www.charlottemagazine
.com/Charlotte-Magazine/May-2008/Sports-Bars/.

"About Queens." Student Programs, Office of Diversity and Inclusion. Accessed
March 22, 2015. http://www.queens.edu/About-Queens/Office-of
-Diversity-and-Inclusion/Student-Programs.html.

"AIDS and Politics—1980 to 1989." OutHistory.org, under "Photograph,
Tower Lounge staff." Accessed May 10, 2012. http://outhistory.org/wiki
/AIDS_and_Politics_-_1980_to_1989.

Albo, Mike. "Gayest Cities in America." *Advocate*, January 13, 2010.
http://www.advocate.com/travel/2010/01/13/gayest-cities-america?page
=full.

Andrews, Nancy. "The Digging Dykes of Decatur, 1993." The Corcoran
Collection, National Gallery of Art. Accessed February 7, 2022. https://www
.nga.gov/collection/art-object-page.170375.html.

"Ansley Square Mall/Cheshire Bridge." Atlanta Convention and Visitors Bureau.
Accessed April 11, 2012. http://www.gay-atlanta.com/ansley_cheshire.aspx.

"Atlanta Companies Falter in Ranking of LGBT Love." *Project Q Atlanta*.
December 8, 2011. https://www.projectq.us/atlanta_companies_falter
_in_ranking_of_their_lgbt_love.

The Atlanta Gay and Lesbian Chamber of Commerce. "History of the AGLCC."
Accessed April 29, 2022. http://www.atlantagaychamber.org.

"Available City Population Data." Population of the 100 Largest Urban Places:
1980. U.S. Bureau of the Census. Internet Release Date, June 15, 1998,
http://physics.bu.edu/~redner/projects/population/cities/1980.txt.

Badenhausen, Kurt. "The Best Places for Business and Careers." *Forbes*, June
27, 2012. http://www.forbes.com/sites/kurtbadenhausen/2012/06/27
/the-best-places-for-business/.

Bowers, Becky. "President Barack Obama's Shifting Stance on Gay Marriage."
PolitiFact, May 11, 2012. https://www.politifact.com/factchecks/2012
/may/11/barack-obama/president-barack-obamas-shift-gay-marriage/.

B'Racz, Emoke. "A History of Malaprop's Bookstore/Café." Malaprop's Bookstore /Café, Inc. Accessed April 17, 2012. http://www.malaprops.com/about-us.

"A Brief History." The FBI Charlotte Division. Accessed January 17, 2015. http://www.fbi.gov/charlotte/about-us/history.

Brock, Emilia, and Virginia Prescott. "South of Stonewall: The Atlanta Police Raid That Sparked Georgia Gay Liberation." Georgia Public Broadcasting, June 28, 2019. http://www.gpbnews.orgwww.gpbnews.org/post /south-stonewall-atlanta-police-raid-sparked-georgia-gay-liberation.

"Buckhead-Atlanta." Atlanta Convention and Visitors Bureau. Accessed June 15, 2012. http://www.atlanta.net/buckhead/.

"Buckhead, Georgia." Atlanta.com, LLC. Accessed June 15, 2012. http://www .atlanta.com/neighborhoods/buckhead.aspx.

Caiazza, Amy, and April Shaw. "The Status of Women in Georgia, 2004: Highlights." Institute for Women's Policy Research, R311, November 2004. Accessed July 1, 2012. http://www.iwpr.org/publications/pubs /the-status-of-women-in-georgia-2004-highlights.

———. "The Status of Women in North Carolina, 2004: Highlights." Institute for Women's Policy Research, R325, November 2004. Accessed July 1, 2012. http://www.iwpr.org/publications/pubs /the-status-of-women-in-north-carolina-2004-highlights.

Cannick, Jasmyne. "Celebrating Black Gay Pride." *News and Notes*, National Public Radio, June 9, 2005. https://www.npr.org/templates/story/story .php?storyId=4696068.

Carolinas LGBT+ Chamber of Commerce. "Our Story." Accessed February 7, 2022. https://www.clgbtcc.org/our-story/.

"Charlotte Area Largest Employers." Charlotte Chamber of Commerce. Accessed April 30, 2012. http://charlottechamber.com/clientuploads/Economic_pdfs /LargestEmployers.pdf.

Charlotte Business Guild. "About Us & History." Accessed February 8, 2015. http://cltbusinessguild.org/about-us-and-history/.

"Charlotte Chaplains Resign over Gay Clergy Member." *Advocate*, November 7, 2010. http://www.advocate.com/news/daily-news/2010/11/07 /charlotte-chaplains-resign-over-gay-clergy-member.

Chenault, Wesley. "Atlanta since Stonewall, 1969–2009." OutHistory .org. Accessed February 9, 2022. http://outhistory.org/exhibits/show /atlanta-since-stonewall/out_in_atlanta.

Chu, Louise. "Conflict Slows Revival Of Historic Black Area Of Atlanta Sweet Auburn, Famous As Martin Luther King Jr.'s Birthplace, Was A Thriving Black Business Community During Segregation." *Greensboro News & Record*, July 17, 2004, Updated Jan 26, 2015. https://greensboro.com/conflict -slows-revival-of-historic-black-area-of-atlanta-sweet-auburn-famous-as -martin-luther/article_0746d9ad-3c1a-52c0-8b0c-fb5c4be299fa.html.

"Coretta Scott King Memorial: Remarks Delivered by Lambda Legal Executive Director Kevin Cathcart, February 23, 2006." Lambda Legal. Accessed May 20, 2020. https://www.lambdalegal.org/news/ny_2006022.

Dolan, Maria Helena. "You Can't Be a People Unless You Have a History." The Body, October 1, 2004. https://www.thebody.com/article/cant-people-unless-history.

Ebeling, Ashlea. "Married or Not, Gays Gain Partner Coverage." *Forbes*, April 4, 2004. http://www.forbes.com/2004/04/07/cz_ae_0407beltway.html.

Ellis, Ralph. "Avondale One of 'Gayest Zip Codes' in U.S." Patch.com, June 20, 2012. https://patch.com/georgia/decatur/avondale-9th-gayest-zip-code-in-u-s.

Ferguson, Moira. "The History of Women's Studies at UNL: Twenty Years Later: 1976–1996." University of Nebraska, Lincoln. Accessed January 23, 2022. http://www.unl.edu/womenssp/about/history.shtml.

"Fourth Tuesday/The Heath Initiative." Accessed May 5, 2012. http://thehealthinitiative.org/programs-resources/programming/fourth-tuesday/ (site discontinued).

"Full Text of Eric Rudolph's Confession." National Public Radio, April 14, 2005. http://www.npr.org/templates/story/story.php?storyId=4600480.

Galloway, Jim. "Charlotte Who? Mayor Kasim Reed Says Atlanta Still on Top." *Political Insider with Jim Galloway* (blog), March 17, 2010. Accessed June 15, 2012. http://blogs.ajc.com/political-insider-jim-galloway/2010/03/17/charlotte-who-mayor-kasim-reed-says-atlanta-still-on-top/ (site discontinued).

Gates, Gary J. "Geographic Trends among Same-Sex Couples in the U.S. Census and the American Community Survey." Williams Institute, November 2007. Accessed July 1, 2012. http://williamsinstitute.law.ucla.edu/wp-content/uploads/Gates-Geographic-Trends-ACS-Brief-Nov-2007.pdf.

Gates, Gary J., et al. "Census Snapshot: Georgia." Williams Institute, January 2008. Accessed July 1, 2002. http://williamsinstitute.law.ucla.edu/wp-content/uploads/GeorgiaCensus2000Snapshot.pdf.

———. "Census Snapshot: North Carolina." Williams Institute, June 2008. Accessed July 1, 2012. http://williamsinstitute.law.ucla.edu/wp-content/uploads/NorthCarolinaCensus2000Snapshot.pdf.

Gates, Gary and Richard Florida. "Technology and Tolerance: The Importance of Diversity to High Technology Growth." Brookings Institution, June 1, 2001. http://www.brookings.edu/research/reports/2001/06/technology-florida.

"Gay and Lesbian March on Washington." C-SPAN, April 25, 1993. https://www.c-span.org/video/?40062-1/gay-lesbian-march-washington.

"Georgia State University History." Georgia State University Library. Accessed April 18, 2012. http://www.library.gsu.edu/spcoll/pages/pages.asp?ldID=105&guideID=549&ID=3670.

Graf, Scott, and Mark Rumsey. "Gay Marriage Amendment Focus of Forum." WFAE, March 29, 2012. www.wfae.org/local-news/2012-03-29/gay-marriage-amendment-focus-of-forum.

Glock, Allison. "Southern Women." *Garden and Gun*, August/September 2011, under "A New Generation of Women Who Are Redefining the Southern Belle." http://gardenandgun.com/article/southern-women.

Hartmann, Heidi, et al. "The Best and Worst State Economies for Women." Institute for Women's Policy Research, R334, November 30, 2006. https://iwpr.org/iwpr-general/the-best-and-worst-state-economies-for-women-2/.

"History." Office of Identity, Equity, and Engagement, UNC Charlotte. Accessed May 1, 2020. https://identity.uncc.edu/about/history.

"Hornets History." National Basketball Association. Accessed May 1, 2012. http://www.nba.com/hornets/history/history_hornets.html.

"Interactive Results Map." WRAL, Capitol Broadcasting Company, Inc. Accessed July 1, 2012. http://www.wral.com/news/political/page/10991843/.

"Inventory of the Atlanta Lesbian Feminist Alliance Periodicals Collection, 1962–1994." Duke University Libraries. Accessed June 20, 2012. http://library.duke.edu/rubenstein/findingaids/alfaperiodicals/.

Ladd, Thomas E., and Benjamin J. Guthrie, eds. *Statistics of the Presidential and Congressional Election of November 6, 1984.* Washington, DC: Government Printing Office, 1985. http://clerk.house.gov/member_info/electionInfo/1984election.pdf.

Levs, Joshua. "Black Gays and Lesbians, at Home in Atlanta." *News and Notes,* National Public Radio, October 7, 2005. https://www.npr.org/templates/story/story.php?storyId=4949165.

Martin, Edward. "Wesley Heights' Decline Halted with New Interest." *Charlotte Business Journal,* March 13, 2000. http://www.bizjournals.com/charlotte/stories/2000/03/13/focus3.html?page=all.

"Mayor Anthony Foxx Speaks Out against Amendment One." CBS Charlotte, April 25, 2012. Accessed July 1, 2012. http://charlotte.cbslocal.com/2012/04/25/mayor-anthony-foxx-speaks-out-against-amendment-one/ (site discontinued).

Mecklenburg County Board of Elections. "Official Results, Primary Election, May 8, 2012." Accessed July 1, 2012. http://results.enr.clarityelections.com/NC/Mecklenburg/36656/85644/en/vts.html?cid=0141 (site discontinued).

"Metro-Area Membership Report: Religious Traditions, 2010." Association of Religious Data Archives. Accessed July 1, 2012. http://www.thearda.com/rcms2010/r/m/12060/rcms2010_12060_metro_family_2010.asp, and http://www.thearda.com/rcms2010/r/m/16740/rcms2010_16740_metro_family_2010.asp.

"Midtown Alliance: Share the Vision." The Midtown Alliance. Accessed March 26, 2012. http://www.midtownalliance.org/.

"Midtown Local Historic District." Midtown Neighbors' Association, Historic Preservation Committee. Accessed March 26, 2012. http://preservemidtownatlanta.org/AboutUs.html.

"News from the Sisterland." *Lavender Woman* 4, no. 4 (1975): 14. Archives of Sexuality and Gender, https://link-gale-com.ezproxy.mtsu.edu/apps/doc/XQKBYF650059367/AHSI?u=tel_middleten&sid=bookmark-AHSI&xid=8379e70b.

"News Reports from the Christians on the Streets of Charlotte." Operation Save America. Accessed June 20, 2012. http://www.operationsaveamerica.org /streets/nc/index-charlotte.htm.html.

Ordoñez, Franco. "Six Volunteer CMPD Police Chaplains Resign Their Posts." WCNC-TV, November 6, 2010. https://www.wcnc.com/article/news/local /six-volunteer-cmpd-police-chaplains-resign-their-posts/275-374197854.

"Our Purpose, Mission and Vision." Southern Fried Queer Pride. Accessed January 18, 2022. http://www.southernfriedqueerpride.com/our-vision.

"Polling Tracks Growing and Increasingly Diverse Support for the Freedom to Marry." Freedom to Marry. Accessed March 20, 2015. http://www .freedomtomarry.org/resources/entry/marriage-polling.

"Population—Regional Reports." Asheville, NC Chamber of Commerce. Accessed June 22, 2012. http://www.ashevillechamber.org/economic-development /research-and-reports/population-regional-reports (site discontinued).

"The Power and the Pride." *Newsweek*, June 20, 1993. https://www.newsweek .com/power-and-pride-193662.

"Pride." Out in the Archives Exhibit, Georgia State University Library. Accessed February 9, 2022. https://exhibits.library.gsu.edu/current/exhibits/show /out-in-the-archives/fun-and-games/fun-and-games—pride.

"Pride History." The Atlanta Pride Committee, Inc. Accessed April 17, 2012. http://atlantaPride.org/about/Pride-history.

"Richard Nixon, Statement on Signing the Comprehensive Employment and Training Act of 1973, December 28, 1973." The American Presidency Project, University of California, Santa Barbara. Accessed February 9, 2022. http://www.presidency.ucsb.edu/ws/index.php?pid=4088.

Saunders, Patrick. "'It's a Raid!' Atlanta's Stonewall Moment 50 Years Ago Today." *Project Q Atlanta*, August 5, 2019. https://www.projectq.us/atlanta /its_a_raid_atlantas_stonewall_moment_50_years_ago_today?gid=20032.

"Sponsorships." Delhaize America, Inc., dba Food Lion. Accessed April 28, 2012. http://www.foodlion.com/CommunityOutreach/Sponsorships.

"State Employment Laws and Policies Map." Human Rights Campaign. Accessed February 8, 2015. http://www.hrc.org/campaigns/employment -non-discrimination-act.

Stiffler, Scott. "Gay Nightlife's Identity Crisis." Edge on the Net, April 6, 2009. http://www.edgeonthenet.com/index.php?ch=entertainment&sc=culture &sc3=&id=89298&pg=1.

Summers, Juana. "Amendment One: North Carolina Gay Marriage Ban Passes." Politico. Accessed July 1, 2012. http://www.politico.com/news/stories/0512 /76081_Page2.html.

Texas Real Estate Research Center at Texas A&M University. "Population MSA: Atlanta–Sandy Springs–Marietta, GA." Accessed June 25, 2012. http://recenter.tamu.edu/data/pop/popm/cbsa12060.asp (site discontinued).

———. "Population MSA: Charlotte-Gastonia-Concord, NC-SC." Accessed June 25, 2012. http://recenter.tamu.edu/data/pop/popm/cbsa16740.asp (site discontinued).

"Top 5 Largest and Fastest-Growing Churches in America." ChurchLeaders.
    com. Accessed July 1, 2012. http://www.churchleaders.com/outreach
    -missions/outreach-missions-articles/154431-top-5-largest-and-fastest
    -growing-churches-in-america.html.

Trova, Judith. "Woman's Space and Male Marauders." *Lesbian Voices*.
    September 1975. https://digitalassets.lib.berkeley.edu/sfbagals/Lesbian
    _Voices/1975_Lesbian_Voices_Vol01_Iss01_Sept.pdf.

"University History." Office of Public Relations, UNC Charlotte. Accessed April
    28, 2012. http://publicrelations.uncc.edu/information-media-kit/university
    -history.

U.S. Bureau of Labor Statistics. "May 2011 Metropolitan and Nonmetropolitan
    Area Occupational Employment and Wage Estimates, Atlanta–Sandy
    Springs–Marietta, GA." Occupational Statistics: Atlanta. Accessed February
    9, 2022. http://www.bls.gov/oes/current/oes_12060.htm#33-0000.

———. "May 2011 Metropolitan and Nonmetropolitan Area Occupational
    Employment and Wage Estimates, Charlotte-Concord-Gastonia, NC-SC."
    Occupational Statistics: Charlotte. Accessed February 9, 2022. http://www
    .bls.gov/oes/current/oes_16740.htm#33-0000.

U.S. Bureau of the Census. *Florida Quick Links*. Accessed July 1, 2012.
    http://quickfacts.census.gov/qfd/states/12000lk.html.

———. *Georgia—Race and Hispanic Origin for Selected Large Cities and Other
    Places: Earliest Census to 1990*. Accessed November 11, 2011. http://www
    .census.gov/population/www/documentation/twps0076/GAtab.pdf.

———. *New York—Race and Hispanic Origin for Selected Large Cities and
    Other Places: Earliest Census to 1990*. Accessed November 11, 2011.
    http://www.census.gov/population/www/documentation/twps0076/NYtab.pdf.

———. *1980 and 1990 Census Counts for Cities with 1990 Population Greater
    than 100,000: Sorted by 1990 Population Size*. Population Distribution
    Branch, October 10, 1995. Accessed June 22, 2012. http://www.census.gov
    /population/www/censusdata/files/c1008090.txt.

———. *1990 Census of Population: General Population Characteristics—North
    Carolina*. Accessed April 28, 2022. https://www2.census.gov/library
    /publications/decennial/1990/cp-1/cp-1-35.pdf.

———. *Population of Counties by Decennial Census: 1900 to 1990: Georgia*.
    Edited by Richard L. Forstall, Population Division. Washington: Government
    Printing Office, March, 27, 1995. Accessed June 11, 2012. http://www
    .census.gov/population/cencounts/ga190090.txt.

———. *Population of Counties by Decennial Census: 1900 to 1990: North
    Carolina*. Edited by Richard L. Forstall, Population Division. Washington:
    Government Printing Office, March, 27, 1995. Accessed June 11, 2012.
    http://www.census.gov/population/cencounts/nc190090.txt.

———. *Population of the Largest 75 Cities: 1900–2000*. HS-7. Accessed
    February 5, 2012. http://www.census.gov/statab/hist/HS-07.pdf.

"User Clip: RuPaul Performs at 1993 Gay and Lesbian March on Washington."
    C-SPAN, April 25, 1993. https://www.c-span.org/video/?c4517776
    /user-clip-rupaul-performs-1993-gay-lesbian-march-washington.

U.S. Small Business Administration Office of Advocacy. *Women in Business.* Office of Economic Research, October 1998. Accessed May 25, 2012. http://archive.sba.gov/advo/stats/wib.pdf.

Venable, Tim. "Hottest Metro Areas for Facility Investments in 1991: Dallas, Charlotte, and Atlanta." *Site Selection*, February 1992. Accessed June 18, 2012. http://www.developmentalliance.com/docu/pdf/41500.pdf (site discontinued).

Weinstein, Steve. "Gay Bars, Gay History." Edge on the Net, June 25, 2010. http://www.edgeonthenet.com/index.php?ch=nightlife&sc=&sc2=&sc3 =&id=107320.

Williams, Geoff. "Ten Businesses Facing Extinction in 10 Years." *Entrepreneur*, September 19, 2007. http://www.entrepreneur.com/article/184288.

Wilson, Evey. "Meet the Generation of Atlantans Who Helped Make Little Five Points What It Is Today." WABE, February 25, 2019. https://www.wabe.org /meet-the-generation-of-atlantans-who-helped-make-little-five-points-what -it-is-today/.

Xenotype [pseud.]. "The Hornet's Nest Stirs against Amendment 1: LGBT Rights in Charlotte, the Site of the 2012 DNC." Daily Kos, May 10, 2012. http://www.dailykos.com/story/2012/05/10/1090184/-The-Hornet-s-Nest -Stirs-Against-Amendment-1-LGBT-Rights-at-the-site-of-the-2012-DNC.

PUBLISHED BOOKS AND ARTICLES

Abbott, Shirley. *Womenfolks: Growing Up Down South.* New Haven: Ticknor and Fields, 1983.

Adair, Nancy, and Casey Adair. *Word Is Out.* New York: New Glide Publications, 1978.

Adelman, Marcy, ed. *Long Time Passing: Lives of Older Lesbians.* Boston: Alyson Publications, 1986.

Allison, Dorothy. *Bastard Out of Carolina.* New York: Plume, 1992.

———. *Skin: Talking about Sex, Class and Literature.* Ithaca, NY: Firebrand, 1994.

Bechdel, Alison. *Dykes to Watch Out For.* Ann Arbor, MI: Firebrand Books, 1986.

Bickley, Rah. "Southern Discomfort: Gays in Charlotte, N.C., Strive for Community Cohesion as They Struggle to Get Back on Track after a Virulent 1997." *Advocate*, March 17, 1998.

Bond, Ken. "Southern Exposure: Atlanta and Its Blossoming Gay Community." *Advocate*, December 9, 1982.

Boyd, Blanche McCrary. *The Redneck Way of Knowledge.* New York: Random House, 1978.

Brown, Rita Mae. *Rubyfruit Jungle.* Plainfield, VT: Daughters, 1973.

Clement, Linda, Jessie Duvall, Vicki Gabriner, Linda Lovell, and Susan Woerner. "Southern Dykes in 'Oppression Sandwich.'" *Lesbian Tide* 8, no. 1 (1978): 5.

Daniell, Rosemary. *Fatal Flowers: On Sin, Sex, and Suicide in the Deep South.* New York: Holt, Rinehart and Winston, 1980.

Davis, Angela. "Joan Little: The Dialectics of Rape (1975)." *Ms. Magazine*, Spring 2002.

Eisenbach, Helen. *Lesbianism Made Easy*. New York: Three Rivers Press, 1996.

Ellis, Havelock. *Sexual Inversion*. Vol. 2 of *Studies in the Psychology of Sex*. 2nd ed. Philadelphia: F. A. Davis, 1921.

Freiberg, Peter. "The March on Washington: Hundreds of Thousands Take the Gay Cause to the Nation's Capital, November 10, 1987." In *Witness to Revolution*, edited by Chris Bull, 205–11. Los Angeles: Alyson Books, 1999.

Jay, Karla. *Tales of the Lavender Menace: A Memoir of Liberation*. New York: Basic Books, 1999.

McCullers, Carson. *The Member of the Wedding*. Boston: Mariner Books, 2004. First published 1946 by Houghton Mifflin (Boston).

Mellor, Earl F. "Investigating the Differences in Weekly Earnings of Women and Men." *Monthly Labor Review Online* 107, no. 6 (June 1984): 17–28.

Mellor, Earl F., and George D. Stamas. "Usual Weekly Earnings: Another Look at Intergroup Differences and Basic Trends." *Monthly Labor Review Online* 105, no. 4 (April 1982): 15–24.

Myron, Nancy, and Charlotte Bunch, eds. *Lesbianism and the Women's Movement*. Baltimore: Diana Press, 1975.

"National Black Gay and Lesbian Leadership Forum: A Conference Report." *Off Our Backs*, April 1990.

Patton, Frances. "Women's Creativity a Priority at Charis." *Pulse*, September 6, 1984.

Pratt, Minnie Bruce. "Out in the South: Writers in Conversation." Reading, White Lecture Hall, Duke University, Durham, NC, September 23, 2011.

Radicalesbians. "The Woman-Identified Woman." In *Dear Sisters*, edited by Rosalyn Baxandall and Linda Gordon, 107–9. New York: Basic Books, 2000.

Rich, Ronda. *What Southern Women Know (That Every Woman Should): Timeless Secrets to Get Everything You Want in Love, Life, and Work*. New York: G. P. Putnam's Sons, 1999.

Sharon, Tanya, Farar Elliott, and Cecile Latham. "The Conference Issue: National Lesbian Conference." *Off Our Backs*, June 1991.

Shaw, Pamela. "Firebirds SouthPark: Polished Casual Dining." *Charlotte Food and Wine*, December/January 2008-9.

Smith, Lillian. *Killers of the Dream*. New York: Norton, 1949.

"Southern Discomfort." *Advocate*, March 17, 1998.

"Spectrum." *Gaze* 5, no. 8 (1984): 10.

Tilchen, Maida. "Lesbians and Women's Music." In *Women-Identified Women*, edited by Trudy Darty and Sandee Potter, 287–303. Palo Alto, CA: Mayfield Publishing, 1984.

"Trials: Joan Little's Story." *Time*, August 25, 1975.

Urquhart, Kim. "Diversity, Equality, Social Justice: LGBT Leader Linked Activism, Academia to Make a Difference." *Emory Report*, July 21, 2008.

Van Gelder, Lindsy, and Pamela Robin Brandt. *The Girls Next Door: Into the Heart of Lesbian America*. New York: Touchstone, 1997.

Secondary Sources

PUBLISHED BOOKS AND ARTICLES

Abelove, Henry, Michele Aina Barale, and David M. Halperin. *The Lesbian and Gay Studies Reader.* New York: Routledge, 1993.

Als, Hilton. "Unhappy Endings: The Collected Carson McCullers." *New Yorker,* November 25, 2001. https://www.newyorker.com/magazine/2001/12/03/unhappy-endings.

Ambrose, Andy. "Atlanta." In *New Georgia Encyclopedia.* Georgia Humanities, University of Georgia Press, 2004–22. Article published March 15, 2004, last modified September 16, 2020. https://www.georgiaencyclopedia.org/articles/counties-cities-neighborhoods/atlanta/.

Anderson, Benedict. *Imagined Communities: Reflections on the Origin and Spread of Nationalism.* London: Verso, 1983.

Applebome, Peter. *Dixie Rising: How the South Is Shaping American Values, Politics, and Culture.* New York: Times Books, 1996.

Atwell, Elizabeth. "*Feminary*: A Feminist Journal for the South Emphasizing the Lesbian Vision." OutHistory.org. Accessed August 9, 2019. http://outhistory.org/exhibits/show/nc-lgbt/periodicals/Feminary.

Beemyn, Brett, ed. *Creating a Place for Ourselves: Lesbian, Gay, and Bisexual Community Histories.* New York: Routledge, 1997.

Bender, Thomas. *Community and Social Change in America.* Baltimore: Johns Hopkins University Press, 1978.

Bennett, Judith. "'Lesbian-Like' and the Social History of Lesbianisms." *Journal of the History of Sexuality* 9, no. 1–2 (January/April 2000): 1–24.

Bernhard, Virginia, Betty Brandon, Elizabeth Fox-Genovese, Theda Perdue, and Elizabeth Hayes Turner, eds. *Hidden Histories of Women in the New South.* Columbia: University of Missouri Press, 1994.

Bérubé, Allan. *Coming Out under Fire: The History of Gay Men and Women in World War Two.* New York: Free Press, 1990.

Boyd, Nan Alamilla. "Sex and Tourism: The Economic Implications of the Gay Marriage Movement." *Radical History Review* 100 (January 1, 2008): 223–37.

———. *Wide Open Town: A History of Queer San Francisco to 1965.* Berkeley: University of California Press, 2003.

Brown-Saracino, Japonica. *How Places Make Us: Novel LBQ Identities in Four Small Cities.* Chicago: University of Chicago Press, 2017.

Buring, Daneel. *Lesbian and Gay Memphis: Building Communities behind the Magnolia Curtain.* New York: Routledge, 1997.

———. "Softball and Alcohol: The Limits of Lesbian Community in Memphis from the 1940s through the 1960s." In *Carryin' On in the Lesbian and Gay South,* edited by John Howard, 203–23. New York: New York University Press, 1997.

Campbell, Gavin James. "Up Beat Down South: The Southern World of Britney Spears." *Southern Cultures* 7 (Winter 2001): 81–97.

Canaday, Margot. "'Finding a Home in the Army': Women's Integration, Homosexual Tendencies, and the Cold War Military, 1947–1959." In *The Straight State: Sexuality and Citizenship in Twentieth-Century America*, 174–213. Princeton, NJ: Princeton University Press, 2009.

Carr, Virginia Spencer. *The Lonely Hunter: A Biography of Carson McCullers*. Garden City, NY: Doubleday, 1975.

Chasin, Alexandra. *Selling Out: The Gay and Lesbian Movement Goes to Market*. New York: Palgrave, 2000.

Chauncey, George. *Gay New York: Gender, Urban Culture, and the Making of the Gay Male World, 1890–1940*. New York: Basic Books, 1994.

———. "The Unspoken Past: Atlanta's Lesbian and Gay History." *Perspectives on History*, December 1, 2006. http://www.historians.org/perspectives /issues/2006/0612/07AMSupplement/07AMSup19.cfm.

Chenault, Wesley, and Stacy Braukman. *Gay and Lesbian Atlanta*. Charleston, SC: Arcadia Publishing, 2008.

Chenault, Wesley, Andy Ditzler, and Joey Orr. "Discursive Memorials: Queer Histories in Atlanta's Public Spaces." *Southern Spaces*, February 26, 2010. https://doi.org/10.18737/M7XG7D.

Chesnut, Saralyn, and Amanda C. Gable. "'Women Ran It': Charis Books and More and Atlanta's Lesbian-Feminist Community, 1971–1981." In *Carryin' On in the Lesbian and Gay South*, edited by John Howard, 241–84. New York: New York University Press, 1997.

Chesnut, Saralyn, Amanda C. Gable, and Elizabeth Anderson. "Atlanta's Charis Books and More: Histories of a Feminist Space." *Southern Spaces*, November 3, 2009. http://southernspaces.org/2009/atlantas-charis-books-and-more -histories-feminist-space.

Clemente, Deirdre. *Dress Casual: How College Students Redefined American Style*. Chapel Hill: University of North Carolina Press, 2014.

Clinton, Catherine. *The Plantation Mistress: Woman's World in the Old South*. New York: Pantheon, 1984.

Cobb, James C. *Away Down South: A History of Southern Identity*. New York: Oxford University Press, 2005.

———. *Industrialization and Southern Society, 1877–1984*. Lexington: University Press of Kentucky, 1984.

———. *The Most Southern Place on Earth: The Mississippi Delta and the Roots of Regional Identity*. New York: Oxford University Press, 1992.

———. *Redefining Southern Culture: Mind and Identity in the Modern South*. Athens: University of Georgia Press, 1999.

———. *The Selling of the South: The Southern Crusade for Industrial Development, 1936–90*. 2nd ed. Urbana: University of Illinois Press, 1993.

———. *The South and America since World War II*. New York: Oxford University Press, 2011.

Cooper, Brittney C. "Queering Jane Crow: Pauli Murray's Quest for an Unhyphenated Identity." In *Beyond Respectability: The Intellectual Thought of Race Women*, 87–114. Women, Gender, and Sexuality in American History. Urbana: University of Illinois Press, 2017.

Cragin, 'Becca. "Post-Lesbian-Feminism: Documenting 'Those Cruddy Old Dykes of Yore.'" In *Carryin' On in the Lesbian and Gay South*, edited by John Howard, 285–328. New York: New York University Press, 1997.

Crenshaw, Kimberlé. "Demarginalizing the Intersection of Race and Sex: A Black Feminist Critique of Antidiscrimination Doctrine, Feminist Theory and Antiracist Politics." *University of Chicago Legal Forum* 1989, no. 1 (1989): 139–68.

Crone, Michelle. "Women's Music Festivals and Lesbian Feminist Process." *Sinister Wisdom* 104 (Spring 2017): 185–87.

Daniel, Pete. *Lost Revolutions: The South in the 1950s*. Chapel Hill: University of North Carolina Press, 2000.

De Hart, Jane Sherron. "Feminism(s) and the South: The Difference That Differences Make." In *Women of the American South: A Multicultural Reader*, edited by Christie Anne Farnham, 273–301. New York: New York University Press, 1997.

De la Canal, Nick. "FAQ City: Why Is Charlotte Pride in August, Not June?" WFAE, August 14, 2018. https://www.wfae.org/local-news/2018-08-14/faq-city-why-is-charlotte-pride-in-august-not-june.

D'Emilio, John. *Sexual Politics, Sexual Communities: The Making of a Homosexual Minority in the United States, 1940-1970*. Chicago: University of Chicago Press, 1983.

D'Emilio, John, and Estelle B. Freedman. *Intimate Matters: A History of Sexuality in America*. Chicago: University of Chicago Press, 1988.

Dews, Carlos L., and Carolyn Leste Law, eds. *Out in the South*. Philadelphia: Temple University Press, 2001.

Dillman, Caroline Matheny, ed. *Southern Women*. New York: Hemisphere, 1988.

Dolance, Susannah. "'A Whole Stadium Full': Lesbian Community at Women's National Basketball Association Games." *Journal of Sex Research* 42 (February 2005): 74–83.

Drucker, Peter. *Warped: Gay Normality and Queer Anti-capitalism*. Chicago: Haymarket Books, 2015.

Duberman, Martin. *Stonewall*. New York: Dutton, 1993.

Duberman, Martin, Martha Vicinus, and George Chauncey Jr., eds. *Hidden from History: Reclaiming the Gay and Lesbian Past*. New York: Meridian, 1990.

Duggan, Lisa. "The New Homonormativity: The Sexual Politics of Neoliberalism." In *Materializing Democracy: Toward a Revitalized Cultural Politics*, edited by Russ Castronovo, Dana D. Nelson, and Donald E. Pease, 175–94. Durham, NC: Duke University Press, 2002.

Eaves, LaToya. "Outside Forces: Black Southern Sexuality." In *Queering the Countryside: New Frontiers in Rural Queer Studies*, edited by Mary L. Gray, Colin R. Johnson, and Brian Joseph Gilley, 146–60. New York: New York University Press, 2016.

Echols, Alice. *Daring to Be Bad: Radical Feminism in America, 1967-1975*. Minneapolis: University of Minnesota Press, 1989.

Enke, Finn. *Finding the Movement: Sexuality, Contested Space, and Feminist Activism*. Durham, NC: Duke University Press, 2007.

Eng, David L., with Judith Halberstam and José Esteban Muñoz. "What's Queer about Queer Studies Now?" *Social Text* 23 (Fall–Winter 2005): 1–17.

Estes Blair, Melissa. "'A Dynamic Force in our Community': Women's Clubs and Second-Wave Feminism at the Grassroots." *Frontiers: A Journal of Women's Studies* 30, no. 3 (Winter 2009): 30–51.

Faderman, Lillian. *Odd Girls and Twilight Lovers: A History of Lesbian Life in Twentieth-Century America.* New York: Penguin, 1991.

Farnham, Christie Anne, ed. *Women of the American South: A Multicultural Reader.* New York: New York University Press, 1997.

Faust, Drew Gilpin. "Clutching the Chains That Bind: Margaret Mitchell and *Gone with the Wind*." *Southern Cultures* 5 (Spring 1999): 6–20.

"Feminary (Newsletter)." 1970s North Carolina Feminisms, March 2011. Accessed May 10, 2012. http://sites.duke.edu/docst110s_01_s2011_bec15 /print-culture/feminary-newsletter/ (site discontinued).

Ferguson, Karen. *Black Politics in New Deal Atlanta.* Chapel Hill: University of North Carolina Press, 2001.

Filene, Peter G. Review of *Sexual Politics, Sexual Communities: The Making of a Homosexual Minority in the United States, 1940–1970*, by John D'Emilio. *Journal of American History* 70 (December 1983): 735–36.

Fink, Leon. *The Maya of Morganton: Work and Community in the Nuevo New South.* Chapel Hill: University of North Carolina Press, 2003.

"A First for Famed Peachtree Street." *Advocate*, 1972.

Florida, Richard. *The Rise of the Creative Class: And How It's Transforming Work, Leisure, Community and Everyday Life.* New York: Basic Books, 2003.

Florida, Richard, and Gary Gates. "Technology and Tolerance: The Importance of Diversity to High Technology Growth." Brookings Institute, June 1, 2000.

Foucault, Michel. *The History of Sexuality: An Introduction.* Vol. 1. New York: Random House, 1978.

Freedman, Estelle. "'The Burning of Letters Continues': Elusive Identities and the Historical Construction of Sexuality." *Journal of Women's History* 9, no. 4 (Winter 1998): 181–200.

Freedman, Estelle B., Barbara Charlesworth Gelpi, Susan L. Johnson, and Kathleen M. Weston, eds. "The Lesbian Issue." Special issue, *Signs: Journal of Women in Culture and Society* 9, no. 4 (Summer 1984).

Freeman, Susan K. "From the Lesbian Nation to the Cincinnati Lesbian Community: Moving toward a Politics of Location." *Journal of the History of Sexuality* 9, no. 1/2 (January 2000): 137–74.

Furuseth, Owen J. "Epilogue: Charlotte at the Globalizing Crossroads." In *Charlotte, NC: The Global Evolution of a New South City*, edited by William Graves and Heather A. Smith, 284–90. Athens: University of Georgia Press, 2010.

Gaillard, Frye. *With Music and Justice for All: Some Southerners and Their Passions.* Nashville: Vanderbilt University Press, 2008.

Gallo, Marcia M. *Different Daughters: A History of the Daughters of Bilitis and the Birth of the Lesbian Rights Movement.* New York: Carroll and Graf, 2006.

Garber, Linda. "Where in the World Are the Lesbians?" *Journal of the History of Sexuality* 14, no. 1/2 (2005): 28–50.

Gelfand, Rachel. "'Come Out Slugging!' The Atlanta Lesbian Feminist Alliance, 1972–1975." *Southern Cultures* 26 (Fall 2020): 86–103.

Ghaziani, Amin. "There Goes the Gayborhood?" *Contexts* 9, no. 4 (2010): 64–66.

Gibson, Michelle, and Deborah T. Meem, eds. *Femme/Butch: New Considerations of the Way We Want to Go*. New York: Harrington Park Press, 2002.

Gieseking, Jen Jack. "On the Closing of the Last Lesbian Bar in San Francisco: What the Demise of the Lex Tells Us about Gentrification." *HuffPost Gay Voices* (blog), October 28, 2014. http://www.huffingtonpost.com/jen-jack -gieseking/on-the-closing-of-the-las_b_6057122.html.

———. *A Queer New York: Geographies of Lesbians, Dykes, and Queers*. New York: New York University Press, 2020.

Gilmore, Stephanie. "The Dynamics of Second-Wave Feminist Activism in Memphis, 1971–1982: Rethinking the Liberal/Radical Divide." *NWSA Journal* 15, no. 1 (2003): 94–117.

———. *Groundswell: Grassroots Feminist Activism in Postwar America*. New York: Routledge, 2013.

Gilmore, Stephanie, and Elizabeth Kaminski. "A Part and Apart: Lesbian and Straight Feminist Activists Negotiate Identity in a Second-Wave Organization." *Journal of the History of Sexuality* 16, no. 1 (2007): 95–113.

Gladney, Margaret Rose. "Personalizing the Political, Politicizing the Personal: Reflections on Editing the Letters of Lillian Smith." In *Carryin' On in the Lesbian and Gay South*, edited by John Howard, 93–103. New York: New York University Press, 1997.

———, ed. *How Am I to Be Heard? Letters of Lillian Smith*. Chapel Hill: University of North Carolina Press, 1993.

Gluckman, Amy, and Betsy Reed, eds. *Homo Economics: Capitalism, Community, and Lesbian and Gay Life*. New York: Routledge, 1997.

Goldfield, David. *Black, White, and Southern: Race Relations and Southern Culture, 1940 to the Present*. Baton Rouge: Louisiana State University Press, 1990.

———. "A Place to Come To." In *Charlotte, NC: The Global Evolution of a New South City*, edited by William Graves and Heather A. Smith, 10–23. Athens: University of Georgia Press, 2010.

———. *Region, Race, and Cities: Interpreting the Urban South*. Baton Rouge: Louisiana State University Press, 1997.

———. *Still Fighting the Civil War: The American South and Southern History*. Baton Rouge: Louisiana State University Press, 2002.

Goldfield, David, and Blaine Brownell. *Urban America: From Downtown to No Town*. Boston: Houghton Mifflin, 1979.

Graves, William, and Heather A. Smith, eds. *Charlotte, NC: The Global Evolution of a New South City*. Athens: University of Georgia Press, 2010.

Gutterman, Lauren Jae. *Her Neighbor's Wife: A History of Lesbian Desire within Marriage*. Philadelphia: University of Pennsylvania Press, 2020.

Haber, Honi Fern. *Beyond Postmodern Politics: Lyotard, Rorty, Foucault*. New York: Routledge, 1994.

Halberstam, Judith. *Female Masculinity*. Durham, NC: Duke University Press, 1998.

Hale, Grace Elizabeth. *Making Whiteness: The Culture of Segregation in the South, 1890–1940*. New York: Vintage Books, 1999.

Hall, Jacquelyn Dowd. "Documenting Diversity: The Southern Experience." *Oral History Review* 4 (1976): 19–28.

Hanchett, Thomas W. "Salad-Bowl Suburbs: A History of Charlotte's East Side and South Boulevard Immigrant Corridors." In *Charlotte, NC: The Global Evolution of a New South City*, edited by William Graves and Heather A. Smith, 247–62. Athens: University of Georgia Press, 2010.

———. *Sorting Out the New South City: Race, Class, and Urban Development in Charlotte, 1875–1975*. Chapel Hill: University of North Carolina Press, 1998.

Hanhardt, Christina B. *Safe Space: Gay Neighborhood History and the Politics of Violence*. Durham, NC: Duke University Press, 2013.

Hankin, Kelly. "'Wish We Didn't Have to Meet Secretly?': Negotiating Contemporary Space in the Lesbian-Bar Documentary." *Camera Obscura* 15, no. 3 (2000): 34–69.

Harker, Jaime. *The Lesbian South: Southern Feminists, the Women in Print Movement, and the Queer Literary Canon*. Chapel Hill: University of North Carolina Press, 2018.

Harris, Laura, and Elizabeth Crocker, eds. *Femme: Feminists, Lesbians and Bad Girls*. New York: Routledge, 1997.

Hegarty, Marylin E. "The Other War: Gay Men and Lesbians in the Second World War." In *Understanding and Teaching U.S. Lesbian, Gay, Bisexual, and Transgender History*, 2nd ed., edited by Leila J. Rupp and Susan Kathleen Freeman, 178–85. The Harvey Goldberg Series for Understanding and Teaching History. Madison: University of Wisconsin Press, 2017.

Hicks, Cheryl. *Talk with You Like a Woman: African American Women, Justice, and Reform in New York, 1890–1935*. Chapel Hill: University of North Carolina Press, 2010.

Higginbotham, Evelyn Brooks. *Righteous Discontent: The Women's Movement in the Black Baptist Church, 1880–1920*. Cambridge, MA: Harvard University Press, 1994.

Hobson, Maurice J. *The Legend of the Black Mecca: Politics and Class in the Making of Modern Atlanta*. Chapel Hill: University of North Carolina Press, 2017.

Holloway, Pippa. "Searching for Southern Lesbian History." In *Women of the American South: A Multicultural Reader*, edited by Christie Anne Farnham, 258–72. New York: New York University Press, 1997.

———, ed. *Other Souths: Diversity and Difference in the U.S. South, Reconstruction to Present*. Athens: University of Georgia Press, 2008.

Howard, John. "The Library, the Park, and the Pervert: Public Space and Homosexual Encounter in Post–World War II Atlanta." In *Carryin' On in the*

Lesbian and Gay South, edited by John Howard, 107–31. New York: New York University Press, 1997.

———. *Men Like That: A Southern Queer History.* Chicago: University of Chicago Press, 1999.

———, ed. *Carryin' On in the Lesbian and Gay South.* New York: New York University Press, 1997.

Hunter, Tera W. *To 'Joy My Freedom: Southern Black Women's Lives and Labors after the Civil War.* Cambridge, MA: Harvard University Press, 1997.

Inscoe, John C. *Writing the South through the Self: Explorations in Southern Autobiography.* Athens: University of Georgia Press, 2011.

Jacobsen, Joyce, and Adam Zeller, eds. *Queer Economics: A Reader.* New York: Routledge, 2008.

Johnson, Colin R. *Just Queer Folks: Gender and Sexuality in Rural America.* Philadelphia: Temple University Press, 2013.

Johnson, E. Patrick. *Black. Queer. Southern. Women.* Chapel Hill: University of North Carolina Press, 2018.

———. *Honeypot: Black Southern Women Who Love Women.* Durham, NC: Duke University Press, 2019.

———. "Southern (Dis)Comfort: Creating and Consuming Homosex in the Black South." In *Creating and Consuming the American South*, edited by Martyn Bone, Brian Ward, and William A. Link, 97–116. Gainesville: University Press of Florida, 2015.

Johnson, George E. "Intermetropolitan Wage Differentials in the United States." In *The Measurement of Labor Cost*, edited by Jack E. Triplett, 327. Chicago: University of Chicago Press, 1983.

Joseph, Miranda. *Against the Romance of Community.* Minneapolis: University of Minnesota Press, 2002.

Kennedy, Elizabeth Lapovsky. "'But We Would Never Talk about It': The Structure of Lesbian Discretion in South Dakota, 1928–1933." In *Inventing Lesbian Cultures in America*, edited by Ellen Lewin, 15–39. Boston: Beacon Press, 1996.

Kennedy, Elizabeth Lapovsky, and Madeline D. Davis. *Boots of Leather, Slippers of Gold: The History of a Lesbian Community.* New York: Routledge, 1993.

Kenschaft, Lori J. "Homoerotics and Human Connections: Reading Carson McCullers 'As a Lesbian.'" In *Critical Essays on Carson McCullers*, edited by Beverly Lyon Clark and Melvin J. Friedman, 220–33. New York: G. K. Hall, 1996.

King, Florence. *Confessions of a Failed Southern Lady.* New York: St. Martin's Press, 1985.

———. *Southern Ladies and Gentlemen.* New York: St. Martin's Press, 1975.

Knowlton, Elizabeth W. "'Only a Woman Like Yourself'—Rebecca Alice Baldy: Dutiful Daughter, Stalwart Sister, and Lesbian Lover of Nineteenth-Century Georgia." In *Carryin' On in the Lesbian and Gay South*, edited by John Howard, 34–53. New York: New York University Press, 1997.

Krahulik, Karen. *Provincetown: From Pilgrim Landing to Gay Resort.* New York: New York University Press, 2005.

Kruse, Kevin. *White Flight: Atlanta and the Making of Modern Conservatism.* Princeton, NJ: Princeton University Press, 2005.

Kuhn, Clifford. *Living Atlanta: An Oral History of the City, 1914–1948.* Athens: University of Georgia Press, 1990.

Kunzel, Regina. "The Power of Queer History." *American Historical Review* 123, no. 5 (December 2018): 1577–79.

Lassiter, Matthew D. "Searching for Respect: From 'New South' to 'World Class' at the Crossroads of the Carolinas." In *Charlotte, NC: The Global Evolution of a New South City,* edited by William Graves and Heather A. Smith, 24–49. Athens: University of Georgia Press, 2010.

———. *The Silent Majority: Suburban Politics in the Sunbelt South.* Princeton, NJ: Princeton University Press, 2006.

Lassiter, Matthew D., and Joseph Crespino, eds. *The Myth of Southern Exceptionalism.* New York: Oxford University Press, 2009.

Liu, Yvonne Yen. "Trained to Fail." *Colorlines,* April 13, 2010. https://www.colorlines.com/articles/trained-fail.

Lockard, Denyse. "The Lesbian Community: An Anthropological Approach." *Journal of Homosexuality* 11 (January 1986): 83–95.

Lorde, Audre. *Sister Outsider.* Freedom, CA: Crossing Press, 1984.

———. *Zami: A New Spelling of My Name; A Biomythography.* Berkeley: Crossing Press, 1982.

Manion, Jen. *Female Husbands: A Trans History.* Cambridge: Cambridge University Press, 2020.

———. "The Performance of Transgender Inclusion: The Pronoun Go-Round and the New Gender Binary." Public Seminar, 2018. http://www.publicseminar.org/2018/11/the-performance-of-transgender-inclusion/.

Marshall, Catherine, and Gary L. Anderson. "Rethinking the Public and Private Spheres: Feminist and Cultural Studies Perspectives on the Politics of Education." *Journal of Education Policy* 9, no. 5 (1994): 169–82.

Mathews, Donald G., and Jane Sherron De Hart. *Sex, Gender, and the Politics of ERA: A State and the Nation.* New York: Oxford University Press, 1990.

May, Elaine Tyler. *Homeward Bound: American Families in the Cold War Era.* New York: Basic Books, 1988.

Maynard, Steven. "'Without Working?' Capitalism, Urban Culture, and Gay History." *Journal of Urban History* 30, no. 3 (March 2004): 378–98.

McClintock, Anne. *Imperial Leather: Race, Gender and Sexuality in the Colonial Conquest.* New York: Routledge, 1995.

McNaron, Toni A. H., Gloria Anzaldúa, Lourdes Argu lles, and Elizabeth Lapovsky Kennedy, eds. "Theorizing Lesbian Experience." Special issue, *Signs: Journal of Women in Culture and Society* 18, no. 4 (Summer 1993).

Meeker, Martin. *Contacts Desired: Gay and Lesbian Communications and Community, 1940s–1970s.* Chicago: University of Chicago Press, 2006.

"Metro-Area Membership Report: Religious Traditions, 2010." Association of Religious Data Archives. Accessed July 1, 2012. http://www.thearda.com/rcms2010/r/m/12060/rcms2010_12060_metro_family_2010.asp, and

http://www.thearda.com/rcms2010/r/m/16740/rcms2010_16740_metro
_family_2010.asp.

Meyer, Leisa D. *Creating G.I. Jane: Sexuality and Power in the Women's Army
Corps during World War II*. New York: Columbia University Press, 1997.

———. "Roundtable: Lesbian Generations." Conference reports by CLGBTH,
Fifteenth Berkshire Conference on the History of Women, June 10, 2011.

Meyerowitz, Joanne. *Not June Cleaver: Women and Gender in Postwar America,
1945–1960*. Philadelphia: Temple University Press, 1994.

Mickelson, Roslyn Arlin, Stephen Samuel Smith, and Amy Hawn Nelson, eds.
*Yesterday, Today, and Tomorrow: School Desegregation and Resegregation in
Charlotte*. Cambridge, MA: Harvard Education Press, 2015.

Mims, La Shonda. "Gay Pride in the Urban New South: Politics, Neighborhood,
and Community in Atlanta and Charlotte." *Journal of Urban History*,
published ahead of print, October 11, 2021. https://journals.sagepub.com
/doi/abs/10.1177/00961442211047553.

Mumford, Kevin. *Interzones: Black/White Sex Districts in Chicago and New
York in the Early Twentieth Century*. New York: Columbia University Press,
1997.

Murphy, Kevin P. "Gay Was Good: Progress, Homonormativity, and Oral
History." In *Queer Twin Cities*, edited by Twin Cities GLBT Oral History
Project, 305–18. Minneapolis: University of Minnesota Press, 2010.

Murphy, Kevin P., Jennifer L. Pierce, and Jason Ruiz. "What Makes Queer Oral
History Different." *Oral History Review* 43, no.1 (February 2016): 1–24.
DOI: 10.1093/ohr/ohw022.

Nestle, Joan. *A Restricted Country*. Ithaca, NY: Firebrand Books, 1987.

———, ed. *The Persistent Desire: A Femme-Butch Reader*. Boston: Alyson
Publications, 1992.

Nestle, Joan, Clare Howell, and Riki Wilchins, eds. *Genderqueer: Voices from
Beyond the Sexual Binary*. Los Angeles: Alyson Publications, 2002.

Newman, Harvey K. *Southern Hospitality: Tourism and the Growth of Atlanta*.
Tuscaloosa: University of Alabama Press, 1999.

Ownby, Ted. "Evangelical but Differentiated: Religion by the Numbers." In
Religion and Public Life in the South: In the Evangelical Mode, edited by
Charles Reagan Wilson and Mark Silk, 31–62. Walnut Creek, CA: AltaMira
Press, 2005.

Portelli, Allesandro. *The Death of Luigi Trastulli and Other Stories: Form and
Meaning in Oral History*. Albany: State University of New York Press, 1991.

———. *S/HE*. Ithaca, NY: Firebrand Books, 1995.

Rivas, Jorge. "The Association of Black Women Historians Says 'The Help' Is
Distorted." *Colorlines*, January 17, 2012.

Rosenthal, Gregory Samantha. "Make Roanoke Queer Again." *Public Historian*
39, no. 1 (February 2017): 35–60.

Rotenstein, David S. "The Decatur Plan: Folklore, Historic Preservation, and
the Black Experience in Gentrifying Spaces." *Journal of American Folklore*
132, no. 526 (Fall 2019): 431–51.

Rupp, Leila J. "'Imagine My Surprise': Women's Relationships in Historical Perspective." *Frontiers: A Journal of Women's Studies* 5, no. 3 (Autumn 1980): 61–70.

Sanford, Ken. *Charlotte and UNC Charlotte: Growing Up Together.* Charlotte: UNC Charlotte Press, 1996.

Scherzer, Kenneth A. "Southern Cities—How Exceptional?" *Journal of Urban History* 26, no. 5 (July 2000): 692–705.

Schulman, Sarah. "Grappling with Carson McCullers: 100 Years." OutHistory. org (blog), July 20, 2017. http://outhistory.org/blog/grappling-with-carson -mccullers-100-years/.

Scott, Anne Firor. *The Southern Lady: From Pedestal to Politics, 1830–1930.* Chicago: University of Chicago Press, 1972.

Scott, Thomas A. "Bell Bomber." In *New Georgia Encyclopedia.* Georgia Humanities, University of Georgia Press, 2004–22. Article published October 17, 2003, last modified November 3, 2020. https://www .georgiaencyclopedia.org/articles/government-politics/bell-bomber/.

Sears, Alan. "Queer Anti-capitalism: What's Left of Lesbian and Gay Liberation?" *Science and Society* 69, no. 1 (January 2005): 92.

Sears, James T. *Growing Up Gay in the South: Race, Gender, and Journeys of the Spirit.* New York: Harrington Park Press, 1991.

———. *Rebels, Rubyfruit, and Rhinestones: Queering Space in the Stonewall South.* New Brunswick, NJ: Rutgers University Press, 2001.

Segrest, Mab. *Memoir of a Race Traitor.* Boston: South End Press, 1994.

———. *My Mama's Dead Squirrel: Lesbian Essays on Southern Culture.* Ithaca, NY: Firebrand, 1985.

Shapland, Jenn. *My Autobiography of Carson McCullers.* Portland, OR: Tin House Books, 2020.

Shockley, Megan. "Southern Women in the Scrums: The Emergence and Decline of Women's Rugby in the American Southeast, 1974–1980s." *Journal of Sport History* 33, no. 2 (2006): 127–55.

Shopes, Linda. "Oral History and the Study of Communities: Problems, Paradoxes, and Possibilities." *Journal of American History* 89 (September 2002): 588–98.

Sismondo, Christine. *America Walks into a Bar: A Spirited History of Taverns and Saloons, Speakeasies and Grog Shops.* New York: Oxford University Press, 2011.

Smith, Clint. "The Desegregation and Resegregation of Charlotte's Schools." *New Yorker,* October 3, 2016.

Smith, Donna Jo. "Queering the South: Constructions of Southern/Queer Identity." In *Carryin' On in the Lesbian and Gay South,* edited by John Howard, 370–85. New York: New York University Press, 1997.

———. "Same Difference: My Southern Queer Stories." In *Out in the South,* Carlos L. Dews, and Carolyn Leste Law, eds., 127–43. Philadelphia: Temple University Press, 2001.

Smith, Stephen Samuel. "Development and the Politics of School Desegregation and Resegregation." In *Charlotte, NC: The Global Evolution of a New South*

City, edited by William Graves and Heather A. Smith, 189–219. Athens: University of Georgia Press, 2010.

Smith-Rosenberg, Carroll. "The Female World of Love and Ritual: Relations between Women in Nineteenth-Century America." *Signs: Journal of Women in Culture and Society* 1, no. 1 (Autumn 1975): 1–29.

Sokol, Jason. *There Goes My Everything: White Southerners in the Age of Civil Rights, 1945–1975.* New York: Knopf, 2006.

Somerville, Siobhan B. "Queer." In *Keywords for American Cultural Studies*, edited by Bruce Burgett and Glenn Hendler, 203–7. New York: New York University Press, 2014.

———. *Queering the Color Line: Race and the Invention of Homosexuality in American Culture.* Durham, NC: Duke University Press, 2000.

Stein, Arlene. "The Incredible Shrinking Lesbian World and Other Queer Conundra." *Sexualities* 13, no. 1 (2010): 21–32.

Stephens, Charles. "Maynard Jackson and the Black Gay Mecca." *Advocate*, February 1, 2018. https://www.thefreelibrary.com/Maynard+Jackson +and+the+Black+Gay+Mecca%3a+How+a+straight+ally+helped... -a0524611018.

Stewart-Winter, Timothy. *Queer Clout: Chicago and the Rise of Gay Politics.* Philadelphia: University of Pennsylvania Press, 2016.

Taylor, Verta, and Leila J. Rupp. "Women's Culture and Lesbian Feminist Activism: A Reconsideration of Cultural Feminism." *Signs: Journal of Women in Culture and Society* 19, no. 1 (1993): 32–61.

Thorpe, Rochella. "'A House Where Queers Go': African-American Lesbian Nightlife in Detroit, 1940–1975." In *Inventing Lesbian Cultures in America*, edited by Ellen Lewin, 40–61. Boston: Beacon Press, 1996.

Turner, Jae. "A Death without Cause: Mary E. Hutchinson's Un-archived Life in Certified Death." In *Un-archived Histories: The "Mad" and the "Trifling" in the Colonial and Postcolonial World*, edited by Gyanendra Pandey, 41–57. New York: Routledge, 2014.

———. "Mary E. Hutchinson, Intelligibility, and the Historical Limits of Agency." *Feminist Studies* 38, no. 2 (June 2012): 375–414.

———. "Mary E. Hutchinson (1906–1970)." In *New Georgia Encyclopedia*. Georgia Humanities, University of Georgia Press, 2004–22. Article published September 22, 2006, last modified August 2, 2018. https://www .georgiaencyclopedia.org/articles/arts-culture/mary-e-hutchinson -1906–1970/.

Urquhart, Alex T., and Susan Craddock. "Private Cures for a Public Epidemic: Target(ing) HIV and AIDS Medications in the Twin Cities." In *Queer Twin Cities*, edited by Twin Cities GLBT Oral History Project, 269–304. Minneapolis: University of Minnesota Press, 2010.

Valk, Anne M. "Living a Feminist Lifestyle: The Furies Collective." *Feminist Studies* 28, no. 2 (Summer 2002): 303–32.

Vicinus, Martha. "Lesbian History: All Theory and No Facts or All Facts and No Theory?" *Radical History Review* 60 (Fall 1994): 57–75.

————. "'They Wonder to Which Sex I Belong': The Historical Roots of the Modern Lesbian Identity." In *Lesbian Subjects: A Feminist Studies Reader*, edited by Martha Vicinus, 233–59. Bloomington: Indiana University Press, 1996.

Vider, Stephen. "Consumerism." In *The Routledge History of Queer America*, edited by Don Romesburg, 344–58. New York: Routledge, 2018.

Walker, Lisa. *Looking Like What You Are: Sexual Style, Race, and Lesbian Identity*. New York: New York University Press, 2001.

Walters, Suzanna Danuta. *All the Rage: The Story of Gay Visibility in America*. Chicago: University of Chicago Press, 2001.

Warner, Sara. *Acts of Gaiety: LGBT Performance and the Politics of Pleasure*. Ann Arbor: University of Michigan Press, 2013.

Waters, Michael. "The Stonewall of the South That History Forgot." *Smithsonian Magazine*, June 15, 2019. https://www.smithsonianmag.com /history/stonewall-south-history-forgot-180972484/.

Watkins, Jerry. *Redneck Riveria: Sexuality and the Rise of Florida Tourism*. Gainesville: University Press of Florida, 2018.

Weeks, Gregory B., John R. Weeks, and Amy J. Weeks. "Latino Immigration in the U.S. South: 'Carolatinos' and Public Policy in Charlotte, North Carolina." *Latino(a) Research Review* 6, no. 1–2 (2006–7): 50–71.

Whitlock, Reta Ugena, ed. *Queer South Rising: Voices of a Contested Place*. Charlotte, NC: Information Age Publishing, 2013.

Whitt, Jan. "Living and Writing in the Margins: Lesbian Desire and the Novels of Carson McCullers." In *Reflections in a Critical Eye: Essays on Carson McCullers*, edited by Jan Whitt, 87–106. Lanham, MD: University Press of America, 2008.

Williams, Kathie D. "Louisville's Lesbian Feminist Union: A Study in Community Building." In *Carryin' On in the Lesbian and Gay South*, edited by John Howard, 224–40. New York: New York University Press, 1997.

Winner, Lauren F. "Pauli Murray: 'Gifts of the Holy Spirit to Women I Have Known.'" In *North Carolina Women: Their Lives and Times*, edited by Michele Gillespie and Sally G. McMillen, 334–53. Athens: University of Georgia Press, 2015.

Yockey, Ross. *McColl: The Man with America's Money*. Atlanta: Longstreet, 1999.

MOTION PICTURES

Ingram, Malcolm, dir., and Kevin Smith, Scott Mosier, Andre Canaparo, Sarah Gibson, and Matthew Gissing, prods. *Small Town Gay Bar*. Red Bank, NJ: View Askew Productions, 2006.

Poirier, Paris, dir., and Karen Kiss and Paris Poirier, prods. *Last Call at Maud's*. Venice, CA: The Maud's Project, 1993.

Ross, Herbert, dir., and Ray Stark, prod. *Steel Magnolias*. Culver City, CA: TriStar Pictures, 1989.

Scagliotti, John and Greta Schiller, dirs. *Before Stonewall: The Making of a Gay and Lesbian Community*. New York: First Run Features, 1985.

DISSERTATIONS AND THESES

Chenault, Wesley. "An Unspoken Past: Atlanta Lesbian and Gay History, 1940–1970." PhD diss., University of New Mexico, 2008.

Cole, Ashley D. "'I Wanted to Be Just What I Was': Documenting Queer Voices in the South." Master's thesis, Middle Tennessee State University, 2016.

Combs, Barbara Harris. "The Ties That Bind: The Role of Place in Racial Identity Formation, Social Cohesion, Accord, and Discord in Two Historic, Black Gentrifying Atlanta Neighborhoods." PhD diss., Georgia State University, 2010.

Del Rio, Chelsea. "'That Women Could Matter': Building Lesbian Feminism in California, 1955–1982." PhD diss., University of Michigan, Rochester, 2016.

Gilbert, Jennifer L. *Feminary* of Durham–Chapel Hill: Building Community through a Feminist Press." Master's thesis, Duke University, 1993.

Hamilton, Aretina Rochelle. "'I Thought I Found Home': Locating the Hidden and Symbolic Spaces of African American Lesbian Belonging." PhD diss., University of Kentucky, 2018.

Huff, Christopher. "A New Way of Living Together: A History of Atlanta's Hip Community, 1965–1973." PhD diss., University of Georgia, 2012.

Marini, Angelica Danielle. "'Looking for a City': Community, Politics, and Gay and Lesbian Rights in Atlanta, 1968–1993." PhD diss., Auburn University, 2018.

Pope, Andrew. "Living in the Struggle: Black Power, Gay Liberation, and Women's Liberation Movements in Atlanta, 1964–1996." PhD diss., Harvard University, 2018.

Schultz, Hooper. "The Carolina Gay Association, the Southeastern Gay Conferences, and Gay Liberation in the 1970s South." Master's thesis, University of Mississippi, 2019.

Wright, Christina. "'How Could Love Be Wrong?' Gay Activism and AIDS in Charlotte, 1970–1992." Master's thesis, University of North Carolina at Charlotte, 2017.

INDEX

Page numbers in italics refer to illustrations.

invisibility, 25, 36, 39. *See also* visibility

isolation, 77, 79, 136

Jackson, Maynard, 92, *95*, 96–98, 112, 130, 132, 152

Jay, Karla, 77

Jill and Marty, 55

jobs. *See* corporations; employment; workplace discrimination; workplace protections

Johnson, E. Patrick, 133, 134, 160; *Black. Queer. Southern. Women.*, 160

Johnson C. Smith University, 136

Jones, Jennifer D., 159

Justice, Jennifer, 78

Justice, Joy, 64, 65, 74, 76, 79, 80, 86

Kelly, Sarrah, 56, 104

Kennedy, Elizabeth, 17, 23, 25, 34, 35, 38, 42

Kenschaft, Lori J., 17

King, Don, 100, 104–5, 119–20

King, Dorothy, 14, 18, 19, 22, 23–24, 25, 35, 36

King, Lisa, 110

Kirsch, Dan, 112, 113, 114, 115, 118, 119, 120, 144

Knotts, Gloria, 81

Knowlton, Elizabeth, 86

Kuhn, Clifford, 27

Ku Klux Klan, 13, 77

Kushner, Tony, 140; *Angels in America*, 140

L5P (Little Five Points) neighborhood, 83, 84, 88–89, 90, 134, 155

labels, 31

labor, unpaid, 81

Ladder, The (journal), 100

Lambda Community Center, 108

Lambda Political Caucus, 98, 105

lang, k.d., 2

Lanza, Joanna, 18

Lassiter, Matthew D., 3, 5

Latina lesbians, 125, 130, 155

law enforcement, 55–56, 86–87, 106, 125, 126–27, 150; Atlanta Pride and, 126–27; bars and, 47; in Charlotte compared to Atlanta, 149; Lesbian and Gay Police Advisory Committee, 126, 127; *Lonesome Cowboys* raid, 93–94; murder of African Americans, 161; in Piedmont Park, 44; Stonewall riots and, 92; supportive of gay people, 91. *See also* safety

Layton, Ruth, 18, 19, 25

Lesbian and Gay Police Advisory Committee, 126, 127

Lesbian Avengers, 110, 114

Lesbian Center Group, 78–79

Lesbian Center Journal, 78

lesbian identity, in South, 1

lesbianism, private, 23

lesbianism, quiet, 17, 23, 25, 90. *See also* respectability

lesbians: identity and, 1, 2, 7, 49, 89; separation from gay men, 10 (*see also* gender); in southern U.S. history, 9

lesbians, Black, 128, 129–34; anonymity and, 34–35; archives of, 159–60; in Atlanta, 124; exclusion from category of lesbian, 133; at Great Southeast Lesbian Conference, 86; health and, 131, 134; intersectionality and, 133; invisibility of, 58; issues facing, 134; National Lesbian Conference and, 129–31; Pride and, 123–24; priorities of, 160; safety for, 45; separation from white lesbians, 14, 133–34; social spaces and, 34, 38, 45, 46–47; vulnerability of, 33; ZAMI, 134, 159–60. *See also* African Americans; women, Black

lesbians, Latina, 125, 130, 155

Lewis, Sonya, 115

LGBTQ Health Initiative, 128

Liaisons Restaurant, 61

wage statistics, 148. *See also* earnings, women's; financial power of queer community
Washington Post (newspaper), 31, 140
Weston, Don, 107
whiteness: queer opportunities and, 14; research and, 159; visibility and, 135
white privilege, 25, 33
white supremacy, 35
Williamson, Cris, 89, 103, 104
Winter Woman Music, 104
WNBA (Women's National Basketball Association), 144
women, Black, 8; earnings of, 148; in history of women's activism, 32; murder of, 161; social spaces for, 29, 38. *See also* lesbians, Black
women, Hispanic, 125, 130, 155; earnings of, 148
women, southern: culturally created identities, 7, 8; shared sense of common past, 9. *See also* belle, southern
women of color: invisibility of, 130. *See also* lesbians, Black; lesbians, Latina
Women's Army Corps, 28–30
women's centers: unpaid labor of lesbians and, 81. *See also* Charlotte Women's Center

women's liberation movement, 65–66, 80, 82, 83. *See also* feminist movement
Women's National Basketball Association, 144
working class, 14. *See also* Boyd, Ginny; employment
workplace discrimination, 142–43, 157; visibility and, 49, 50, 94
workplace protections, 142–43, 156, 157
Works Progress Administration, 18, 19
World War II era, 22, 23, 27; cultural changes, 30; efforts to quash lesbian activity during, 29; fear of mannishness during, 28–29, 31. *See also* Boyd, Ginny; military
Wright, Richard, 13
writers' workshops, 71, 72
writing, queer, 90. *See also* publications, queer; *and names of individual publications*

Young, Andrew, 107–8
Youth Against War and Fascism, 69

ZAMI, 134, 159–60
ZAMI NOBLA, 159